D1606844

Great Lakes Ships We Remember II

Rev. Peter J. Van der Linden
AUTHOR & EDITOR

IN COOPERATION WITH
John H. Bascom
John N. Bascom
Rev. Edward J. Dowling, S.J.
C. Patrick Labadie
Edward N. Middleton
Marine Historical Society of Detroit

Published by
FRESHWATER PRESS, INC.
334 The Arcade, P.O. Box 14009,
Cleveland, Ohio 44114

I.S.B.N. 0-912514-25-6

3 9082 03691010 0

JUN 25 1991

Others there are who go to sea in ships
and make their living on the wide waters.
These men have seen the acts of the Lord
and his marvellous doings in the deep.

Ps. 107; 23, 24.

EXPLANATION

The ships depicted in this book were creatures of engineering art. The following explanations about the dimensions and statistics of these vessels should be understood to follow accurately the chronology of each individual ship story.

Unless otherwise noted, the length of a vessel is that length found in the official documents of the country in which the vessel was constructed. The length dimension nearly universally used in these documents is *length between perpendiculars*. This is defined as "the length of the vessel as measured on the Summer load line from the foreside of the stem to the afterside of the rudder post." Other lengths which apply to vessel statistics and which typically are used in the maritime field are: 1) *keel length*, which is the length of the vessel measured along the keel plate, and 2) *overall length*, which is the extreme length of the vessel as measured from its forward most to aftermost perpendicular extensions. The beam and depth of the vessel as shown refer to the greatest breadth measured over the frames and the moulded vertical hold depth measured on the center line of the vessel amidships, respectively. *IN ALL CASES, THE TECHNICAL INFORMATION SHOWN WITH EACH VESSEL STORY IS THE ORIGINAL STATISTICAL DATA WHEN THE SHIP WAS PUT INTO SERVICE WITH THE EXCEPTION OF ANY SUBSEQUENT OFFICIAL NUMBERS. ANY SALIENT SUBSEQUENT CHANGES TO THIS ARE NOTED IN THE TEXT.*

Each ship is given an official number when first documented in a country. The vessel might have many different names in its lifetime, but the official number rarely changes unless she is transferred to another nation, in which case she is given a new official number according to the system used in that particular country.

The types of engines used in various steam and diesel vessels have particular significance to an enthusiast of the shipping world. Each engine is a little different than the next. The dimensions of each engine are given for sake of completeness. The diameter of cylinders used can vary during a ship's lifetime. The engine can be re-bored to make it more economical, thus changing the diameter. The stroke is the vertical distance that a piston takes to make one up or down movement. If an engine is a "triple expansion" (the most popular) type, it will have three cylinders, the low pressure, the intermediate, and the high pressure. The steam flows from the high pressure cylinder to the low, giving added power with each stroke. Propulsion machinery data are, of course, not shown in this book for non-self-propelled vessels such as barges and schooners.

The hull numbers are noted because they are a means of determining just how many ships a shipyard built during its lifetime. The numbering will differ from one firm to another, but most keep an accurate record of the ships they have built. Although uncommon, some yards preferred not to assign hull numbers and, where this is the case, the data line is omitted.

Gross registered tonnage (GRT) applies to vessels, not to cargo. It is determined by dividing by 100 the area, in cubic feet, of the vessel's closed-in spaces. A vessel ton is 100 cubic feet. This tonnage is determined by hull inspectors of the classification society for each ship. This may change from time to time in a ship's life according to the measurement system and governing rules under which the calculation is made. GRT is included in the statistical record of each vessel. The tonnages listed are taken from the American and Canadian records found in the annual reports issued by these nations. The American vessels will be in the "Merchant Vessels of the United States," the Canadian in the "List of Shipping."

Launch dates, when available, have usually come from articles appearing in daily newspapers when the vessel was christened. Specifications of the engines and other dimensions were traced back through the various classification society records such as "Lloyds Register of Shipping." "The Record" of the American Bureau of Shipping, older issues of "Inland Lloyds." "Beeson's Marine Directory" and "Underwriters Insurance" records. Today, such statistics may be found in "Greenwood's Guide to Great Lakes Shipping," an annual publication by the publishers of this volume.

To any enthusiast or "Boat Collector," everything about a ship is of utmost importance. So that the reader may see the effort of pleasureful research that goes into a hobby such as this, we have attempted to share herein all we know about any given vessel's history. Particularly interesting sidelights have been added whenever possible.

Renaming of ships often causes difficulty. To make it easier to understand the time sequence and order in which the ship was given various names, the first name a ship is given in official records is listed as the "a" name. Each successive name and the date it is changed are mentioned. The second name, therefore, becomes the "b" name, etc. Some ships were originally destined to be named one way but were given a name change before the official records were made. These cases are noted wherever possible.

WE REMEMBER . . .

Down through the ages, the fascination and romance of ships has captivated the thousands who have watched the leviathans plow through calm or troubled global waters. Great Lakes ships, as well as the men who have labored aboard them, have had their enthusiasts since La Salle's GRIFFON first sailed these inland waters. We remember these ships, old and new, and now recall in story and pictures some of the fascination we have felt for them.

This volume is a sequel to the first, but unlike it in so far as it is not a continuation of the "Ships That Never Die" columns that appear ever so often in the monthly journal, *The Detroit Marine Historian*. These are entirely new vessels and the photographs come from various sources listed below. Again, we have selected these vessels as a representative group. Not all the ships that have sailed these Great Lakes can be included. We hope that these are familiar to many enthusiasts and fascinating to those uninitiated.

We dedicate this volume to the many historians and ship buffs who have led the way to a more comprehensive study of the vessels which sailed and still sail our "Inland Seas." These dedicated men have now passed to their eternal reward, but we would like to remember them for giving us the incentive and the fruits of their research. We remember Eugene Cote, Tom Dancy, Captain Frank Hamilton, Erik Hyle, Fred Landon, Robert E. Lee, William A. McDonald, Neil Morrison, John Poole, Rev. Franklin C. St. Clair, Kenneth and Keith Smith, Captain W. J. Taylor, Herman Runge and others who have been the forerunners of the many historians of today.

Our thanks go to those who have been so instrumental in putting this second volume to press. Our co-authors have been especially helpful. These are: Tim Blackwell, who helped research and write some of the stories; John H. and John N. Bascom of Toronto, whose specialty is the Canadian old-timers; Father Edward J. Dowling, S.J., without whose help hardly any of us would be where we are now as Great Lakes ship enthusiasts; C. Patrick Labadie, whose fascination with the older ships prior to 1900 has greatly enhanced the stories in this volume; Edward N. Middleton, though living far from our Great Lakes in Kansas City, is THE dedicated scholar of Lake Michigan passenger ships; Peter B. Worden, whose business acumen and expertise in handling delicate situations besides printing the best black and white photos of ships for this volume . . . my personal thanks.

Our special thanks go to those who supplied the photographs for this new volume: Leonard Barr II, John and "Jay" Bascom, Duff Brace, Rev. Edward J. Dowling, John W. Frost, Dave Glick, Stephen Gmelin, Wes Harkins, Don Jardine, Robert E. Kennington, Jim Kidd, C. Patrick Labadie, Capt. John Leonard, Skip Gilham, John O. Greenwood, Bill Luke, Harry McDonald, Robert W. Pocotte, Ralph Roberts, Ken Thro, David Vaughan, Peter B. Worden, and Dr. Richard Wright. Others, including *Lake Log Chips*, the *Scanner* of the Toronto Marine Historical Society, the VALLEY CAMP Museum at Sault Ste. Marie, the Canal Park Museum at Duluth, the Dossin Marine Museum at Belle Isle and the Great Lakes Museum at Vermilion, Ohio have been most helpful in promoting this second volume.

Special thanks go to the Steamship Historical Society, the Library of Congress, and Mariners Museum in Norfolk, Virginia and the U.S. Naval Institute for use of their photographs.

The staff of Freshwater Press and that of the Great Lakes Research Center at Bowling Green State University, the Center for Archival Collections under the able director Dr. Richard J. Wright have been exceedingly helpful in making this work a success.

Lastly, to those who typed the manuscript, especially Mrs. Donna Pritchard and to Bill Luke, who handled the pre-publication efforts, many thanks.

Rev. Peter J. Van der Linden
Editor/Author

NORTH AMERICAN SOCIETY FOR OCEANIC HISTORY

1979

John Lyman Book Award

for

NORTH AMERICAN OCEANIC HISTORY

PRESENTED TO

Marine Historical Society of Detroit
for
GREAT LAKES SHIPS WE REMEMBER

William A. Baker
President

F. Jack Bauer
Chairman,
Awards Committee

Dr. John Lyman, 1915-1977, a founder of NASOH, described himself as a Consultant on Maritime History, Nautical Vexillology, and the Ocean Environment. He wrote extensively for maritime journals and for many years published *Log Chips*, which recorded the histories of ships and shipyards.

SOUTHGA.. ERANS
MEMORIAL LIBRARY
14680 DIX-TOLEDO ROAD
SOUTHGATE, MI 48195

Other Publications
of
Freshwater Press, Inc.

Greenwood's Guide to Great Lakes Shipping . . . . *(annual)*
Greenwood's and Dills' Lake Boats . . . . *(annual)*
Namesakes of the 80's . . . . *by John O. Greenwood*
(current ships)
Namesakes 1956-1980 . . . . *by John. O. Greenwood*
(former ships: 1956-1980)
Namesakes 1930-1955 . . . . *by John O. Greenwood*
Namesakes of the Lakes (Original edition) . . . . *by John O. Greenwood*
Lore of the Lakes . . . . *by Dana Thomas Bowen*
Memories of the Lakes . . . . *by Dana Thomas Bowen*
Shipwrecks of the Lakes . . . . *by Dana Thomas Bowen*
Our Inland Seas . . . . *by James Cooke Mills (1910 reprint)*
The Lower St. Lawrence . . . . *by Ivan S. Brookes*
Great Lakes Ships We Remember (Revised 1984) . . . . *Marine Hist. Society of Detroit*

Over 400 Fine Ship Photographs Available For Sale

First Printing, March, 1984
Copyright, 1984, Marine Historical Society of Detroit, Inc.
Copyrighted in the United States of America
and the Dominion of Canada

No material may be excerpted or copied from
this book without express written permission
from the publisher.

SOUTHGATE VETERANS
MEMORIAL LIBRARY
14680 DIX-TOLEDO ROAD
SOUTHGATE, MI 48195

ACE

LAKE FROHNA at an East Coast coal dock

BRIG. GEN. M. G. ZALINSKI in the Pacific after service on the Lakes

During World War I, the standard type of freighter built for ocean service was called a "Laker". The LAKE FROHNA was launched on April 14, 1919, at Lorain, Ohio, by the American Shipbuilding Company for the U.S. Shipping Board. She saw little service on the high seas and in 1924 was purchased by the McDougall-Duluth Company. The steel vessel was incorporated in the Minnesota-Atlantic Transit fleet and renamed b) ACE, that same year.

The "Poker Fleet", as this company was commonly known, ran its fleet of ships in the package freight trade to various ports from Duluth to Buffalo and Chicago. All the vessels were named for the high cards in a deck: ACE, KING, QUEEN, JACK, TEN and NINE. The ACE, KING, QUEEN, JACK and TEN were similar in design, all being of the "Laker" type. The NINE was of conventional Great Lakes freighter design.

The onset of World War II, and the need for ocean vessels to supply the troops overseas, demanded that every available vessel be sought to augment the dwindling tonnage afloat due to the great success of the German "U" Boat campaign. ACE, taken over by the US Army Quartermasters Corps in 1942, was taken to the coast for use by the War Department. She saw service in the Atlantic and Pacific, after being renamed c) BRIG. GEN. M. G. ZALINSKI in 1942.

At the end of hostilities in 1945, she was refurbished and resumed peaceful pursuits, but her usefulness was near an end. On September 29, 1946, she struck a rock and stranded near Pitt Island, British Columbia. The vessel did not sink and no crew were lost but she was unfit for further service and, taken to Seattle, Washington, was scrapped in 1948.

a) Lake Frohna
b) ACE
c) Brig. Gen. M.G. Zalinski

BUILT:	1919
	American Shipbuilding Co., Lorain, Ohio
HULL NUMBER:	759
LENGTH:	251.0
BREADTH:	43.6
DEPTH:	26.2
GRT:	2,616
REGISTRY NUMBER:	US 218268
ENGINES:	20", 33", 54" Diameter x 40" Stroke, Triple Expansion
ENGINE BUILDER:	American Shipbuilding Co., Lorain, Ohio

ACE downbound in the Detroit River

AGAWA (1)

The Algoma Central Railway has operated three vessels named for the Agawa Canyon area of Northern Ontario, a famous tourist spot served by the railroad. Two straight-deckers bore the shortened name AGAWA, while a self-unloader christened AGAWA CANYON still serves the fleet.

The first AGAWA was a three-masted steel barge which was launched at Collingwood on July 19, 1902, by the Collingwood Shipbuilding Company. She was built to the order of the Algoma Central Steamship Company, of Sault Ste. Marie, Ontario, and was usually towed by the line's steamer MONKSHAVEN. By 1907, it had been decided to convert her to a powered bulk carrier, and the work of boiler and engine installation was carried out at Collingwood. After reconstruction, her dimensions were: 377.0 x 46.1 x 22.1, and tonnage was 3,759 GRT.

On December 7, 1927, AGAWA stranded on Advance Shoal at St. Michael's Bay, on the shore of Manitoulin Island, while downbound with a cargo of grain. Abandoned to the underwriters, she spent the winter on the shoal and was salvaged the next spring by the Reid Wrecking Company. On May 16, 1928, she was towed to South Baymouth for temporary repairs. AGAWA was awarded to Reid as payment for the salvage job and the steamer left South Baymouth, in tow, for Collingwood. The vessel encountered more misfortune, however, in that it sank just outside the entrance to Collingwood harbor. Reid was in no hurry for the ship and it was not raised until January 1929, at which time it was towed to the Collingwood shipyard for a complete rebuild. During the course of the repairs, Canada Steamship Lines Ltd., gained an interest in AGAWA as a result of its connection with the shipyard.

On June 10, 1929, AGAWA was purchased by Arrow Steamships Ltd., Toronto, a concern which was affiliated with Toronto Elevators Ltd. She was renamed b) ROBERT P. DURHAM for her new duties.

ROBERT P. DURHAM was sold on December 2, 1939, to the Quebec and Ontario Transportation Company Ltd., which renamed her c) HERON BAY (1) in 1940. Carrying mostly pulpwood and grain, she operated in the Q & O fleet until her retirement at the end of the 1962 navigation season. Federal Commerce and Navigation Company Ltd., Montreal, acquired the hull, which was used as a storage barge for salt at Port Cartier, Quebec, under the name d) FEDERAL HUSKY.

This veteran steamer was eventually sold to Spanish ship-breakers in October, 1965. Towed across the Atlantic, she arrived safely at Bilbao, Spain, on November 26, 1965, and was subsequently cut up for scrap.

AGAWA as a barge at Fort William

AGAWA as a steamer upbound at the Soo

ROBERT P. DURHAM unloading grain at Toronto Elevators

a) **AGAWA (1)**
b) **Robert P. Durham**
c) **Heron Bay (1)**
d) **Federal Husky**

BUILT:	1902
	Collingwood Shipbuilding Co.,
	Collingwood, Ontario
HULL NUMBER:	2
LENGTH:	376.0
BREADTH:	46.0
DEPTH:	26.0
GRT:	3,516
REGISTRY NUMBER:	C 111807
ENGINES:	20", 33½", 55" Diameter x
	40" Stroke
	Triple Expansion
	Received in 1907
ENGINE BUILDER:	Shipyard

HERON BAY being shifted in winter quarters at Toronto

ALGONAC

SYRACUSE as a package freighter

Built by the Detroit Dry Dock Company at Wyandotte, Michigan in 1884 as a package freighter for the Western Transit Company, this iron and steel vessel saw a variety of services for twelve owners from its launching until 1975. As the SYRACUSE, she was in regular service from Buffalo, New York to Chicago, Illinois and various other ports. SYRACUSE was a duplicate of the steamer ALBANY, which was lost in 1893.

In 1912, she was sold to the Port Huron and Duluth Steamship Company and renamed b) LAKEWOOD. The following year, she was converted to a passenger and freight vessel to operate between Port Huron, Michigan, and Duluth, Minnesota, by the Reid Dry Dock Company at Port Huron. However, passenger traffic was too light to support the cost of the ship in a combined trade and the vessel was reconverted to freight only in 1915 at Toledo, Ohio, by the Toledo Shipbuilding Company.

In 1917, the LAKEWOOD was sold to the Northwestern Steamship Company. In 1918, the Minnesota Loan & Trust Company became her owners and the following year she was purchased by the Peterson & Collinge firm known as the Lakes & St. Lawrence Transit Company. This same year, she was converted to a bulk freighter and shortened at Wyandotte, Michigan, by the Detroit Dry Dock Company. (246.0 x 38.5 x 16.0; 1,351 gross tons.)

Ruben W. Eberly of Buffalo, New York purchased the vessel in 1924 and the Buffalo Gravel Corporation took over in 1925. The LAKEWOOD was then converted, at Buffalo by the Buffalo Dry Dock Co., to a sand dredge. (1,326 gross tons.) For more than twenty years, the vessel operated in the Buffalo vicinity until she was purchased in 1947 by Ira J. Lyons' Schwartz Sand & Gravel Corp., of Detroit, Michigan. The newly acquired vessel was made into a self-unloader at River Rouge, Michigan, by the

6

Nicholson firm and renamed c) K.V. SCHWARTZ. She was a familiar sight to Detroiters and those living along the St. Clair River from then on.

The Construction Materials Corp., which purchased the vessel in 1953, renamed her d) ALGONAC, and continued service in the Detroit area. In 1962, the vessel was sold to the Detroit Marine Disposal Co. (Seaway Cartage Company), which had her engines removed the following year (1,394 gross tons) and took the vessel to Toledo, Ohio. From then on, her career was definitely downhill. In 1965, she sank at her dock on the Maumee River but was raised in short time. Toth Transportation Company was her owner in 1965; C.I.T. Corp. of New York in 1968; James W. O'Rourke in 1971, for one day (June 29th); and finally, Walter Kolbe of Port Clinton, Ohio, her last owner, June 30, 1971.

The old iron and steel vessel was removed from documentation in January of 1974 and was scrapped in Toledo in 1975.

BUILT:	1884
	Detroit Dry Dock Co.,
	Wyandotte, Michigan
HULL NUMBER:	70
LENGTH:	267.0
BREADTH:	38.5
DEPTH:	13.8
GRT:	1,917
REGISTRY NUMBER:	US 116025
ENGINES:	28", 48½" Diameter x 48" Stroke, Fore & Aft Compound
ENGINE BUILDER:	Dry Dock Engine Works, Detroit, Michigan

a) Syracuse
b) Lakewood
c) K.V. Schwartz
d) ALGONAC

LAKEWOOD in the ice at the Soo in 1917

K. V. SCHWARTZ downbound in the St. Clair River in 1950

ALGONAC downbound in the Detroit River

ANN ARBOR NO. 1

The wooden railroad carferry, ANN ARBOR NO. 1 was launched at Toledo, Ohio by the Craig Shipbuilding Company, on September 28, 1892, for the Ann Arbor Railroad for service across Lake Michigan from Frankfort, Michigan to Manistique and Menominee, Michigan and Manitowoc and Kewaunee, Wisconsin. She was the first railroad carferry built for Great Lakes service. ANN ARBOR NO. 1 served many years faithfully with few serious mishaps. In 1907, the vessel received large repairs to her hull and machinery and was quickly put back into service.

The railroad cars were loaded aboard the vessel at the stern and unloaded the same way. Carefully, each track was serviced separately to avoid capsizing the vessel or tearing it away from the dock lines.

Fire broke out on the vessel on Tuesday, March 8, 1910, at Manitowoc, Wisconsin while she was loaded with twenty railroad cars of lumber. Fire fighters immediately fought the growing blaze while the vessel was tied to her dock. Her twenty-three crewmen and fire companies from Manitowoc fought the inferno throughout the night but their efforts proved to be unsuccessful. The vessel and cars were totally destroyed, but no one was seriously injured.

BUILT:	1892
	Craig Shipbuilding Co.,
	Toledo, Ohio
HULL NUMBER:	55
LENGTH:	260.4
BREADTH:	53.0
DEPTH:	14.7
GRT:	1,127
REGISTRY NUMBER:	US 106974
TWIN ENGINES:	20", 40" Diameter x 36" Stroke
	Horizontal Compound
ENGINE BUILDER:	Samuel F. Hodge & Company,
	Detroit, Michigan

ANN ARBOR NO. 1 outbound into Lake Michigan

ANN ARBOR NO. 1 and ANN ARBOR NO. 2 (right) in an ice jam

ANN ARBOR NO. 1 docked

ANN ARBOR NO. 1 afire at Manitowoc March 8, 1910

ARGO

ARGO as a Booth Liner

In early September of 1900, Duluth, Minnesota newspapers announced that the A. Booth Packing Company had awarded a contract to the Craig Shipbuilding Company, of Toledo, to build a new steel passenger steamer to run out of Duluth along the north shore. The new boat was to replace the Booth steamer HIRAM R. DIXON. Costing $100,000, she was to be ready for service about April 1, 1901.

ARGO was launched on April 4, 1901. She sailed two seasons between Duluth and Port Arthur and, in November, 1902, was traded to Graham & Morton, of Benton Harbor, for their steamers SOO CITY and the smaller C.W. MOORE.

Graham & Morton used the ARGO as an independent boat, transferring it between their two divisions and using it to supplement or substitute for their larger, regularly scheduled boats. For the season of 1904, G. & M. chartered ARGO to Peoples' Transit Company, of Chicago, to run opposite their FRONTENAC (a) LAWRENCE, between Chicago and White Lake, Michigan. In the spring of 1905, the

ARGO, and the chartered steamer WILLIAM H. GRAT-WICK, were put on a new G. & M. freight route between Chicago and Duluth. In late November of that year, ARGO, on a run to Holland in a full gale, "smelled the bottom" in trying to enter, and ended up hard aground on a bar north of the piers. After several futile attempts to get her off, a salvage contract was awarded to the Reid Wrecking Company, of Sarnia, who pumped her out and got her off during the last week of January, 1906.

Graham & Morton sued the insurance company for cash settlement. While the boat lay idle at Manitowoc, litigation continued until 1910, when she was sold by the insurers to the Chicago, Racine and Milwaukee line. She was repaired and renamed b) RACINE. She served another decade on Lake Michigan, on the run between Chicago and Milwaukee, and then was sold to the French government, during the first world war. She was converted to a tug and sailed out of Brest, France for many more years, renamed c) RENÉ. She was last in the record in 1938 out of Brest.

ARGO in Graham & Morton colors in 1905

ARGO just before her release from her icy grip at Holland

a) **ARGO**
b) **Racine**
c) **René**

BUILT:	1901 Craig Shipbuilding Co., Toledo, Ohio
HULL *NUMBER:*	81
LENGTH:	173.5
BREADTH:	31.6
DEPTH:	20.8
GRT:	1,089
REGISTRY *NUMBER:*	US 107627
ENGINES:	15", 25", 42" Diameter x 24" Stroke, Triple Expansion
ENGINE *BUILDER:*	Shipyard

RACINE at Milwaukee

RACINE caught in the ice, March 7, 1912

ATHABASCA

The first vessels built especially for the Great Lakes service of the Canadian Pacific Railway were the sistership ALGOMA, ALBERTA and ATHABASCA. These were steel-hulled passenger and package freight steamers which, originally, were equipped with auxiliary sail.

ATHABASCA was launched at Whiteinch, Scotland, at noon on July 3, 1883, by Aitken & Mansell and she was christened by Miss Govan. The name was originally reported as being ATHABASKA. However, there is no indication that this spelling was ever entered into official records.

ATHABASCA sailed from Glasgow on August 23, 1883, with a cargo of coal for Montreal, but had to put back to Glasgow for repairs to her two leaking boilers. She finally arrived at Montreal on September 23 and, after unloading, went to Cantin's Shipyard at Montreal to be cut in two for the passage up the old canals. Towed to Buffalo, she was rejoined by the Union Dry Dock Company and went to Port Colborne, where the cabins and passenger accommodations were fitted. The addition of the superstructure increased her Gross Registered Tonnage from 1,774 to 2,269. ATHABASCA arrived at Owen Sound, Ontario on May 13, 1884, and cleared for the Lakehead on her first trip on May 15.

On July 14, 1891, ATHABASCA was upbound in the Sugar Island Channel of Little Lake George in the St. Mary's River. She met the Cleveland-Cliffs steamer PONTIAC, which was downbound with a cargo of iron ore. The two vessels collided head-on. PONTIAC settled in shallow water with her bow stove in, and ATHABASCA arrived at Sault Ste. Marie with PONTIAC's foredeck balanced across her bow. This was not ATHABASCA's first or last mishap. On July 20, 1889, she had been slightly damaged by a fire which broke out while she was moored at Owen Sound.

On October 13, 1909, ATHABASCA cleared Owen Sound for the Lakehead and, once past Cove Island Light and out into Lake Huron, encountered very heavy weather. Capt. Alex Brown put about to seek shelter in Georgian Bay, but ATHABASCA got off course and, about 10:30 p.m., went hard aground on the beach at Flowerpot Island. Despite immediate salvage efforts, it was not until October 17 that the vessel was refloated and returned to Owen Sound. Later taken to Collingwood, she was repaired and lengthened to 298.8 feet. This reconstruction increased her GRT to 2,784.

On November 3, 1910, ATHABASCA collided with the tug GENERAL near Lime Island in the St. Mary's River. As a result of the accident the GENERAL sank.

In 1913, ATHABASCA was repowered by the Western Drydock and Shipbuilding Company Ltd., Port Arthur. She was given a new fore-and-aft compound engine, 30", 64" x 48", and two new Scotch boilers, 14' x 11'.

ATHABASCA ceased to carry passengers in 1916, but continued in the package freight trade, running from Port McNicoll to the Lakehead, until the 1930's. She operated only periodically during the Depression. As business improved, she and her surviving sistership, ALBERTA, were placed on a new package freight run from Port McNicoll to Milwaukee and Chicago.

When ATHABASCA reached the age of sixty years in 1944, the C.P.R. withdrew her from service and laid up the ship at Port McNicoll. She remained there until 1947, when she was sold to the Steel Company of Canada Ltd. and towed to Hamilton for scrapping. She passed down the Welland Canal on May 27, 1947, and was dismantled during 1948.

ATHABASCA and OSCEOLA at the Soo Locks

with PONTIAC's bow on her deck, July 1891

ATHABASCA in 1905

ATHABASCA in dry dock at Collingwood in 1910

ATHABASCA cut in two for lengthening

16

BUILT: 1883
Aitkon & Manooll,
Whiteinch, Scotland
HULL
NUMBER: 123
LENGTH: 262.8
BREADTH: 38.2
DEPTH: 23.3
GRT: 1,774
REGISTRY
NUMBER: C. 85764
ENGINES: 35", 70" Diameter x
48" Stroke, Fore &
Aft Compound
ENGINE
BUILDER: David Rowan
Glasgow, Scotland

ATHABASCA in her later years upbound in the St. Mary's River

Tug HELENA towing ATHABASCA down the Welland Canal May 27, 1947

AVONDALE (2)

This steel bulk freighter, built in 1908 at St. Clair, Michigan, was launched on May 2nd, 1908 and went into operation for the Boland and Cornelius fleet as the ADAM E. CORNELIUS (1), (US 205239). In 1942, she was converted into a self-unloader at Manitowoc, Wisconsin by the Manitowoc Shipbuilding Company and at the same time was lengthened to 425 feet with a new gross tonnage of 4,939. On March 10, 1948, she was renamed DETROIT EDISON (1) for the major consumer of the coal she carried. On September 7, 1954, she was again renamed, this time to GEORGE F. RAND (2).

The RAND was purchased in 1962 by the Reoch Steamship Company of Canada, which was managed by Leadale Shipping Limited. At the same time she received her final name d) AVONDALE (2). In 1974, management was assumed by Westdale Shipping Ltd.

AVONDALE's career ended when she was retired at the end of the 1975 season, and taken to Port Colborne, Ontario where she lay in the old section of the Welland Ship Canal below Humberstone, Ontario. In 1978, she was set afire by vandals and her forward end was completely gutted. In 1979, she was towed overseas to Spain for scrapping. On July 6, 1979, she departed Quebec in tow of the Polish tug, JANTAR. With her in tow was the steamer FERNDALE. AVONDALE arrived at Santander, Spain on August 3, 1979 to be cut up.

a) Adam E. Cornelius (1)
b) Detroit Edison (1)
c) George F. Rand (2)
d) AVONDALE (2)

BUILT:	1908 Great Lakes Engineering Works, St. Clair, Michigan
HULL NUMBER:	53
LENGTH:	420.0
BREADTH:	52.0
DEPTH:	24.0
GRT:	4,900
REGISTRY NUMBER:	C. 316352
ENGINES:	21", 34½", 57" Diameter x 42" Stroke, Triple Expansion
ENGINE BUILDER:	Great Lakes Engineering Works, St. Clair, Michigan

ADAM E. CORNELIUS (1) as a straight-decker, October 1, 1939

ADAM E. CORNELIUS (1) as a self-unloader, July 10, 1947 at Port Huron, Mich.

DETROIT EDISON (1) upbound in the Detroit River

GEORGE F. RAND (2) at Cleveland

AVONDALE (2) upbound in the St. Clair River

AYCLIFFE HALL

This vessel was one of the many steel canal-type freighters built overseas during the 1920's. The AYCLIFFE HALL was built by Smith's Dock Co. Ltd. in 1928 at South Bank-on-Tees, Great Britain for the Hall Corporation of Canada, of Montreal, P.Q. Her cargoes of coal, grain, pulpwood and other varieties of bulk freight were transported from lower lake ports through the old series of locks of the St. Lawrence River to ports as far away as Halifax, Nova Scotia and St. John, New Brunswick.

While off Long Point on Lake Erie, during a dense fog in the early hours of June 11, 1936, the AYCLIFFE HALL and the 612-foot ore-laden steamer EDWARD J. BERWIND collided. The BERWIND sustained only slight damage, but the AYCLIFFE HALL plunged to the bottom almost immediately. Her entire crew of 19 was saved by the BERWIND. The hull of the AYCLIFFE HALL rested in 78 feet of water, about 18 miles, 233 degrees from Long Point Lighthouse.

Salvage operations were carried on by Sin-Mac Lines Ltd. until heavy weather set in that fall. AYCLIFFE HALL was temporarily raised to the surface but could not be kept afloat. Further attempts at salvage proved unsuccessful. On July 18, 1939, the hull was again found in 12 fathoms of water by divers from the U.S. Coast Guard vessel CROCUS and the Canadian Department of Transport's steamer GRENVILLE. It was decided that further salvage attempts were useless and the steamer's cabins and rigging were blown up to prevent damage to passing vessels. The end of the little canaller was sudden, and she lies there to this day.

BUILT:	1928
	Smith's Dock Co. Ltd.,
	South Bank-on-Tees, England
HULL NUMBER:	845
LENGTH:	253.0
BREADTH:	44.1
DEPTH:	18.5
GRT:	1,900
REGISTRY NUMBER;	C. 147800
ENGINES:	15", 25", 40" Diameter x 33"
	Stroke, Triple Expansion
ENGINE BUILDER:	Smith's Dock Co. Ltd.

AYCLIFFE HALL at Port Colborne

BADGER STATE

BADGER STATE upbound at the Soo

The wooden passenger and package freight steamer BADGER STATE, built at Buffalo, New York by Mason & Bidwell, was launched April 17, 1862 for Charles Ensign of the same city. One of twin sisters, the other being EMPIRE STATE, she left Buffalo on May 22, 1862 on her maiden voyage to Milwaukee, Wisconsin. On June 6, 1864, the vessel experienced a serious engine breakdown on Lake Huron and was towed to Detroit where her engine was thoroughly overhauled. The former engine was rebuilt as a Steeple Compound; 25¼" and 54" diameter x 68" stroke. That same year, the vessel passed into the control of the Western Transportation Company (incorporated in New York). This firm was reincorporated as the Western Transit Company in 1884.

In 1865, the BADGER STATE measured 213.0 x 33.0 x 12.1; and was readmeasured to 1,115 gross tons. Her main route was from Buffalo to Lake Michigan ports for the New York Central Railroad.

During the seasons of 1879, 1883, 1889, and 1892, the BADGER STATE was in the pool of vessels called the Lake Superior Transit Company.

In 1898, The Northern Transit Company of Cleveland purchased the vessel to run from Cleveland, Ohio to upper lake ports. In 1902, she was purchased by the Barry Brothers Transportation Company of Chicago, Illinois to run between Chicago and Muskegon, Michigan. During the season of 1903, the BADGER STATE ran for the Cleveland to Detroit Division of the Barry Brothers. Hugh R. Havey of Detroit purchased the vessel in November of that year. The vessel had a tonnage change, at Detroit on April 25, 1904, to 987 gross tons. The same day, Charles W. Kotcher, also of Detroit, entered into a partnership with Mr. Havey which lasted until May 12, 1905; thereafter Mr. Havey remained in sole control, at least until September 30th.

On May 20, 1905, the Detroit Free Press had a most interesting article concerning the BADGER STATE. "The steamer BADGER STATE, the floating poolroom . . . is already anchored in the Detroit River near Peche Island, on the Canadian side, and is ready for business. Jerry Falvey, the promoter of the enterprise, says that nothing but the poolroom form of gambling will be tolerated. The upper deck is fitted with a blackboard and all the paraphernalia necessary for an up-to-date establishment, including a buffet and a bar. The steamer HATTIE will make regular trips to the BADGER STATE and all small boats will be welcome, of course. That is, providing the Canadian Government does not break up the little scheme." The very next day the "enterprise" was halted by the American and Canadian governments. What became of the venture is not stated, but we can be sure that whoever was involved was made to change his mind. The next owner of the "Poolroom Ship" was H. N. Loud of AuSable, Michigan who purchased the boat September 30, 1905, after it had been rebuilt at Detroit in August to a lumber carrier. The upper decks, probably including the poolroom, were removed. The new dimensions were: 213.0 x 33.0 x 11.8; 686 gross tons.

Another tonnage change was made at Port Huron on June 2, 1906, to 802 gross tons. During February of 1908, The Badger State Transportation Company (Archibald McBean, secretary) took over the lumber carrier. John G. Boyle of Detroit took over in 1909 as trustee. The BADGER STATE caught fire at her dock at Marine City, Michigan on December 6, 1909. The lines were cut and the vessel drifted down the St. Clair River, stranding just below Fawn Island, where she burned to the water's edge. Of the six crew on board at the time, no one was injured. Her final document was surrendered in Detroit on December 31, 1909.

BADGER STATE in 1904

BADGER STATE downbound with pulpwood in the St. Clair River

BUILT: 1862
Mason & Bidwell,
Buffalo, N.Y.
LENGTH: 210.4
BREADTH: 32.4
DEPTH: 13.3
GRT: 860
REGISTRY
NUMBER: U.S. 2111
ENGINES: 44" Diameter x
42" Stroke,
Direct-Acting
ENGINE
BUILDER: King Iron Works,
Buffalo, N.Y.

BARKHAMSTEAD

BARKHAMSTEAD downbound in the St. Mary's River

One of the steel tugs ordered by the U.S. Shipping Board in the first World War was the BARKHAMSTEAD which was built by the Bethlehem Shipbuilding Company in 1919 at Elizabeth, New Jersey.

Idled by the end of hostilities, the BARKHAMSTEAD was finally sold to the Pringle Barge Line of Detroit, Michigan in 1923. She came to the Lakes and began operations as the tug for the many wooden barges that Pringle owned. She was engaged in towing these in the lumber trade for three years. BARKHAMSTEAD then towed barges MAIDA and CONSTITUTION between Toledo, Ohio and Detroit in the coal trade for many years. Replaced in 1950 by the new tug S.M. DEAN, the old timer was placed in ordinary at Detroit. Her cabins and engines were removed shortly after and her intended use was to be as a barge. Mr. M. Ritter of Muskegon, Michigan purchased the old vessel in 1951, but she was soon reduced to a scrap pile, being dismantled at River Rouge, Michigan in 1953.

The old workhorse of the Pringle Barge Line served many years between Toledo and Detroit, hauling the towline of either of the two barges in the Pringle fleet and remains just a memory of faithful service to all who knew her. Operating about 230 days a year for 27 years, a total of 6,210 round trips and hauling approximately 5,000 net tons of coal per trip, the BARKHAMSTEAD towed nearly 31 million net tons of coal in her career; quite an impressive record for a tug that was such a common sight to residents of Toledo and Detroit!

BUILT:	1919
	Bethlehem Shipbuilding Co.,
	Elizabeth, New Jersey
HULL NUMBER:	2124
LENGTH:	142.0
BREADTH:	27.6
DEPTH:	14.8
GRT:	437
REGISTRY NUMBER:	U.S. 211889
ENGINES:	17", 25", 43" Diameter x 30"
	Stroke, Triple Expansion
ENGINE BUILDER:	Shipyard

BARKHAMSTEAD in the Detroit River

After being cut down at River Rouge

U.S.S. ROBERT L. BARNES

The steel canal-type steamer R.L. BARNES was built by the McDougall-Duluth Company, Duluth, Minnesota in 1917 as a prototype vessel designed for lake-coast trading, using the barge canals instead of the St. Lawrence River canals to get to the East coast. The company had been organized in January 1916 by Alexander McDougall, the originator of the whaleback vessels, and Julius Barnes of Duluth. This ship bore a striking resemblance to the earlier whalebacks, having engines and superstructure aft and a small turret forward. The only departure from the whaleback design was the use of straight steel plates in the hull instead of the curved plates of the whalebacks.

Completed in June of 1917, the vessel was appropriated by the U.S. Shipping Board for transfer to the U.S. Navy. Her engines had been in the 1889-built wooden steamer OLYMPIA which Captain McDougall had purchased for $1,200. He had the cylinders rebored to 18", 30", 50" diameter x 42" stroke. On October 19, 1918, the ship was commissioned in the U.S. Navy as b) USS ROBERT L. BARNES and designated as AK-11, an auxiliary cargo ship. Her travels began soon after.

The BARNES went from New York to Guantanamo Bay, Cuba and thence to the Pacific, arriving at Apra, Guam on the 27th of April, 1920. Here she remained as part of the "Guam Navy" as a station ship with a few trips to Cavite in the Philippines for drydocking and repairs. During 1936 her designation was changed to AO-14, an oiler, having been converted for such tasks at Cavite Naval Base. Her new dimensions and tonnage now were: 258.6 x 43.2 x 18.6; 2015 gross tons. On July 1, 1938, her designation was again changed to AG-27, miscellaneous auxiliary.

On December 8, 1941, she was bombed and strafed by Japanese planes and on December 10, 1941, along with the USS YP-16, USS YP-17 and the USS PENGUIN (Am-33), she was captured by the Japanese at Guam. She now began the war years as part of the Japanese Navy. (We do not know if she was given another name for this service.) The ship was stricken from the US Navy list on July 24, 1942.

When Guam was recaptured in 1944, the BARNES was still there and was recovered, apparently having suffered little damage. After the war, the vessel was transferred to the British Ministry of Transport and renamed c) FORTUNE. A few years later (date unknown), she was listed as owned by Ek Liong Hin of Singapore as d) M.T.S. No. 2. The vessel was scrapped in 1950 somewhere in the Orient.

R.L. BARNES entering Superior harbor

a) R.L. Barnes   b) USS ROBERT L. BARNES   c) Fortune   d) M.T.S. No. 2

BUILT:	1917
	McDougall-Duluth Co.,
	Duluth, Minn.
HULL NUMBER:	1
LENGTH:	251.10
BREADTH:	43.2
DEPTH:	23.8
GRT:	1,914
REGISTRY NUMBER:	US 215115
ENGINES:	20", 32", 52" Diameter x 42"
	Stroke, Triple Expansion
ENGINE BUILDER:	Globe Iron Works
	Cleveland, Ohio 1889

U.S.S. ROBERT L. BARNES AG-27

BATTLEFORD

GLENROSS downbound in 1936 in the St. Mary's River

In 1925, the steel canaller GLENROSS was built by the Swan, Hunter & Wigham Richardson Ltd., shipbuilders at Wallsend-on-Tyne, England for Great Lakes service. Destined to be lengthened after she crossed the ocean to 343.1 x 43.7 x 22.9; 3219 gross tons, the little canaller carried her new midsection in her hold on the voyage over. Upon arrival at Collingwood, Ontario, work commenced by the Collingwood Shipyard to increase her original length.

GLENROSS was officially registered to Frank Ross of Montreal. Ross was an associate of James Playfair, Midland, Ontario, and the steamer was accordingly operated by Playfair's Great Lakes Transportation Company Ltd. In 1927, the operation of GLENROSS was taken over by Canada Steamship Lines Ltd., Montreal, and she was later purchased by that firm. Her usual service was in the grain trade between the Lakehead ports on Lake Superior to Georgian Bay ports.

In 1939, the GLENROSS was taken back to Collingwood and shortened to her original dimensions (2,357 gross tons) for use in the St. Lawrence through the old canal system. Her duties were now in the fast package freight trades. In

1941, the GLENROSS was renamed b) BATTLEFORD.

On June 1, 1943, BATTLEFORD collided with the Paterson steamer PRINDOC (1) in a dense fog, at 1:43 a.m., 30 miles southeast of Passage Island in Lake Superior. BATTLEFORD, upbound, struck the PRINDOC, which was downbound with grain, on her starboard quarter, wounding her fatally. PRINDOC went down at 2:25 a.m., and her entire complement of 21 crew members was safely taken aboard by BATTLEFORD.

After service on the lakes and in World War II, BATTLE-FORD operated even after the opening of the St. Lawrence Seaway in 1959. She also served on a short-lived CSL service to Newfoundland.

With the arrival of brand new package freighters built for Canada Steamship Lines during the 1960's, the smaller BATTLEFORD was withdrawn from service and sold to Bahama Shipowners, Ltd. of Nassau, The Bahamas in 1966, and renamed by this firm as c) REAL GOLD. In 1967, her owners were Bahama Package Carriers, and in 1971, Antilles, Lines, Ltd., of Nassau. In 1975, she was scrapped.

a) Glenross	BUILT:	1925
b) BATTLEFORD		Swan, Hunter & Wigham Richardson, Ltd., Wallsend-on-Tyne, England
c) Real Gold	HULL NUMBER:	1275
	LENGTH:	248.1
	BREADTH:	43.8
	DEPTH:	22.9
	GRT:	2,309
	REGISTRY NUMBER:	C 148134
	ENGINES:	18", 30", 49" Diameter x 36" Stroke
		Triple Expansion
	ENGINE BUILDER:	McColl & Pollock Ltd.
		Sunderland, England

GLENROSS after being shortened at Collingwood

BATTLEFORD upbound in the St. Mary's River

W.K. BIXBY

Launched on November 15, 1905, the steel bulk freighter W. K. BIXBY was built by the Detroit Shipbuilding Company at Wyandotte, Michigan in 1906 for Hugh McMillan's National Steamship Company. Employed in the iron ore, coal and grain trades for much of her life, the BIXBY was a common sight on the St. Mary's, St. Clair and Detroit Rivers.

In 1920, the vessel was purchased by the Minnesota Transit Company, a division of the North American Steamship Company, which in turn became known as the Reiss Steamship Company in 1921. Her main upbound cargo was coal from lower lake ports to Sheboygan, Wisconsin, home of the Reiss Coal Company, and iron ore downbound. She was renamed b) J. L. REISS in 1920.

In 1933, the J. L. REISS was converted into a self-unloader at Manitowoc, Wisconsin by the Manitowoc Shipbuilding Company. Her dimensions now were 489.0 x 52.2 x 26.5; 5,398 gross tons. For many years thereafter the ship was well known around the lakes, not so much for her speed, but for the heavy clouds of black smoke that poured from her funnel.

In 1969, the American Steamship Company, Boland & Cornelius Managers, took over the Reiss fleet. In 1972, the J. L. REISS was sold to the Erie Sand Steamship Company of Erie, Pennsylvania, who renamed her c) SIDNEY E. SMITH, JR. (2) during the spring of 1972. Unfortunately the newly painted (green hull, white cabins, orange stack) vessel did not last long in the service of her new owners.

On June 5, 1972, at 1:46 A.M., the SMITH, upbound with coal, sank near the Blue Water Bridge, on the east edge of the channel of the St. Clair River, the result of collision with the Canadian bulk freighter PARKER EVANS, downbound with grain. No crewmen were lost. Since the SMITH represented a hazard to navigation, she was abandoned to the U.S. Corps of Engineers on June 22. Wrecking operations continued throughout the summer months. At one point in time, the hull split into two sections, making salvage even more hazardous. The forward section was finally removed on September 25, and the stern section later. Both halves were sunk as a dock on the Point Edward side of the River the following year and there she rests, the name on her stern still visible.

W. K. BIXBY in her early years

J.L. REISS as a straight-deck bulk freighter

J.L. REISS as a self-unloader

a) W.K. BIXBY   b) J.L. Reiss   c) Sidney E. Smith, Jr. (2)

BUILT:	1906
	Detroit Shipbuilding Co.,
	Wyandotte, Mich.
HULL NUMBER:	161
LENGTH:	480.0
BREADTH:	52.2
DEPTH:	26.5
GRT:	5,712
REGISTRY NUMBER:	U.S. 202875
ENGINES:	22½", 36", 60" Diameter x 42" Stroke
	Triple Expansion
ENGINE BUILDER:	Shipyard

J.L. REISS in Boland & Cornelius colors

SIDNEY E. SMITH, JR. upbound in the Detroit River, just hours before the accident

The wreck at Port Huron after it broke in two

BOSTON

BOSTON in 1924

In 1913, the Western Transit Company, part of the New York Central Railroad, ordered a steel package freighter from the Great Lakes Engineering Works at Ecorse, Michigan to be named BOSTON. She began her voyages that same season.

In 1915, the railroad controlled steamship companies were forced to disband, and all ships involved went over to other owners. The BOSTON was transferred to the Great Lakes Transit Corporation in 1916, and ran successfully for this fleet. In 1925 the ship was renamed J.M. DAVIS.

Even though her career as a package freighter was uneventful, she proved a valuable asset to the company. She was converted for ocean service due to the war emergency in 1943, and transferred to the War Shipping Administration.

After the war, in 1946, the Pratt Steamship Company of Los Angeles bought her for the West Coast Trade. In 1949, an Argentine Company, Cia Argentinia De Transportes Maritimas, bought the DAVIS and the next year renamed her CANOPUS. Another Argentine Company, Acenaz Bragado, bought the now aging freighter in December of 1972. Service for this company was limited however, for she was sold for scrap and her demolition began at LaPlata, Argentina, on December 7, 1976. A staunch vessel she proved to be and a world traveller, too.

a) **BOSTON**   b) **J.M. Davis**   c) **Canopus**

BUILT:	1913
	Great Lakes Engineering Works,
	Ecorse, Mich.
HULL NUMBER:	106
LENGTH:	350.0
BREADTH:	48.1
DEPTH:	30.9
GRT:	4,184
REGISTRY NUMBER:	U.S. 210990
ENGINES:	19", 27½", 40", 58" Diameter x
	42" Stroke
	Quadruple Expansion
ENGINE BUILDER:	Shipyard

BOSTON at Duluth

J.M. DAVIS in the Detroit River

J.M. DAVIS as an Army Repair Ship at Yokohama, Japan in 1945

Another view of the J.M. Davis at Yokohama in 1945

BRAZIL

The steel package freighter BRAZIL was built by the Union Dry Dock Company at Buffalo, New York in 1890, for M.M. Drake of the Drake & Maytham firm of Buffalo. On Sunday, November 22, 1891, at 3 A.M., she sank the steamer SAMUEL MATHER (1) eight miles out from Whitefish Point, Lake Superior in a dense fog. The wooden MATHER sank in 25 minutes but all hands were rescued by the BRAZIL and taken to a safe haven.

In 1896, the vessel was sold to John Kelderhouse and William Berriman. In 1898, she was again sold, this time to George W. Maytham's Republic Steamship Company, and converted to a crane-equipped package freighter. In 1904, the BRAZIL was sold to the Wisconsin Transportation Company of Sheboygan, Wisconsin. Most of her cargoes were coal from lower lake ports. In 1913, she was taken over by the North American Steamship Company from the same home port.

James Playfair of Midland, Ontario took over her ownership in 1916 for his Great Lakes Transportation Company. For this firm, incorporated in the U.S. from 1916, and in Canada from 1919, she remained in the bulk grain trade, being renamed b) GLENBRAE (C 138217) when she came into Canadian registry. When Playfair got rid of his entire fleet in 1925-1927, the GLENBRAE was again renamed back to her former name, c) BRAZIL. In 1929, the idle vessel was purchased by the Illinois Ship & Dredge Company of Chicago, Illinois and converted to a sand dredge at Toledo, Ohio by the Toledo Shipbuilding Company after again coming into U.S. registry. Her work was dredging the rivers and harbors in lower Lake Michigan.

The rest of the now aging vessel's years were spent in the sand trade. The BRAZIL was abandoned in 1944, and finally reduced to scrap in South Chicago in 1949.

BRAZIL — an early view in Wisconsin Transportation colors

a) **BRAZIL**   b) Glenbrae   c) Brazil

BUILT:	1890
	Union Dry Dock Co.,
	Buffalo, N.Y.
HULL NUMBER:	51
LENGTH:	276.1
BREADTH:	40.0
DEPTH:	21.6
GRT:	2,186
REGISTRY NUMBER:	U.S. 3467
ENGINES:	19½", 32", 52" Diameter x 45"
	Stroke, Triple Expansion
ENGINE BUILDER:	H.G. Trout
	Buffalo, New York

GLENBRAE upbound at Mission Point near the Soo in 1923

BRAZIL as a sand dredge

37

F.R. BUELL

F.R. BUELL at the Soo Locks

F.R. BUELL in the drydock at Buffalo in 1918

a) **F.R. BUELL**   b) Nagaho

BUILT:	1888
	William DuLac,
	Mount Clemens, Mich.
LENGTH:	194.0
BREADTH:	36.4
DEPTH:	22.8
GRT:	1,438
REGISTRY NUMBER:	U.S. 120720
ENGINES:	28½", Diameter x 36"
	Stroke
	High Pressure
	Non-condensing
ENGINE BUILDER:	S.F. Hodge & Company
	Detroit, Mich.

Built as a schooner barge until engines could be acquired, the wooden bulk freight vessel, F. R. BUELL, was completed by William DuLac at Mount Clemens, Michigan in 1888. The engine was installed a year later in Detroit, Michigan by the Frontier Iron Works (Samuel F. Hodge). Reportedly, the old engine from the tug GOODNOW was used and steeple compounded to have the following dimensions: 20" and 40" diameter of the cylinders by a 36" stroke.

In 1899, the BUELL was chartered from her owners, the Tonawanda Barge Line (Wm. DuLac, owner) to the Grand Trunk Railway's Botsford Line for the entire season. That same year, on September 5th, the steamer DOUGLASS HOUGHTON was rammed by her tow barge, the JOHN FRITZ in the lower St. Mary's River. As a result of this collision, which sank the HOUGHTON, the traffic became so jammed that the ships following the HOUGHTON and coming to meet her in the narrow channel, had to scatter in all directions. The BUELL was one of the closest to the accident and stranded violently, causing considerable damage. She was released but had to be taken to Detroit for repairs which were completed by the Detroit Dry Dock Company.

In 1903, the Tonawanda Barge Company was listed as her owners. In 1904, she was altered at the Dunford & Alverson Dry Dock, Port Huron, Michigan, to a single deck steamer to be used in the lumber trade from Manistique, Michigan to Tonawanda, New York. In 1913, the A. Weston & Son company took over her ownership. In 1916, the Hamilton Transportation Company, also a lumber firm, acquired ownership. In 1920, she changed ownership for the final time. Mr. John J. O'Hagan of Buffalo, New York, became her owner and renamed the vessel b) NAGAHO, which is O'Hagan spelled backwards.

On October 27, 1922, the old lumber vessel succumbed to the angry waves of Lake Ontario off Port Collins, Ontario. The crew was rescued, but the aging NAGAHO could not tolerate the stresses to her planking and subsequently sank.

NAGAHO

EUGENE J. BUFFINGTON

The Launching — March 6, 1909

Late in 1908, the Pittsburgh Steamship Company ordered a steel bulk freighter to be named EUGENE J. BUFFINGTON. The American Shipbuilding Company at Lorain, Ohio laid the keel on December 10, 1908, launched the vessel on March 6, 1909, and delivered the BUFFINGTON on May 4, 1909.

During their lifetime, ships usually undergo many changes. The BUFFINGTON was not an unusual vessel, but did have some terrifying moments in her career. Her only major accident occurred on June 21, 1942, when she slammed onto Boulder Reef in Lake Michigan, in a dense fog, and broke in half. It took salvagers 25 days to get her off. Had it not been wartime, the vessel would probably have never been recovered. Under the circumstances, however, she was raised and towed to South Chicago, where she was repaired and completely rebuilt. In 1943, the beleaguered steamer returned to service for the United States Steel Corporation (Pittsburgh Steamship Company), her original owners.

Three decades passed until she was finally retired at Duluth, Minnesota at the close of the 1974 season. There she remained until July of 1980. The BUFFINGTON and another six "Pittsburghers" were sold for scrap to various buyers. Her final voyage began with a tow from Duluth to Port Huron, Michigan. From there she was towed to Buffalo, New York in the fall of 1980. In late 1980, she and the J.P. MORGAN, JR., were towed together from Quebec to Bilbao, Spain where they arrived on October 22, and were subsequently cut up for scrap.

BUILT:	1909
	American Shipbuilding Co.,
	Lorain, Ohio
HULL NUMBER:	366
LENGTH:	580.0
BREADTH:	58.0
DEPTH:	32.0
GRT:	7,528
REGISTRY NUMBER:	US 206147
ENGINES:	24", 39", 65" Diameter x 42"
	Stroke, Triple Expansion
ENGINE BUILDER:	Shipyard

EUGENE J. BUFFINGTON upbound in the St. Clair River in 1916

Broken in two on Boulder Reef, Lake Michigan

EUGENE J. BUFFINGTON upbound in the Detroit River

On the way to the scrap yard under tow of BARBARA ANN, 1980

CALCITE (1)

This steel self-unloader was built in 1912 at Wyandotte, Michigan by the Detroit Shipbuilding Company and was launched March 30th, for the Calcite Transportation Company of Calcite, Michigan. Its principal duties were to carry limestone from the quarry near Rogers City, Michigan to lower lake ports where it was fed into the huge steel blast furnaces to make steel from the iron ore brought down by the other ships. In 1923, the Bradley Transportation Company was formed for the transporting of the limestone for the Michigan Limestone and Chemical Company. This firm was later incorporated into the United States Steel Corporation. The CALCITE, was the first vessel to join the former firm and the first to be retired. After many years of faithful service, the CALCITE was retired in November, 1960. She was scrapped at Conneaut, Ohio in 1961. CALCITE's pilot-house was removed and placed on display at the Rogers City plant, where it can still be visited today.

CALCITE in the ice in the St. Clair River

CALCITE downbound at Mission Point

CALCITE downbound with limestone

BUILT:	1912	*DEPTH:*	29.0
	Detroit Shipbuilding Co.,	*GRT:*	3,996
	Wyandotte, Mich.	*REGISTRY NUMBER:*	US.209763
HULL NUMBER:	188	*ENGINES:*	19", 27½", 40", 58" Diameter x
LENGTH:	416.0		42" Stroke, Quadruple Expansion
BREADTH:	54.2	*ENGINE BUILDER:*	Shipyard

The Pilothouse Memorial at Rogers City

CANISTEO (1886)

Large numbers of sailing craft and steambarges were products of small backwater ports around the lakes. CANISTEO was built at the Dulac shipyard in Mount Clemens, Michigan, four miles up the Clinton River from Lake St. Clair. At 182 feet, she was among the largest craft built there. Even without her machinery, the river would barely float her. She was outfitted at Detroit.

CANISTEO was a good carrier, with the capacity for 700,000 feet of lumber, and usually towed two good-sized barges besides. The ship was owned by the Tonawanda Barge Line from 1886 to 1903, a firm in which her builder, Mr. Dulac, held a principle interest. During this time she hauled lumber from the Upper Lakes down the Niagara River to Tonawanda, towing the consorts ELEANOR and A. STEWART.

The ship changed hands in 1904 (James Madigan, Buffalo and A.B. MacLaren, Toledo) and in 1908 she was acquired by Eli Jacques & Sons of Duluth, who outfitted her for the sand trade with an A-frame and clamshell rig. The firm moved to Detroit in 1914 and sold-out to United Fuel & Supply Company in 1918, at which time CANISTEO joined a whole fleet of "sand-suckers" and tugs working Lake St. Clair and Western Lake Erie out of Detroit, furnishing sand and gravel for the construction trades. Finally, too old to be useful any longer, the CANISTEO was laid up at Detroit in 1921 and subsequently abandoned and dismantled.

CANISTEO leaving the locks in 1909

CANISTEO downbound, passing a steel barge upbound

BUILT:	1886	*GRT:*	595
	William DuLac,	*REGISTRY NUMBER:*	US.126360
	Mount Clemens, Mich.	*ENGINES:*	20", 40" Diameter x 36" Stroke
LENGTH:	182.2		Steeple Compound
BREADTH:	34.3	*ENGINE BUILDER:*	S. F. Hodge & Company
DEPTH:	12.2		Detroit, Michigan

CANOPUS

GEORGE H. RUSSEL in Gilchrist colors upbound at the Soo

Originally designed to be 50 feet shorter when ordered by the Gilchrist Transportation Company from the Columbia Iron Works at St. Clair, Michigan, the GEORGE H. RUSSEL was completed by the Great Lakes Engineering Works at the same yard in St. Clair. It was launched on April 25, 1905. The latter firm took over the yard after Columbia Iron Works went bankrupt. The RUSSEL's trade included carrying cargoes of iron ore, coal and grain.

When the Gilchrist Transportation Company folded in 1913, the RUSSEL was bought by Pickands Mather and Company's Interlake Steamship Company and renamed b) CANOPUS. In 1945, she was purchased by the Nicholson Transit Company and converted to a combination bulk freighter and auto carrier the following year. In 1950, she was converted to a full auto carrier with a flight deck so that the ship could carry more cars from Detroit, Michigan to Cleveland, Ohio and Buffalo, New York. When the carrying of autos by boat became unprofitable early in the 1960's, the trim craft was sold for scrap and dismantled at Ashtabula, Ohio during the winter of 1961-62.

CANOPUS in Interlake colors, July 5, 1940

BUILT:	1905
	Great Lakes Engineering Works,
	St. Clair, Mich.
HULL NUMBER:	11
LENGTH:	462.0
BREADTH:	50.0
DEPTH:	24.0
GRT:	4,978
REGISTRY NUMBER	US 202149
ENGINES:	22", 36", 60" Diameter x 40"
	Stroke, Triple Expansion
ENGINE BUILDER:	Shipyard

a) **George H. Russel**
b) **CANOPUS**

CANOPUS without the "Flight Deck" downbound under the Blue Water Bridge

CANOPUS arriving at E. 55th Street in Cleveland

48

CAPE TRINITY

GERONIA was a steel, twin-screw, passenger steamer built at Collingwood in 1911 by the Collingwood Shipbuilding Company for the Ontario and Quebec Navigation Company Ltd., Picton, Ontario, an enterprise of the Hepburn Family. Her design was altered during construction, but the vessel never proved to be a success.

She ran her trials on July 18, 1911, and entered service on August 3 after a stormy delivery voyage from Collingwood to Toronto. GERONIA was intended for operation between Lake Ontario ports and Quebec City. On the upbound return leg of her first trip, she lost a propeller while passing through the Cornwall Canal, and was forced to go on drydock at Kingston to have it replaced. The delay and repair work cost the owners about $10,000.

At the close of the summer of 1911, GERONIA returned to Collingwood for machinery adjustments and repairs, for she had not been able to operate at her designed speed. However, bad luck continued and, on July 15, 1912, she struck a rock while shooting the Lachine Rapids. It was necessary to beach her on Heron Island, where she settled to the bottom. Fortunately, the passengers were removed safely. GERONIA was later salvaged and towed to Tait's drydock at Montreal, where it was repaired.

During the 1912-13 winter lay-up, auxiliary boilers were installed because the two original boilers were unable to provide sufficient steam. Even with the additional boilers, she was not successful, and the ship was withdrawn from service before the end of the 1913 season.

During 1913, the Ontario and Quebec Navigation Company Ltd. had been acquired by Aemilius Jarvis and Company, Toronto, and it was operated in conjunction with the Canada Interlake Line Ltd., Toronto. It was absorbed into Canada Steamship Lines Ltd., Montreal, later the same year.

Over the winter of 1913-14, all GERONIA's boilers were removed and replaced by new and larger watertube boilers. She went back into service in 1914 under the C.S.L. flag and carried the name b) SYRACUSE. She operated between Lewiston and Ogdensburg, with stops at way ports. Laid up in 1918, she was transferred in 1919 to the C.S.L. service from Montreal to the Saguenay River, and was renamed c) CAPE TRINITY in honor of one of the famous promontories which overlook the Saguenay.

CAPE TRINITY was brought back to Lake Ontario in 1925 for the route from Toronto to the Thousand Islands and the Bay of Quinte. She laid up at Toronto at the close of the 1928 season and never ran again. She was sold in 1937 to Frankel Bros. Ltd., a Toronto scrap dealer. She was then resold and, after leaving Toronto under tow on September 28, 1937, she was broken up at North Tonawanda, New York.

GERONIA in the Soulanges Canal

Geronia, b) Syracuse, c) CAPE TRINITY

BUILT:	1911	GRT:	2,105
	Collingwood Shipbuilding Co.,	REGISTRY NUMBER:	C. 111964
	Collingwood, Ont.	ENGINES:	Twin 22½", 18", 26", 40"
HULL NUMBER:	29		Diameter x 18" Stroke
LENGTH:	219.6		Quadruple Expansion
BREADTH:	42.0	ENGINE BUILDER:	Shipyard
DEPTH:	10.4		

SYRACUSE

CAPE TRINITY passing DALHOUSIE CITY at Toronto's Eastern Gap

CARROLLTON

MARQUETTE AND BESSEMER NO. 1

Designed as a special loading bulk freighter with railroad tracks on deck, the MARQUETTE AND BESSEMER NO. 1 (2) was built in 1903 at Buffalo, New York by the Buffalo Dry Dock Company for the Marquette & Bessemer Dock and Navigation Company to haul cargoes of coal from Conneaut, Ohio to Erieau, Ontario. Railroad cars were pushed onto the deck of the ship and unloaded through hoppers at the bottom of the cars into the hold of the vessel. At Erieau the hatches and tracks were removed and the cargo taken out with clamshell buckets. The unusual loading procedure was not as successful as planned. Even more unusual was her stern configuration. She had an angular stern designed to go into the carferry slips to facilitate the loading of cargo. She had twin thin stacks, one located on each side of her stern. So she looked like a grasshopper and was so nicknamed.

In 1921, the Lake Erie Navigation Company was her nominal owner. The vessel was converted into a conventional bulk carrier at Buffalo by the original builders, the Buffalo Dry Dock Company, (1,526 GRT) in 1928. One engine and one stack were removed at that time.

Only one serious accident occurred to the MARQUETTE AND BESSEMER NO. 1. In October 1918, she collided with the steamer MANITOU on Lake Erie about 30 miles north of Fairport, Ohio. The damage was severe but no one was hurt.

Traffic with the coal cargoes was not sufficient to keep the little boat busy, so she was used to transport cargoes to various other ports including some on the St. Lawrence River. In 1935, the Peterson Terminal Company of Saginaw, Michigan became her owners. In 1937, the Saginaw Dock and Terminal Company purchased the vessel and renamed her b) CARROLLTON. In 1942, during the crisis of World War II, the U.S. War Shipping Administration took over the vessel. The CARROLLTON saw limited war service and was returned to the Saginaw Dock and Terminal Company in 1945.

The Columbia Transportation Company took over complete control of the vessel in 1957, absorbing its affiliate, the Saginaw Dock and Terminal Company, to consolidate its operations. It was not long before the old-timer was sold in 1958 to the Marine Iron and Shipbuilding Company of Duluth, Minnesota. These owners intended to convert the vessel to carry oil in drums to the taconite processing plants on the north shore of Lake Superior. This project was abandoned and the ship lay idle in Duluth harbor until sold in 1961 to Fraser-Nelson Shipyard, Superior, Wisconsin. She was dismantled in the drydock later that same year. The bottom part of her hull was still visible at the shipyard until the summer of 1982, when it also was dismantled.

Deck view of MARQUETTE AND BESSEMER NO. 1 looking aft

CARROLLTON just above Belle Isle in the Detroit River, June 10, 1940

CARROLLTON downbound in the Detroit River June 26, 1949

CARROLLTON being burned out at Superior July 1961

a) Marquette And Bessemer No. 1
b) CARROLLTON

BUILT:	1903
	Buffalo Dry Dock Co.
	Buffalo, N.Y.
HULL NUMBER:	206
LENGTH:	241.0
BREADTH:	43.0
DEPTH:	22.4
GRT:	1,732
REGISTRY NUMBER:	US.200537
ENGINES:	Twin 17", 27½", 46"
	Diameter x 36" Stroke
	Triple Expansion
ENGINE BUILDER:	Detroit Shipbuilding
	Company
	Detroit, Michigan -
	1904

CENTURION

The one-hundreth vessel built by F. W. Wheeler at West Bay City, Michigan, was the CENTURION, a steel package freighter which was launched August 31, 1893 on shipyard account and later chartered to Mitchell and James Corrigan. In 1898, she was sold to the Hopkins Transportation Company, Cleveland Cliffs Iron Company, Managers, and in 1918, to the Mentor Transit Company, W. C. Richardson, Manager. In 1919, the vessel was converted to a bulk carrier by the Great Lakes Engineering Works at their Ashtabula, Ohio yard, and renamed b) ALEX B. UHRIG.

The Milwaukee & Western Coal Company of Sheboygan, Wisconsin purchased the vessel in 1923. This firm was an affiliate of The C. Reiss Coal Company. All wholly-owned vessels were merged into the Reiss Steamship Company in 1924. In 1927, the UHRIG was reconverted to a combination package freighter and bulk carrier by William Kennedy & Sons at Owen Sound, Ontario. The Reiss Steamship Company changed their minds again about the use of the UHRIG in 1931 when the vessel was again converted to a bulk carrier at Toledo, Ohio by the Toledo Shipbuilding Company.

In 1943, the UHRIG was traded to the U.S. Maritime Commission in exchange for new tonnage during World War II. Upon cessation of the hostilities, the vessel was laid up in Erie Bay along with some 46 other old vessels and was finally towed, in 1946, to Hamilton, Ontario, where she was scrapped.

CENTURION in Hopkins Steamship colors, upbound at the Soo

CENTURION in Cleveland Cliffs colors in 1916

ALEX B. UHRIG unloading coal

BUILT:	1893
	F. W. Wheeler & Co.,
	W. Bay City, Mich.
HULL NUMBER:	100
LENGTH:	360.0
BREADTH:	45.2
DEPTH:	21.9
GRT:	3,401
REGISTRY NUMBER:	US 126994
ENGINES:	20", 33", 54" Diameter x 44"
	Stroke, Triple Expansion
ENGINE BUILDER:	Shipyard

a) **CENTURION**

b) **Alex B. Uhrig**

ALEX B. UHRIG in Reiss colors, downbound in the Detroit River

Downbound with a load of lumber

56

CERISOLES

During the hectic efforts to build-up the warship fleets in World War I, the Canadian Car and Foundry Company, whose guiding light was the financier Francis Clergue, was awarded the contract to build 12 steel trawler minesweepers for the French Navy. Among these were the CERISOLES, launched on September 25, 1918, and the INKERMAN, launched on October 10, 1918, which were ready to leave their builders yard at Fort William, Ontario (now called Thunder Bay), both having been completed November 21, 1918. Each vessel was armed with a 100 mm cannon on the forward deck and one on the stern. The French Navy crew and officers went aboard the new vessels and prepared to sail for France. Captain LeClerc, on board the third vessel, the SEBASTOPOL, was in charge of the journey to Boston, Massachusetts.

The gales of November swept across Lake Superior as the vessels left Fort William bound for the locks at Sault Ste. Marie on November 23, 1918. Two of them were never heard from again. Lake Superior had swallowed them up even as it had so many vessels before their time and since.

The ships had become separated during the storm and were presumed still afloat when the SEBASTOPOL reached the Soo on November 26. Rescue efforts began immediately by searchers on the south shore by the U.S. Coast Guard and on the north shore by Captain LeClerc in the tug FRANK WESTON. They found nothing! 76 officers and men of the French Navy and their two Canadian pilots had vanished.

According to the official statement made by Capt. LeClerc, all three vessels had sailed southward from Port Arthur toward the Keweenaw Peninsula and eastward to Bete Grise Bay, where LeClerc last observed CERISOLES and INKERMAN.

As a result of the loss of the two ships, the ten surviving trawlers were disarmed at Boston before sailing for Europe because their heavy armament caused stability problems. Perhaps the heavy 100 mm cannon was to blame for the loss, but sailors on the lakes theorized that the vessels might have struck shoals which ripped out their bottoms.

NAVARIN (sister to the CERISOLES) leaving for overseas

BUILT:	1918 Canadian Car & Foundry Co., Fort William, Ont.
HULL NUMBER:	9
LENGTH:	135.6
BREADTH:	26.2
DEPTH:	12.7
GRT:	345
ENGINES:	13", 20", Diameter x 24" Stroke Triple Expansion
ENGINE BUILDER:	Nordberg Manufacturing Company Milwaukee, Wis.

CHAMPION

CHAMPION at her dock at Duluth

In the days of sailing ships, the Detroit and St. Clair Rivers sustained a whole flotilla of powerful tugs, most of them big double-deckers fitted for the open Great Lakes as well as the rivers. They hauled enormous log rafts or long strings of schooners as the occasion required. None was better known than the old CHAMPION.

This handsome ship was built in 1868 for a syndicate of Detroit vessel men (Merrick & Company), including her famous builders, Campbell and Owen (later the Detroit Dry Dock Co.), John Edwards, tugman Thomas Murphy, machinist William Cowie, and boilermakers Desotelle & Hutton. Her design employed all of the advantages which could be devised by the experienced partners, and she was also one of the largest vessels of her class and one of the most powerful. The ship was made doubly famous when she was pictured by Detroit area artist Seth Whipple towing eight big schooners in 1869 or 1870 . . . and hundreds of lithographs were reproduced from the original painting to become modern-day collectors' item. The schooners in this famous illustration were the WELLS BURT, MICHIGAN, ELIZABETH A. NICHOLSON, JAMES F. JOY, FRANCIS PALMS, SWEETHEART, SUNNYSIDE, and EMMA L. COYNE.

CHAMPION passed into the hands of the N. N. Strong interests in 1871. From 1883 to 1884, she was in the hands of Thomas Ditts, the executor of the Strong Estate. In 1884, she went to the Grummond Tug Line, also of Detroit. Captain C. E. Benham, the wrecking master of Cleveland, Ohio, used the CHAMPION when he was involved in the salvage operations of the ROBERT WALLACE and barge DAVID WALLACE at Marquette, Michigan in 1886.

On March 26, 1896, S. B. Grummond sold the tug to Harris W. Baker and C. A. Chamberlain of Detroit who used her in wrecking operations and towing the barges TYCOON and MIKADO on Lake Erie. In 1899, her cabins were raised 18" and her engine was rebuilt to 26" and 44" x 36" stroke. Harris W. Baker of Detroit took over her control completely in 1902.

On September 15, 1903 she burned to the waterline while at anchor at Put-in-Bay, Ohio. No one was injured but the vessel was a total loss. The hull was raised in 1904 by Baker, but it was disposed of as useless. The proud old CHAMPION was as beautiful at the time of her fire as she was the day she was launched.

S. A. Whipple lithograph of the CHAMPION in 1878 entering the Detroit River

BUILT:	1868	*DEPTH:*	10.7
	Campbell & Owen,	*GRT:*	263
	Detroit, Mich.	*REGISTRY NUMBER:*	US 5720
HULL NUMBER:	5	*ENGINES:*	26", 26" Diameter x 33" Stroke
LENGTH:	134.6		Two Cylinder High Pressure
BREADTH:	21.4	*ENGINE BUILDER:*	Dry Dock Engine Works
			Detroit, Michigan

CHAMPION afire September 15, 1903 at Put-in-Bay, Ohio

CHEMUNG

The steel package freighter CHEMUNG was launched at Buffalo, New York on Wednesday, February 29, 1888, by the Union Dry Dock Company for the Union Steamboat Company, which employed her in connection with the Erie Railroad Lake Line to the various ports serviced by the railroad.

Along with the OWEGO, the CHEMUNG was the fastest freight vessel on the lakes for almost a decade. On June 30, 1896 the Union Steamboat Company was merged into the Erie Railroad Company. In 1898 she was rebuilt at Buffalo to 14'6" depth. No gross tonnage change was recorded.

In 1913, the CHEMUNG was given new boilers and draft system together with engine modifications, new propeller, new houses throughout and complete new electric instal-lation. At this time, she was renamed b) GEORGE F. BROWNELL.

When the railroads were divested of their shipping fleets by the Panama Canal Act in 1915, the BROWNELL was sold to the Staten Island Shipbuilding Company who took her to the coast and rebuilt her for ocean service to 326.7 x 41.2 x 23.0; 3,061 gross tons, and then sold her to the Harby Steamship Company who again renamed her c) CHEMUNG.

On November 26, 1916, she was sunk by gunfire and torpedo by an Austrian submarine off Cabo de Gata, Spain in the Mediterrean Sea at 36°37', N 1°35' W. No lives were lost. She was on a voyage from New York, N.Y. to Genoa, Italy at the time.

CHEMUNG in Erie colors, downbound in the St. Clair River

a) CHEMUNG, b) George F. Brownell, c) CHEMUNG

GEORGE F. BROWNELL

BUILT:	1888
	Union Dry Dock Co.,
	Buffalo, N.Y.
HULL NUMBER:	44
LENGTH:	325.7
BREADTH:	41.2
DEPTH:	14.8
GRT:	2,615
REGISTRY NUMBER:	US.126495
ENGINES:	28", 42½",
	72" Diameter
	x 54" Stroke,
	Triple Expansion
ENGINE BUILDER:	Quintard Iron Works
	New York, New York

CHICORA

CHICORA entering Benton Harbor

The wooden passenger and freight steamer CHICORA was launched at Detroit, Michigan on June 25, 1892 by the Detroit Drydock Company for the Graham and Morton Transportation Company. Most of the G & M steamers had been sidewheelers, but this smart vessel, a propeller, would make close to 16 knots carrying passengers to Michigan ports and fruit and vegetables back to Chicago, Illinois and Milwaukee, Wisconsin.

Late in December 1894, Milwaukee shippers asked that the CHICORA be pressed into service again, after the vessel had already been laid up, to carry one more cargo of bagged flour out of Milwaukee to Benton Harbor, Michigan. Captain Stines readied his vessel and sailed for Milwaukee on the 19th of January, 1895.

A freak winter storm was brewing when the vessel cleared Milwaukee about 5 A.M. on January 21st. The barometer had been falling steadily all the previous day, but the captain and his crew were anxious to complete the trip and return to their homes. Pounded by ice and tossed like a cork by the great waves, the CHICORA undoubtedly fought the storm for hours that afternoon and lost. The CHICORA was never heard from again. She carried 23 crewmen and one passenger to their deaths somewhere in icy Lake Michigan. Rescue crews spent days out in the lake but to no avail.

Captain Henry E. Stines of the Goodrich steamer, CITY OF LUDINGTON, spent two days looking for his brother Edward on the CHICORA after the storm, but found no trace of the vessel or its crew. All that came ashore later that year were a few bags of flour, part of the cargo of the ill-fated CHICORA, some of the bulwarks with the ship's name and the ship's mast which washed ashore near Saugatuck, Michigan. The mast now stands at Glenn, Michigan, a sad reminder of the proud CHICORA, the first G & M vessel ever to be lost in the fleet's many years of service.

BUILT:	1892
	Detroit Dry Dock Co.,
	Detroit, Mich.
HULL NUMBER:	111
LENGTH:	198.5
BREADTH:	35.0
DEPTH:	13.6
GRT:	1,122
REGISTRY NUMBER:	US.126902
ENGINES:	20", 33", 54" Diameter x 42"
	Stroke, Triple Expansion
ENGINE BUILDER:	Dry Dock Engine Works
	Detroit, Michigan

CHIEFTAIN

One of the longest wooden ships ever built on the Lakes, the CHIEFTAIN was launched from James Davidson's yard at Bay City, Michigan on the 11th of October in 1902. James Davidson built CHIEFTAIN for his own steamship company and used her and her near sister MONTEZUMA in the lumber trade for many years.

The CHIEFTAIN was involved in a few accidents in her lifetime. On October 23, 1906, she collided with the steamer TROY on Lake Superior and ran aground at Portage Entry near Houghton, Michigan. There was a large gash in her bow which extended down to the waterline. The CHIEFTAIN was towed to Marquette, Michigan on October 30th for repairs and narrowly escaped foundering while enroute.

On September 18, 1909, she collided with the steamer LACKAWANNA at Point Edward, Ontario. The steamer's wheel chains had parted and she floated down stream broadside. The CHIEFTAIN, which was in tow of the steamer SHENANDOAH, hit the LACKAWANNA on her starboard side abreast of No. 3 gangway, breaking a number of plates. The LACKAWANNA was caught by the tug REID and towed to shallow water where she sank. Damage to the CHIEFTAIN was heavy, but she did not sink.

In 1928, both the CHIEFTAIN and MONTEZUMA were laid up at Bay City. The lumber trade had dwindled down to almost nothing, the forests around the lakes having been almost completely denuded. In June of 1941, the CHIEFTAIN was purchased by the W.J. Meagher Construction Company to be used as part of a dock. In May of 1942, she was pumped-out and towed up the Saginaw River to the foot of 38th Street in Bay City and allowed to sink to the bottom. The CHIEFTAIN continued to rest quietly through the years, while children explored her hull and pigeons found her a handy place to rest.

On October 1, 1953, the rotting hull of the once proud wooden schooner was destroyed by a fire of "undetermined" origin. For almost eight hours the flames slowly devoured the vessel. Firemen were called to the scene shortly after 4:30 P.M. only to find the CHIEFTAIN too far offshore to fight the fire.

Hurried phone calls soon brought the Meagher tug, MIKIE, to the scene. The fire department's portable pump was rushed aboard along with four firemen, and two lines were pouring water on the burning hulk within a matter of minutes. Shortly before midnight, the firemen left the smoldering hulk. The final ignominy for the once longest wooden vessel on the lakes came in the Fire Chief's estimate of damages: "It wasn't worth a nickel, except for some possible salvage from iron, so our records will carry no loss at all. It just wasn't worth anything."

CHIEFTAIN, the hundredth ship built by Davidson. Workers pose for their picture.

CHIEFTAIN upbound at the Soo in 1910

BUILT:	1902
	James Davidson, W. Bay City, Mich.
HULL NUMBER:	100
LENGTH:	342.0
BREADTH:	46.0
DEPTH:	21.6
GRT:	2,704
REGISTRY NUMBER:	US.127703

CHIEFTAIN at Bay City summer of 1953

T. S. CHRISTIE

The T. S. CHRISTIE was a wooden steambarge built in 1885 for the Bay City & Cleveland Transportation Company of Detroit, one of the earliest of the Great Lakes' lumber fleets. As was common in her day, she was given the second-hand machinery from the earlier (1866) hooker B. W. JENNESS, although the engine was much improved when it was put into the newer ship.

The CHRISTIE was built as a typical well-decked lumber carrier, but she was given a second deck in 1886 to suit her for the grain trade, which proved more remunerative at the time than the lumber trade (769 gross tons). She served a variety of owners during the next 15 years, including Cunningham et al, Detroit (1889); P. Peterson, Green Bay (1890); P. Larson et al, Chicago (1902); and George Engelking of the same place. During the 90's she often towed the barges ROSA SONSMITH and the MATTIE C.

BELL in the grain, ore and lumber trades, largely from Lake Michigan ports. In 1902 the ship was cut down to a lumber hooker again (517 gross tons), and in 1907 she became a part of the Herman H. Hettler Lumber Company fleet, based at Chicago. Under the Hettler houseflag, she usually towed the barge INTERLAKEN.

In 1932, the T. S. CHRISTIE was purchased by the Marinette Transportation Company of Marinette, Wisconsin. With a cargo of 350 cords of pulpwood from Marinette to lower Lake Michigan ports, and while trying to make the harbor at Manistee, the vessel was driven ashore on November 8, 1933, stranded in the heavy seas and pounded to pieces four miles northeast of the harbor. Her crew of 12 made it to shore safely and watched the waves dash the 48-year-old ship onto the beach.

T. S CHRISTIE laid up with many other vessels at Duluth

BUILT:	1885	GRT:	533
	F. W. Wheeler & Co.,	REGISTRY NUMBER:	US.145402
	W. Bay City, Mich.	ENGINES:	19", 34" Diameter x 30" Stroke
HULL NUMBER:	22		Steeple Compound
LENGTH:	160.0	ENGINE BUILDER:	Christie & DeGraff
BREADTH:	30.3		Detroit, Michigan, 1866
DEPTH:	12.0		Rebuilt in 1884

T. S. CHRISTIE with a deckload of lumber

On the beach near Manistee November 8, 1933

CITY OF CLEVELAND III

The steel sidewheel passenger boat CITY OF CLEVE-LAND was launched on the 5th of January, 1907 at the Wyandotte, Michigan yard of the Detroit Shipbuilding Company for the Detroit and Cleveland Steam Navigation Company. Designed by Frank E. Kirby, the renowned ship designer, the stately vessel was destined for a fiery birth and death.

Around 4:30 A.M. on the 13th of May, 1907 a fire broke out aboard the nearly completed "largest passenger steamer on lake, river or sound" as she lay in the Orleans slip of the Detroit Shipbuilding Company. Fireboats and land engines were quickly called but the fire raged uncontrolled through the beautiful mahogany and walnut furnishings. Soon, in less than two hours, flames ate through the newly varnished cabins and reduced the ship to a blackened hulk from stem to stern. The superstructure had to be rebuilt at a cost of $1.25 million and the ship was not ready until the start of the 1908 season.

In 1912 the Roman numeral III was added to the name of the palatial steamer and she sailed her usual route between Detroit and Cleveland, Ohio.

On June 26, 1950, disaster struck the vessel again, this time it was a collision in fog. Downbound on foggy Lake Huron, on a chartered cruise, the CITY OF CLEVE-LAND III was five miles off Harbor Beach, Michigan. Looming up suddenly out of the mist, the Norwegian freighter RAVNEFJELL angled into the port side of the "C-3." The upper rail was ripped off, cabins were smashed and a gaping hole was torn in the upper lounge. Five passengers were killed and a dozen other passengers and crew members were injured. Yet the impact was not great enough to wake some cruisers sleeping in other parts of the ship. Both ships managed to make port but this was the end of the palatial passenger vessel.

Nothing went right for the old ship after that. Tied at Windsor, Ontario, she was swept by fire on October 20, 1954. Towed to Toledo, Ohio, she sank when vandals boarded her and opened the seacocks. The vessel, minus her superstructure, was taken to Buffalo where she was reduced to scrap in 1956. She began and ended her career in a blaze.

CITY OF CLEVELAND entering Cleveland harbor, tug WILLIAM KENNEDY assisting

CITY OF CLEVELAND III bound for Detroit

BUILT:	1907
	Detroit Shipbuilding Co.,
	Wyandotte, Mich.
HULL NUMBER:	168
LENGTH:	390.0
BREADTH:	54.2
DEPTH:	22.3
GRT:	4,568
REGISTRY NUMBER:	US. 204080
ENGINES:	54", 82", 82" Diameter x 96"
	Stroke, Inclined Compound
ENGINE BUILDER:	Shipyard

Upbound in the St. Clair River at Marine City

Entering Midland, Ontario harbor

Heading for Detroit after the collision

Details of the damage to the ship's port side

CITY OF GENOA

CITY OF GENOA downbound in the St. Clair River

BUILT:
1892
James Davidson,
W. Bay City,
Mich.
HULL NUMBER:
49
LENGTH:
301.0
BREADTH:
42.5
DEPTH:
20.1
GRT:
2,109
REGISTRY NUMBER:
US.126897
ENGINES:
20", 33", 54"
Diameter x 42"
Stroke, Triple
expansion
ENGINE BUILDER:
Dry Dock
Engine Works
Detroit,
Michigan

Sunk August 26, 1911

On July 27, 1892 James Davidson launched a new wooden bulk carrier from his yard in West Bay City, Michigan for his own company to haul grain and ore. In the next few years this vessel and the others of his fleet would earn him more dollars to keep his shipyard busy building even more wooden freighters and barges when most other shipbuilders were turning to steel to fabricate their new ships. In 1894, Davidson sold the CITY OF GENOA to J. C. Gilchrist for his Gilchrist Transportation Company. In 1901, her upper works burned and she was completely repaired at Detroit, Michigan by the Detroit Shipbuilding Company. The vessel was deepened to 22.9 feet and her gross tonnage increased to 2,446.

At daybreak on August 26, 1911, the downbound ore-carrying, steel steamer W. H. GILBERT rammed the CITY OF GENOA just 100 feet from the Canadian shore at Sarnia, Ontario, just below where the Blue Water Bridge over the St. Clair River rapids now stands. The CITY OF GENOA, carrying 125,000 bushels of wheat and corn, was waiting for the fog that enshrouded the river and lower Lake Huron to lift when she was struck on her port bow,

gouging a large hole in it. The wooden steamer went down immediately. The GILBERT was able to turn around and rescue its crew.

The CITY OF GENOA lay in the river, with just her wheel house and stack showing, for several weeks before the Reid Wrecking Company could put a cofferdam around her to pump her out. When she finally began to emerge from the depths on September 20, 1911, her cargo of water-soaked grain had already begun to ferment. By the time the vessel was moved downstream to the wrecking company's dock and the grain unloaded and spread out to dry, the variable winds carried the extremely unpleasant (or pleasant depending on the person) odors of fermenting grain over Sarnia and Port Huron, Michigan. The furor in the press over this "odor" was unprecedented, and intoxicating. Repercussions felt in these earlier days were of a much different kind compared to those of recent shipwrecks where concern has been over oil pollution. However, the collision of the GILBERT (which was soon repaired and put back into service) and the CITY OF GENOA (which was found to be irrepairable) was not soon forgotten by the residents of Port Huron and Sarnia. The engines and boilers of the GENOA were removed, and she reportedly burned at the dock on October 9, 1915. Later the hull was taken out into Lake Huron and scuttled. The "smell" of the fermented grain did remain around the Blue Water cities for some time, if even only in the memory of great imbibers.

CITY OF GRAND RAPIDS OF 1879

The wooden passenger steamer CITY OF GRAND RAPIDS was built at Grand Haven, Michigan by Duncan Robertson and was launched on April 19, 1879, for Hannah, Lay & Co., of Traverse City, Michigan. She appears to have spent the first fourteen seasons of her existence plying quietly and peacefully between Traverse City and Mackinac Island, Michigan with stops at intermediate ports.

She spent the seasons of 1893, 1894 and 1895, under the ownership of Oscar E. Wilbur, of Charlevoix, running between that port, Marquette and Grand Marais, Michigan.

In the spring of 1897, she was sold to the South Haven and Chicago Transportation Co., a company formed to compete with the H. W. Williams Transportation line between those two ports. She ran between South Haven, Michigan and Chicago, Illinois the seasons of 1897 and 1898, and was then rebuilt to 399 gross tons. In the spring of 1899, it was rumored she would be chartered by the O'Connor Dock Co., of Chicago, to run St. Joseph to Chicago, but this fell through, and she lay idle at South Haven most of the summer until early August, when she was hastily fitted out for the excursion business between South Haven and Milwaukee, Wisconsin. Her first trip was on August 5, with 200 passengers. Some distance out she was discovered to be leaking badly. She very nearly foundered before she could be turned around to regain the safety of South Haven. The following March, she was sold to the Barry Brothers, of Chicago, who used her between Chicago and Waukegan, Illinois.

On July 9, 1903 the little steamer was purchased by Daniel F. Toomey of Dunkirk, New York to run the excursion business in and around Buffalo, New York. The Cleveland, Rondeau and Port Stanley Navigation Company purchased the vessel on April 7, 1905, with great intentions of operating her from Cleveland, Ohio to Rondeau (a park on the Canadian side of Lake Erie) and Port Stanley, Ontario nearby. This adventure also did not pan out and the CITY OF GRAND RAPIDS was once again sold on May 25, 1907, to William G. Fitzpatrick of Detroit, Michigan. He in turn sold her to Ontario parties of Gillies and Rutherford on September 30, 1907 (C. 116922).

The CITY OF GRAND RAPIDS was to run between the many islands of Georgian Bay, with Owen Sound her main port. On October 29, 1907 while bound from Wiarton, Ontario to Providence Bay, the vessel stopped at Tobermory overnight. There she was set afire by vandals and burned to the water's edge. The vessel was cut loose and drifted into Big Tobermory Bay where she grounded and sank.

A very early view of the CITY OF GRAND RAPIDS

BUILT:	1879
	Duncan Robertson,
	Grand Haven, Mich.
LENGTH:	125.6
BREADTH:	26.4
DEPTH:	9.3
GRT:	335
REGISTRY NUMBER:	US.125743
ENGINES:	30" Diameter x 30" Stroke
	High Pressure Non-Condensing
ENGINE BUILDER:	Ottawa Iron Works
	Ferrysburg, Michigan

CITY OF GRAND RAPIDS at Owen Sound, late in her career

COLLINGWOOD

COLLINGWOOD in Farrar Transportation colors

The steel bulk freighter COLLINGWOOD was launched by the Collingwood Shipbuilding Company on October 5, 1907 for the Farrar Transportation Company. This economical vessel was used in the grain trade for many years from the Lakehead cities of Port Arthur and Fort William, Ontario. When launched she had 3 steel masts with booms and rigging for handling cargo. Later, these were removed. Even though her career was not unsullied, the steamer lived a long life.

Among the incidents that befell her were these: In 1909 she stranded at Michipicoten Harbor. On August 24, 1909 she was rammed amidships by the steamer GEORGE L. CRAIG on the Detroit River. On October 2, 1909 she was raised and later repaired at Detroit, Michigan. On April 23, 1916 she again stranded, this time on Whitefish Bay, Lake Superior. From this accident she was released on the 25th of the same month. On September 10, 1918, the COLLINGWOOD was purchased by the Canada Steamship Lines

— a great "incident" because she came under progressive and modern ownership.

Her fortunes seemed to be better under CSL. On May 1, 1940 she rescued 16 of the 17 crewmen of the steamer ARLINGTON which had foundered near Superior Shoals on Lake Superior.

In 1950, the COLLINGWOOD was converted to a package freighter, 4545 gross tons, to carry, among other things, Heinz's 57 varieties up the lakes. In 1966, she was laid up at Kingston, Ontario because of slow times. She was reactivated during the 1967 season but then permanently retired at the end of that year.

Sold for scrap in 1968, to Steel Factors, she was towed from Kingston to Quebec on September 17, 1968 by the tugs GRAEME STEWART and JAMES BATTLE. With the steamer HAGARTY, she arrived at Santander, Spain on October 28, 1968 to be reduced to scrap.

BUILT:	1907
	Collingwood Shipbuilding Co.,
	Collingwood, Ont.
HULL NUMBER:	17
LENGTH:	386.0
BREADTH:	50.0

DEPTH:	23.0
GRT:	4,529
REGISTRY NUMBER:	C.117089
ENGINES:	21", 33½", 57" Diameter x 42"
	Stroke, Triple Expansion
ENGINE BUILDER:	Shipyard

COLLINGWOOD as a bulk freighter downbound at Mission Point

COLLINGWOOD as a package freighter downbound in Lake Huron

CHESTER A. CONGDON

The steel bulk freighter SALT LAKE CITY was built by the Chicago Shipbuilding Company in 1907, for the Holmes Steamship Company, managed by W. A. and A. H. Hawgood, mainly for the iron ore and grain trade. The Acme Transit Company took over her ownership a few years later. On February 2, 1912, the vessel was sold to the Tomlinson Fleet, operated by G. A. Tomlinson and received her second name: b) CHESTER A. CONGDON.

The CONGDON, with a cargo of 390,154 bushels of wheat, left Fort William, Ontario at 2:28 a.m. on November 6, 1918, and proceeded a little way outside Thunder Cape. Encountering a southwest gale and heavy sea, she turned at 4 a.m. and ran back seven or eight miles and went to anchor. The wind having subsided, the voyage was resumed at 10:15 a.m. There was some sea running when the steamer got outside Thunder Cape again and the weather shut in with a heavy fog. When passing Thunder Cape at 10:40 a.m., a course was set for Passage Island, and the steamer was put on a speed of nine miles per hour, it being the Captain's intention, if it continued foggy, to run 2½ hours and then stop. The ship's officers did not hear the Passage Island fog signal, and at 1:00 p.m. the ship fetched up on the southerly reef of Canoe Island.

Captain Charles J. Autterson said after the accident, "We were running under slow speed, at about nine miles an hour and I figured on stopping on account of the fog until we could locate something. Then at eight minutes after one in the afternoon, she fetched up-grounded."

Capt. Autterson despatched Second Mate Schwab to Port Arthur aboard a fishing vessel from Isle Royale, but engine problems beset them and it took several hours to make the distance. Once the news arrived, local wreckers were quick to respond. Tug A. B. CONMEE and wrecking barge EMPIRE were sent to the scene and began salvaging about 30,000 bushels of wheat from the forward end. Salvors were literally blown off the wreck on November 8 in 55 mph winds. When they returned on the 10th, the CONGDON's back was broken below number 6 hatch. Some 50,000 additional bushels of wheat were salvaged before the vessel was declared a total loss.

James Playfair of Midland, Ontario purchased the CONGDON from the underwriters hoping to make a triumphant salvage of the eleven-year-old vessel. When the salvors arrived the following Spring, however, the CHESTER A. CONGDON was broken in two sections lying on either side of the reef in excess of 100 feet of water. No salvage was attempted.

Today the CHESTER A. CONGDON is an underwater archeological site under the protection of the National Park Service at Isle Royale which prohibits any form of salvage whatsoever on the vessel, its fittings, or contents. Recreational scuba diving is common on the CONGDON and free permits are available at any island ranger station.

SALT LAKE CITY upbound at the Soo in 1907

Salt Lake City,   b) **CHESTER A. CONGDON**

BUILT:	1907
	Chicago Shipbuilding Co., Chicago, Ill.
HULL NUMBER:	74
LENGTH:	532.0
BREADTH:	56.2
DEPTH:	26.5
GRT:	6,530
REGISTRY NUMBER:	US.204526
ENGINES:	23½", 38", 63" Diameter x 42" Stroke
	Triple Expansion
ENGINE BUILDER:	American Shipbuilding Company, Cleveland, Ohio

CHESTER A. CONGDON in 1915

Wreck of the CONGDON, James Playfair and some of his crew aboard

OMAR D. CONGER

OMAR D. CONGER in her early years as a cross-river ferry

Port Huron, Michigan residents past and present have many memories of this wooden passenger ferry which was launched May 3, 1882 at the yard of George Hardison on the Black River for D. N. Runnels and Captain Moffat who owned the cross-river ferry line to Sarnia, Ontario. The reason the little ferryboat is so well remembered is that in some way she affected the lives of so many people during the forty years of her existence.

As well as a cross-river ferry, the CONGER was frequently used as an excursion boat to such events as ship launchings both in Sarnia and Port Huron, occasional summer voyages to Wallaceburg, Ontario and into the St. Clair Flats, and moonlights in the cool breezes of lower Lake Huron. Her daily voyages to Sarnia were often spiked by "everyday" rescues of "Sunday Sailors" whose little craft were swamped by passing larger vessels, or daring rescues of shipwrecked men from the frequent collisions occurring in the upper St. Clair River Rapids. In 1891, the CONGER became a member of the Port Huron and Sarnia Ferry Company (a revised and restructured company).

After a fire which "burned and charred and entirely destroyed" her upper works at midnight, Saturday June 22, 1901, the little vessel was entirely rebuilt. She received new upper cabins, decks and equipment. A new engine, a fore and aft compound 14" and 30" diameter x 28" stroke, built by S. F. Hodge (#293) was installed about this time also but is not recorded in the insurance books as far as we can determine.

On the afternoon of March 26, 1922, at approximately 2:22 P.M., while her captain was returning to his ship docked at her terminal berth on Black River, being readied for her 3 P.M. sailing for Sarnia, the city of Port Huron was rocked by a violent explosion that shook houses and sent people scurrying about in wonderment of the cause.

News that the boiler of the OMAR D. CONGER had exploded swept through the peaceful Sunday afternoon populace. Details soon were learned. Four members of her crew, preparing the vessel for sailing, the Chief Engineer, a fireman and two deck hands had been killed. The explosion not only sank and completely devastated the vessel but had hurled a 125 pound boiler valve through the roof of a store, sent a 200 pound radiator crashing into a funeral parlor and blew parts of the boiler into a nearby house, completely smashing it to rubble.

A lifeboat davit pierced the corner of a brick building, entering one side and protruding out the other like a curved sail needle, so violent was the explosion later blamed on a lack of water in the boiler.

The nearby ferry HIAWATHA, lying at her dock, was badly damaged to the stern. The other ferry, CITY OF CHEBOYGAN, was rocked as it entered the Black River with 100 passengers who panicked when debris shot out from the explosion. Windows were shattered in the nearby business district. Only "chance" and "split timing" had saved scores more from being killed or injured. That tragic explosion of the OMAR D. CONGER is still remembered by many citizens of Port Huron and Sarnia and often recalled by the local historians and the press.

76

OMAR D. CONGER with an excursion crowd aboard

BUILT:	1882	*GRT:*	199
	George Hardison,	*REGISTRY NUMBER:*	US.155055
	Port Huron, Mich.	*ENGINES:*	24½" Diameter x 30" Stroke
LENGTH:	92.2		High Pressure Non-Condensing
BREADTH:	26.0	*ENGINE BUILDER:*	Cuyahoga Furnace Company
DEPTH:	10.6		Cleveland, Ohio

After the explosion

WILLIAM E. COREY

During the early years of the twentieth century, lake shipyards were able to increase greatly the size of the steel hulls that could be built. When the Chicago Shipbuilding Company turned out WILLIAM E. COREY in 1905, she was the largest vessel on the Great Lakes, although she was soon surpassed in size by other steamers. The COREY was built for the Pittsburgh Steamship Company, the lake shipping subsidiary of the United States Steel Corporation. It was the flagship of this fleet when it entered service. There were four ships in her class, but her full forecastle and slightly larger pilothouse always made her readily distinguishable from her near-sisterships, HENRY C. FRICK, ELBERT H. GARY and GEORGE W. PERKINS.

WILLIAM E. COREY sailed from Chicago on her maiden voyage on August 12, 1905, bound for Duluth. On November 28, 1905, she ran aground on Gull Island Shoal in the Apostle Islands of western Lake Superior. She was so hard aground that it took the efforts of the steamers MANOLA, MARINA, SIR WILLIAM SIEMENS and DOUGLASS HOUGHTON, as well as the tugs EDNA G.

and GLADIATOR to free her. She was not refloated until December 10, 1905.

Reboilered in 1937, WILLIAM E. COREY served the Pittsburgh fleet until she was sold in 1963, to Upper Lakes Shipping Ltd., Toronto. Renamed b) RIDGETOWN (C. 305991), she operated until the close of the 1969 season. She arrived at Toronto on November 17, 1969, with storage grain, and was then laid up.

Sold in May 1970, to the Canadian Dredge and Dock Company Ltd., Toronto, she was taken to Nanticoke, Ontario on the north shore of Lake Erie, where she joined several other superannuated steamers as part of a temporary construction breakwater. Later raised from the muddy bottom, she was towed back into Toronto harbor on September 5, 1973. In 1974, she was loaded with stone and sunk as a breakwater at the entrance to Port Credit harbor (on the north shore of Lake Ontario, just west of Toronto). She still lies there, looking much as she did during her years of operation in Upper Lakes Shipping colors.

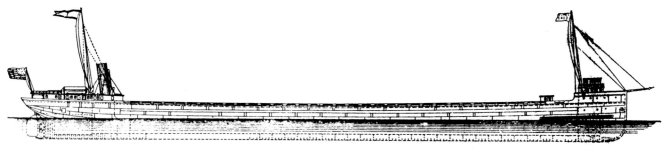

WILLIAM E. COREY — outboard profile

The Launch — the seven masts were used to keep the vessel from capsizing

78

WILLIAM E. COREY upbound at Mission Point

WILLIAM E. COREY upbound light June 1, 1960

BUILT:	1905
	Chicago Shipbuilding Co., Chicago, Ill.
HULL NUMBER:	67
LENGTH:	557.8
BREADTH:	56.0
DEPTH:	26.5
GRT:	6,363
REGISTRY NUMBER:	US.202296
ENGINES:	24", 39-1/8", 65-1/8" Diameter x 42" Stoke
	Triple Expansion
ENGINE BUILDER:	American Shipbuilding Co.
	Cleveland, Ohio

WILLIAM E. COREY,
b) **Ridgetown**

RIDGETOWN upbound in the St. Mary's River

CORONA

On July 15, 1895, the Niagara Navigation Company's passenger steamer CIBOLA burned at Lewiston, New York, where she was moored for the night. It was important that CIBOLA be replaced as soon as possible, and the owner quickly contracted with the Bertram Engine and Shipbuilding Company Ltd., Toronto, for the construction of a new day steamer for the Niagara Route.

The new vessel, named CORONA, was designed by the noted marine architect Arendt Angstrom. The steel-hulled side-wheeler was launched on May 25, 1896, and was christened by Miss Mildred Cumberland and Miss Clara Foy, daughters of Niagara Navigation Company executives.

CORONA was powered by the inclined compound engine which had been built in 1887 at Greenock, Scotland, for CIBOLA. After the fire of 1895, it was removed from the wreck and was reconditioned by Bertram's before being installed in CORONA. It served her well!

CORONA was completed by the Bertram yard during 1896, and, at the opening of the 1897 sailing season, she entered the Niagara Navigation Company's service between Toronto and the ports of the Niagara River. She was one of the most handsome passenger vessels ever to operate on

Lake Ontario, and was the means whereby many Toronto residents found respite on the lake from the summer heat of the city. She ran the route in the company of the veteran CHICORA, the big paddler CHIPPEWA, and, latterly, the propellor CAYUGA.

Early in 1913, control of Niagara Navigation was acquired by the Richelieu and Ontario Navigation Company Ltd., Montreal. Later the same year, the R & O was, itself, swallowed up in the formation of Canada Steamship Lines Ltd., Montreal.

CORONA continued on the Niagara route until the early 1920s, when she spent some time on the run between Toronto and Hamilton. By 1924, she had returned to the Niagara service. She last operated in 1929, and was then laid up in the Toronto Ship Channel, where she remained for eight years.

In 1937, along with many other inactive C.S.L. steamers, CORONA was sold for scrapping. She was purchased by Frankel Bros. Ltd., a Toronto scrap dealer, who resold her to Summer and Company, Buffalo. Towed from Toronto on September 26, 1937, she was taken up the Welland Canal and over to Buffalo where she was dismantled.

CORONA in Niagara Navigation colors

BUILT:	1896	*GRT:*	1,274
	Bertram Engine & Shipbuilding	*REGISTRY NUMBER:*	C. 103673
	Co., Ltd.,	*ENGINES:*	57", 85" Diameter x 66" Stroke
	Toronto, Ont.		Inclined Compound originally
LENGTH:	270.3		fitted in CIBOLA
BREADTH:	32.4	*ENGINE BUILDER:*	Rankin, Blackmore & Co.
DEPTH:	12.5		Greenock, Scotland

CORONA leaving her dock in Toronto

CORONA in CSL colors

JOHN B.COWLE (1)

JOHN B. COWLE being launched, October 2, 1902

JOHN B. COWLE unloading iron ore

The steel bulk freighter JOHN B. COWLE was launched on October 2, 1902 from the Jenks Shipbuilding Company yard on the Black River at Port Huron, Michigan for the Cowle Transit Company, of Fairport, Ohio, a subsidiary of the United States Transportation Company whose president was W. W. Brown of Cleveland, Ohio.

Tragedy struck near Marysville, Michigan early on the morning of May 31, 1906. The COWLE, downbound for Huron, Ohio, collided with the Canadian steamer ERIN, towing the barge F. L. DANFORTH, upbound with coal from Cleveland, Ohio to Algoma Mills, Ontario.

The vessels had exchanged whistle signals when the COWLE suddenly veered and struck the ERIN aft of her forward rigging and nearly cut her in two. The ERIN sank immediately "like a cannon ball", one eye-witness said, trapping five crewmen in the sunken vessel. The men of the F. L. DANFORTH with the help of some fishermen rescued the other nine members of the crew, including the captain, who were clinging to floating parts of the cabin. The COWLE sustained some damage and was soon back in service. The ERIN was abandoned.

At 5:31 A.M. on July 12, 1909, the COWLE was again involved in a tragic collision. This time it was her own end.

In a very thick fog, the COWLE, downbound with iron ore for Lake Erie ports, was struck broadside by the steamer ISAAC M. SCOTT on her maiden voyage to the head of the lakes. The SCOTT had just passed Whitefish Point on Lake Superior, upbound light, and straightened out her course up the lake, when suddenly the JOHN B. COWLE loomed up through the fog only a few feet away. The SCOTT crashed into the side of the heavily laden COWLE. Her bow penetrated twenty feet into the COWLE. Tons of water rushed into the giant hole and in three minutes the COWLE had settled to the bottom. Immediately after the collision, a line was thrown from the deck of the SCOTT to the COWLE, and three members of the crew were rescued out of the water by the SCOTT and the following upbound vessel, FRANK H. GOODYEAR. Fourteen lost their lives in the sinking. Captain Wallace Rogers, his son Alvah (15) and his brother Byron were among those rescued. The SCOTT upbound light was heavily damaged but succeeded in making port. The COWLE, once the pride of Port Huron shipbuilders, lies on the sandy bottom of Lake Superior having been recently "rediscovered" by avid skin divers who have photographed the wreck.

BUILT: 1902
Jenks Shipbuilding Co.,
Port Huron, Mich.
HULL
NUMBER: 19
LENGTH: 420.0
BREADTH: 50.2
DEPTH: 24.0
GRT: 4,731
REGISTRY
NUMBER: US. 77559
ENGINES: 23", 38", 63" Diameter
x 40" Stroke
Triple Expansion
ENGINE
BUILDER: Shipyard

ISAAC M. SCOTT at Superior after sinking the COWLE

DELPHINE

The two million dollar steel yacht DELPHINE was built in 1921 at Ecorse, Michigan by the Great Lakes Engineering Works for Mrs. Anna T. Dodge, wife of one of the Dodge brothers, builders of automobiles. Designed by H.J. Gielow, the naval architect of New York, New York, the vessel had been planned by Horace Dodge for his wife, but he died before its launch.

Without a doubt, the DELPHINE was the grandest and most spectacular yacht ever seen on the lakes before the handsome BRITANNIA of Her Majesty Queen Elizabeth II made its appearance on the lakes in 1959. Besides her fine decks, the DELPHINE was appointed for a real king or queen. The pilot house was panelled in East India teak, her eight guest rooms were done in black walnut and she even carried a $60,000 pipe organ in the "music room."

In 1926, the DELPHINE burned and sank in the Hudson River and lay on the bottom for four months. She was raised and refitted for $750,000. The following year, her owner was registered as Mrs. Hugh Dodge Dillman. The DELPHINE sank again in 1940, off Manitoulin Island in Georgian Bay and was again raised and repaired.

On January 21, 1942, she was acquired by the U.S. Navy to be the flagship of the Commander-in-Chief of the U.S. Fleet. She was repainted in battle grey, renamed b) U.S.S. DAUNTLESS, PG-61, and commissioned on May 11, 1942. She departed Ecorse on May 27, 1942, and arrived on June 16, 1942 at Washington, D.C. The "reconditioning" of the DAUNTLESS meant that the organ was superfluous. It was unfortunately, unceremoniously dumped overboard, and is now lying somewhere at the bottom of Chesapeake Bay.

After the end of World War II, the ship was decommissioned, on May 22, 1946 and returned to Anna Dodge Dillman the same year. "Reconditioned" again, the yacht returned to the Lakes as c) DELPHINE. In 1950, she was listed officially as owned by Mrs. Horace Dodge, and lay in Lake St. Clair just off the Dodge Estate in Grosse Pointe, Michigan.

The DELPHINE was taken to the East Coast in 1962. After Mrs. Dodge died, the ship was sold to Roy A. Swayze "et al" in 1966. The Seafarers International Union purchased the yacht in 1968 and renamed her d) DAUNTLESS for the second time. They used her as a floating training vessel at Norfolk, Virginia until the ship was sold for scrap in 1972. Thus ended the varied career of the largest private yacht ever to sail the Great Lakes.

DELPHINE just prior to her launch

a) **DELPHINE**
b) **U.S.S. Dauntless**
c) **Delphine**
d) **Dauntless**

BUILT:	1921 Great Lakes Engineering Works, Ecorse, Mich.
HULL NUMBER:	239
LENGTH:	241.7
BREADTH:	35.5
DEPTH:	17.3
GRT:	1,255
REGISTRY NUMBER:	US. 221218
2-ENGINES:	14½", 21", 30½", 45" Diameter x 30" Stroke Quadruple Expansion
ENGINE BUILDER:	Shipyard

DELPHINE anchored in Lake St. Clair

U.S.S. DAUNTLESS in her war camouflage

DELPHINE downbound in the St. Mary's River after the war

DAUNTLESS in S.I.U. colors

ROLAND DESGAGNES

The steel canaller FRANKCLIFFE HALL was launched on April 28, 1952 at Montreal by Canadian Vickers Ltd., for the Hall Corporation of Canada. This vessel was the first modern diesel canaller built for the Hall fleet and entered service as one of the largest deadweight carriers on the St. Lawrence canal system. The FRANKCLIFFE HALL was able to carry more tons of cargo without deepening her draft correspondingly. During the winter of 1958-59, her deck was raised by 2'9" by Canadian Vickers, increasing her gross registered tonnage to 2,454.

In 1962, the ship was renamed b) NORTHCLIFFE HALL (2) to free the name for a maximum-size laker which still carries the name FRANKCLIFFE HALL (2). On September 8, 1970, the NORTHCLIFFE HALL suffered four small holes in the hull by striking the bank of the Welland Ship Canal near Allanburg, Ontario, while passing the steamer CAROL LAKE. NORTHCLIFFE HALL laid up at Prescott at the end of the season, and never sailed for Halco again. After being towed to Kingston, Ontario late in the Fall of 1971, NORTHCLIFFE HALL, along with her near sisters, EAGLESCLIFFE HALL, CONISCLIFFE HALL and WESTCLIFFE HALL remained at this port in lay up until 1974. All these ships were sold to other trades. The NORTHCLIFFE HALL (2) was removed from documentation on the Canadian register on December 7, 1973.

The following year, on December 15, 1974, she left the lakes to serve in the Caribbean for the Tara Corporation of Nassau, The Bahamas. Her name was shortened to NORTHCLIFFE at this time, apparently unofficially. (No record of this rename appears in any Lloyd Register throughout this period). In June, 1976, she was purchased by Les Chargeurs Unis, Inc. (managed by Groupe Desgagnes) of Quebec, refurbished for lake service at Houston, Texas and brought back to sail the St. Lawrence River as d) ROLAND DESGAGNES. In 1978, ownership was transferred to Quebec Rail & Water Terminals Company, another Desgagnes affiliate.

Many incidents plagued the ROLAND DESGAGNES in the next few years. On May 25, 1977, ROLAND DESGAGNES went aground in the Detroit River and needed the tug ROUGE to help pull her free. On May 17, 1980, she was in a collision just west of the Eisenhower Lock with the Cuban flag vessel CARLOS MANUEL DE CESPEDES. The latter had lost steering and veered into the DESGAGNES' port bow. Later, on October 18, 1980, while upbound in the St. Lawrence River, the ship suddenly veered to port and ran hard aground about one mile below the Thousand Islands Bridge in the American Narrows. Traffic was tied up for hours. The following day, the tugs DANIEL McALLISTER and ROBINSON BAY freed the vessel and towed her to Kingston, Ontario for temporary repairs. She was back in service on October 22nd.

For about 14 hours on November 2, 1981, the vessel was again aground, this time at the mouth of the St. Clair River in Lake St. Clair. The ROLAND DESGAGNES was upbound with pig iron. The tugs SHANNON, WILLIAM A. WHITNEY and KINSALE succeeded in refloating the ship and she proceeded on her way.

Her final grounding occurred on May 27, 1982. Fifteen crewmen were rescued when the ROLAND DESGAGNES sank in the St. Lawrence River off Pointe-au-Pic, 74 miles northeast of Quebec City. The Canadian Coast Guard ship VILLE MARIE rescued all the crewmen and the captain. She had run aground at 11:40 p.m. on the 26th. The Coast Guard arrived at 1:00 a.m. Shortly after, an attempt was made to move the ship off the rocks out into the river at high tide and she began taking on water. The ship was abandoned and sank in 300 feet of water. The ROLAND DESGAGNES had a cargo of salt from Pugwash, Nova Scotia to Montreal, and had stopped at Pointe-au-Pic, its home port, "to give the crew a few hours ashore." Thus did the newspaper article report the loss of ROLAND DESGAGNES.

FRANKCLIFFE HALL upbound in Lock 5 Welland Ship Canal July 24, 1954

NORTHCLIFFE HALL just below Lock 4, WSC

Frankcliffe Hall (1), b) Northcliffe Hall (2), c) Northcliffe, d) ROLAND DESGAGNES

BUILT:	1952
	Canadian Vickers, Montreal P. Q.
HULL NUMBER:	255
LENGTH:	253.4
BREADTH:	43.8
DEPTH:	19.0
GRT:	2,126
REGISTRY NUMBER:	C. 194320
TWIN ENGINES:	4 cyl. Diesel 8-1/3" x 10" Stroke
ENGINE BUILDER:	Fairbanks Morse Company,
	1951

WESTCLIFFE HALL, EAGLESCLIFFE HALL, CONISCLIFFE HALL and NORTHCLIFFE HALL
laid up at Kingston in 1973

ROLAND DESGAGNES downbound in the St. Clair River June 26, 1977

DONNACONA (1)

DONNACONA on her maiden voyage from Newcastle to Canada

The steel canal-sized bulk freighter DONNACONA was built by Wood, Skinner & Company in 1900, at Bill Quay, Newcastle, England for the Hamilton and Fort William Steamship Company (A.B. MacKay) to operate from the Lakehead to St. Lawrence River ports. In 1908, she was transferred to the Inland Navigation Company, Ltd., which became Inland Lines, Limited in 1910. In 1911, the vessel was converted into a package freighter.

Canada Steamship Lines took over ownership in 1913. When World War I began, the desperate need for vessels drove many small lakers to the oceans. DONNACONA went to sea again. Her war time service was cut short however, on October 16, 1915, when she foundered in heavy seas 760 miles from the Azores at 52°, 25'N. x 80°, 15'W. on passage from Maryport to Sydney, Nova Scotia, light ship. For 16 days the vessel was buffeted about by fierce gales. Suddenly, one mountainous wave smashed her rudder head. A jury gear was fixed up to steer the ship but it soon was also smashed. Leaks appeared and a loud crack was heard as the vessel was at the mercy of the waves. Distress signals were sighted by the steamer ARIEL which stood by to rescue the crew if the ship continued in danger of sinking.

The master of the ARIEL, Captain H. Hyde, soon realized that the DONNACONA was near her end. The sea moderated long enough for the crew of the ill-fated vessel to be ferried across to the ARIEL by means of a small dory, the lifeboats having been smashed by the storm. A crewman of the DONNACONA made eight journeys between the two vessels and brought off the whole crew. This task took approximately four hours to accomplish, and won the admiration and heartfelt thanks of all. The engineers returned to the DONNACONA to open her seacocks when it became evident the vessel would be a derelict and a hazard to navigation.

The captain and crew of the DONNACONA were taken to Plymouth, England by the ARIEL, whose captain was presented with a gold watch by officials of C.S.L. as a token of great esteem and in appreciation for his seamanship in sticking close to the DONNACONA and rescuing her crew.

Upbound in the St. Clair River

BUILT:	1900
	Wood, Skinner & Co.,
	Bill Quay, Newcastle, England
HULL NUMBER:	93
LENGTH:	245.0
BREADTH:	42.6
DEPTH:	20.8
GRT:	1,222
REGISTRY NUMBER:	BR. 110363
ENGINES:	18½", 30½", 51" Diameter
	x 36" Stroke
	Triple Expansion
ENGINE BUILDER:	Ross & Duncan
	Glasgow, Scotland

DONNACONA upbound at the Soo in 1909

DOUGLAS

The DOUGLAS was a small wooden steam barge for the lumber trade. It was built in 1882 by John Martel of Saugatuck, Michigan for R.M. Moore and F. Purdy of the same city, and had quite a varied career. She originally operated between Lake Michigan ports from one end of the lake to the other. A few years after her launch, the DOUGLAS was converted to a passenger and freight steamer, after being decked over with cabins added.

In 1891, the DOUGLAS was sold to the McElroy Transportation Company of Milwaukee, Wisconsin, running between that city and Muskegon, Michigan. Bound from Milwaukee with passengers to Saugatuck on Sunday night, June 12, 1892, the DOUGLAS collided with the steamer ALICE E. WILDS, 18 miles off Milwaukee in smoky weather. The WILDS sank in three minutes but her crew was rescued by the DOUGLAS and taken back to Milwaukee.

The Chicago Daily Inter-Ocean of October 19, 1892 stated: "The action of the Milwaukee Steamboat inspectors in revoking the licenses of Captain Barney Wilds, of the steamer A. E. WILDS, and C. B. Coates, of the steamer DOUGLAS was generally approved by marine men. The two boats were in collision off Milwaukee, and the WILDS went to the bottom. The testimony showed that both boats were running at full speed, and although they sighted each other twenty minutes before the crash, neither changed course. Not even a whistle was sounded."

The DOUGLAS was sold at U. S. Marshall sale to Wells, Brigham & Upham Co., brokers, in behalf of F. D. Underwood of the Soo Line in 1894. She then plied between Gladstone and Traverse City, Michigan in connection with the Minneapolis, St. Paul and Sault Ste. Marie Railway which was called Soo Line.

In 1896, John S. Thomson of St. Clair, Michigan purchased the vessel for operation in his Oscoda and Cleveland Transportation Company to run in the passenger and freight trade between Oscoda, Michigan and Cleveland, Ohio. The ship stopped at almost every port between the two cities.

In 1902, the DOUGLAS' cabin was cut down and the vessel was made into a steam barge for freight traffic only. Her new tonnage was 230 gross tons. After a few minor mishaps, one on July 31, 1907 when she ran aground on Walpole Island in the St. Clair River and another on October 31, 1907 when she broke her stern pipe on Lake St. Clair, the DOUGLAS was sold in 1908 to Harris W. Baker, the wreck master of Detroit. Baker had a derrick spar installed and from this year to 1915 she was used in the wrecking trade on the Detroit River. In 1916, John Ginzel of Wyandotte, Michigan bought her to use in the sand and gravel trade. She ended her days in this trade and was finally abandoned at Detroit on March 30, 1921.

DOUGLAS as she appeared when first built

DOUGLAS in Soo Line colors

BUILT: 1882
John Martel, Saugatuck, Mich.
LENGTH: 120.0
BREADTH: 22.9
DEPTH: 8.7
GRT: 278

REGISTRY NUMBER: US.157064
ENGINES: 20" Diameter x 22" Stroke
High Pressure Non-condensing
ENGINE BUILDER: Grand Haven Iron Works
Grand Haven, Michigan

DOUGLAS running the rivers for the Thompson Line

DAVID DOWS

In 1881, the only five-masted sailing vessel ever built on the Great Lakes was launched on April 21, at the Bailey Brothers shipyard at Toledo, Ohio. She was constructed for M.D. Carrington. Designed to carry 140,000 bushels of grain, the DAVID DOWS, when launched, was the largest schooner in the world. The mainmast was 162 feet high. To all onlookers, she was a giant vessel that stretched out beyond all reason.

The vessel proved to be almost unmanageable in the confined waters of the lakes in spite of her able crew and a small steam donkey engine to raise and lower her gigantic sails. On September 10, 1881, in a heavy westerly squall, she collided with the schooner CHARLES K. NIMS in Lake Erie and sank it. The crew could not handle her fast enough to prevent the collision. After due consideration, her owners decided to convert the DOWS to a tow barge. Her tall masts were reduced in size and a tug boat was hired to tow her around the lakes to carry cargoes.

In June 1887, the DAVID DOWS was sold to John Corrigan of Cleveland, Ohio and the huge vessel was towed behind steamers of the Corrigan fleet. While in tow of the AURORA on November 30, 1889, with a cargo of iron ore, the DOWS came to grief. During a severe gale, the AURORA cast off her tows, the DAVID DOWS and the GEORGE W. ADAMS. Both barges dropped their anchors to ride out the storm on lower Lake Michigan, just off the Chicago, Illinois harbor entrance in 42 feet of water. The DAVID DOWS had previously sprung a leak off Point Au Sable and now began to fill up rapidly. Her steam donkey engine, which had been handling the pumps successfully up to this time, gave out. Seas climbed her decks, finally filling her, driving the crew of 8 into the lifeboat and yawls. The DOWS listed and sank rightside up with her masts sticking out of the water. The tugs T.T. MORFORD and CHICAGO came out to rescue the crew who had suffered immensely in the icy winds and seas. The vessel proved to be unsalvageable and was destroyed the following spring.

DAVID DOWS from a steel engraving

BUILT: 1881
Bailey Brothers, Toledo, Ohio
LENGTH: 265.0
BREADTH: 37.0
DEPTH: 18.0
GRT: 1,418
REGISTRY NUMBER: US.157029

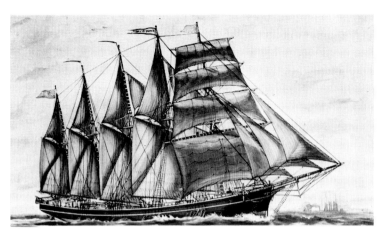
From a painting by Loudon Wilson

Also from a painting by Loudon Wilson

DAVID DOWS as a tow-barge in the Soo Locks

U.S.S. DUBUQUE

DUBUQUE on one of her training cruises in the late 20's

The steel gunboat DUBUQUE was launched August 15, 1904 by the Gas Engine and Power Co., and Charles L. Seabury and Co., Morris Heights, Long Island, New York for the U.S. Navy and commissioned June 3, 1905. Gunboat No. 17 was reclassified AG-6 in 1919, IX-9 in 1922 and PG-17, November 4, 1940.

The DUBUQUE cruised in Atlantic waters until 1911 when she was transferred to the Illinois Naval Militia to be used as a training vessel at Chicago, Illinois. The vessel arrived there on June 29, 1911. She was decommissioned July 22nd.

Recommissioned August 4, 1914, the DUBUQUE sailed three days later for Portsmouth, New Hampshire where she was in reserve. Fitted out as a mine-training ship, she was assigned to the Mining and Minesweeping Division of the Atlantic Fleet in 1915. In 1917, DUBUQUE was a convoy escort, served on patrol duty and trained reserve officers during the rest of World War I.

On June 8, 1922, she sailed from Portsmouth, New Hampshire to Detroit, Michigan where she arrived on June 24. Attached to the 9th Naval District, she took Naval Reservists on cruises from her home port of Detroit into Lakes Superior, Huron and Michigan every summer. The twin stacks were reduced to a single funnel in 1937. On November 14, 1940, the DUBUQUE left Detroit for Boston, Massachusetts where she was modernized and refitted. Throughout World War II, she trained merchant ships' armed guard crews as a gunnery practice ship for the Armed Guard school at Little Creek, Virginia on Chesapeake Bay.

The DUBUQUE was decommissioned September 7, 1945 and transferred to the Maritime Commission for disposal on December 19, 1946. (On that same day Mario Angelo of Miami, Florida bought the PADUCAH, her sistership. Maybe he purchased the DUBUQUE also.) All we have record of is that she was sold in January 1947 and scrapped.

BUILT:	1904
	Gas Engine & Power Co. & Charles Seabury & Co., Morris Heights, Long Island, N.Y.
LENGTH:	200.5
BREADTH:	35.0
DEPTH:	13.4
DISPLACEMENT TONS:	1,084
TWIN ENGINES:	Triple Expansion
ENGINE BUILDER:	Gas Engine & Power Company

DUBUQUE leaving on a cruise, August 16, 1937

In war colors, WWII

DUNELM

The steamer DUNELM was a canaller completed at Sunderland, England in 1907 by the Sunderland Shipbuilding Company as a steel-hulled package freighter. She was originally owned by Dunelm Ltd., of Hamilton, Ontario, which was a company managed by R.O. and A.B. Mackay. In 1908 DUNELM was absorbed into their Inland Navigation Company Ltd., Hamilton. When James Playfair, of Midland, gained control of the company in 1910, it became known as Inland Lines Ltd., Midland, Ontario.

On December 6, 1910, while downbound on Lake Superior with a cargo of grain from the Lakehead for Kingston, DUNELM stranded on the Canoe Rocks at Isle Royale. Attempts to free the steamer failed, and she was abandoned to the underwriters as a total loss on December 14, 1910.

She was later salvaged and towed to Port Arthur for repairs at the yard of the Western Shipbuilding and Drydock Company Ltd. She came out of drydock on June 8, 1911, and was repurchased by her former owner, Inland Lines Ltd.

Canada Steamship Lines Ltd., Montreal, was formed in 1913, and Inland Lines Ltd. was one of the fleets that was absorbed into the new company. As a result, DUNELM operated thereafter under the C.S.L. houseflag.

DUNELM was requisitioned for wartime service on salt water during 1915, but she was not to survive for long. Outbound from Sydney, Nova Scotia, to Manchester, England, on October 17, 1915, she disappeared in the North Atlantic after passing Cape Race, Newfoundland.

DUNELM upbound at Mission Point in 1913

BUILT:	1907
	Sunderland Shipbuilding Co., Sunderland, England
HULL NUMBER:	246
LENGTH:	250.0
BREADTH:	43.2
DEPTH:	23.5
GRT:	2,319
REGISTRY NUMBER:	C.123950
ENGINES:	19½", 33", 54" Diameter x 36" Stroke
	Triple Expansion
ENGINE BUILDER:	North Eastern Marine Engine Works
	Sunderland, England

DUNELM on the Canoe Rocks at Isle Royale December 6, 1910

Just before being refloated

With the tug LAURA GRACE and salvage barge, being towed to Port Arthur

EASTON

The steel passenger steamer EASTON was built in 1896 at Baltimore, Maryland by Charles Reeder for C.C. Wheeler and James W. Holt of Hillsboro, Maryland. On April 8, 1901 her ownership was transferred to the Baltimore, Chesapeake & Atlantic Railway Company of Baltimore, for service between Baltimore and New York City, making three round trips a week. This proved to be unsuccessful and, on June 25, 1901, she was sold to the H.W. Williams Transportation Company of South Haven, Michigan and taken to the Great Lakes. Mr. H.W. Williams passed away in Baltimore and his son took over the vessel.

During 1902, she was chartered to the Graham & Morton Line, being the only vessel still owned by the Williams Transportation Co. to run in the fruit and passenger trade out of South Haven, Michigan. The rest of the vessels of this fleet had been acquired by the newly formed Dunkley Williams Company.

On June 1, 1903, the EASTON was sold to the White Line Transportation Company of Duluth, Minnesota, W.H. Singer, president, to run from Duluth to north shore points on Lake Superior. Singer's White Line merged with Booth's United States & Dominion Transportation Company on March 9, 1905 and the EASTON continued her runs to Two Harbors, Minnesota and the Canadian Lakehead cities of Fort William and Port Arthur with stops in between.

The A. Booth Company became insolvent in 1908 and was reorganized as the Booth Fisheries Company on May 29, 1909. The vessels of the fleet were unaffected.

During the years immediately before the U.S. entry into World War I, J.W. Elwell & Co., New York ship brokers, purchased a number of coastwise and Great Lakes ships for the French Government. EASTON was one of these and her document was surrendered on August 21, 1917. The French renamed her b) APACHE. She survived the war and saw further commercial service. In 1926, the listed owner was Fr. Mongi Bascouche, G. Montefiore and G. Rinauro of Tunis, North Africa. Her final disposition is unknown as she was dropped from the Bureau Veritas (The French Register) in 1926, "presumed scrapped."

EASTON in White Line Transportation colors

EASTON along the north shore

BUILT:	1896
	Charles Reeder & Sons, Baltimore, Maryland
HULL NUMBER:	
LENGTH:	154.8
BREADTH:	30.0
DEPTH:	9.7
GRT:	460
REGISTRY NUMBER:	US.136568
ENGINES:	20", 38" Diameter x 28" Stroke
ENGINE BUILDER:	Fore & Aft Compound
	Charles Reeder & Sons
	Baltimore, Maryland

a) **EASTON**

b) **Apache**

Entering Duluth harbor

EMPRESS OF FORT WILLIAM

MOUNT STEPHEN upbound at Mission Point in 1910

The steel canaller MOUNT STEPHEN was built in 1908, at Wallsend-on-Tyne, England by Swan, Hunter & Wigham Richardson, Ltd. for the Midland Navigation Company, but was soon transferred to a subsidiary, The Empress Transportation Company. This firm was absorbed in 1910 into the Inland Lines Ltd. of Midland, Ontario and the vessel was renamed b) EMPRESS OF FORT WILLIAM that year.

This fleet was absorbed into Canada Steamship Lines in 1913. Previous to this, the EMPRESS OF FORT WILLIAM had been sunk in a collision with the steamer LYMAN C. SMITH near Cedar Reef in the St. Mary's River, but had been raised and repaired.

Chartered on March 10, 1915 to the Nova Scotia Steel and Coal Company for service on salt water, she hauled coal from Sydney, Nova Scotia to Montreal. Damaged by ice near Glace Bay, N.S., on May 6, 1915, the vessel was again sent to the repair yard.

At South Shields, England, the vessel loaded her last cargo and sailed on February 25, 1916. On February 27th, she was in the van of about 200 ships sailing south. The large P & O liner the MALOJA was ahead of the EMPRESS OF FORT WILLIAM and having struck a mine was sinking. The captain of the EMPRESS OF FORT WILLIAM decided to go to her assistance when suddenly the EMPRESS also struck a mine laid by UC-6, Captain Grof Von Schmettow, 2 miles south of Dover Pier in the English Channel. The explosion ripped her stern and at the rate which the stern sank, made it evident that the EMPRESS OF FORT WILLIAM had received her death blow. Most of the crew escaped in the starboard lifeboat while the remainder were taken off by a destroyer. All of the crew were landed at Dover shortly thereafter. The EMPRESS OF FORT WILLIAM, which had been bound for Dunkirk, France, was a peaceful and useful ship which received her deathstroke without any warning while on a rescue mission. The poor MALOJA went down taking 122 lives with her; the rescuer was more fortunate than the original victim.

EMPRESS OF FORT WILLIAM downbound in 1912

a) Mount Stephen		b) EMPRESS OF FORT WILLIAM	
BUILT:	1908	GRT:	2,181
	Swan, Hunter & Wigham	REGISTRY NUMBER:	BR. & C. 125443
	Richardson, Ltd.,	ENGINES:	20½", 33", 54" Diameter
	Wallsend-on-Tyne, England		x 36" Stroke
HULL NUMBER:	813		Triple Expansion
LENGTH:	250.0	ENGINE BUILDER:	North Eastern Machine Engine
BREADTH:	43.0		Company
DEPTH:	23.3		Wallsend-on-Tyne, England

JOHN ERICSSON

The steel whaleback steamer JOHN ERICSSON was launched on July 11, 1896 at W. Superior, Wisconsin by the American Steel Barge Company for its own fleet and transferred to the Bessemer Steamship Company later the same year. She was the only true whaleback steamer to carry her bridge structure forward. All the rest had their cabins aft.

In 1901, the Bessemer fleet was absorbed by the United States Steel Corporation's Pittsburgh Steamship Company, for which the vessel sailed in the iron ore trade until 1926. In 1914, her engines were remodeled to 22½", 36", 60" cylinder diameter x 42" stroke. In 1930, the ERICSSON was transferred to the Schneider Steamship Company, which in turn sold her to James Playfair of Midland, Ontario, for his Great Lakes Transit Corporation, Ltd., the same year. In 1931, she was owned by the Midland Steamship Company who used her in a variety of trades. (C. 154863 Canadian dimensions: 398.5 x 48.2 x 22.0; 3,650 GRT.)

In 1938, the ERICSSON was sold to Upper Lakes and St. Lawrence Transportation Company Ltd., Toronto, which became Upper Lakes Shipping Ltd. in 1961. Her main cargo in those years was grain from the Lakehead to Sarnia, Ontario, Georgian Bay ports and as far east as Toronto, Ontario. Late in 1963, the steamer was retired in Toronto. Upper Lakes officials tried to preserve the ERICSSON, now one of the last whaleback steamers afloat, offering her as a maritime museum first to Toronto and then to Hamilton, Ontario civic groups. The city fathers of Hamilton at first accepted the offer in 1966 but then changed their minds later that year when costs to maintain and convert the vessel and political factors intervened. Upper Lakes took the vessel back and had her towed from her berth at Confederation Park to the scrapyard in Hamilton, where she lay until sold for scrap in 1968. The once largest whaleback on the lakes was dismantled by Strathearne Terminals at Hamilton. Now she is but a memory.

JOHN ERICSSON downbound in the Soo Locks, unidentified barge in tow

BUILT:	1896	GRT:	3,200
	American Steel Barge Co.,	REGISTRY NUMBER:	US.77226
	W. Superior, Wisc.	ENGINES:	25", 40", 68" Diameter x 42"
HULL NUMBER:	138		Stroke
LENGTH:	390.0		Triple Expansion
BREADTH:	48.2	ENGINE BUILDER:	Cleveland Shipbuilding Company
DEPTH:	22.0		Cleveland, Ohio

JOHN ERICSSON downbound at Mission Point in 1922

Upbound in lower Lake Huron June 26, 1960

At Confederation Park July 15, 1966

HARRY T. EWIG

W. W. BROWN alongside the WILLIAM EDENBORN waiting for traffic in the ice

The steel bulk freighter W. W. BROWN was launched February 1, 1902 at Chicago, Illinois by the Chicago Shipbuilding Company for the United States Transportation Company. This firm became the Great Lakes Steamship Company in 1911.

In 1915, the BROWN was purchased by the Jones & Laughlin Steel Corporation's Interstate Steamship Company and renamed b) BALTIC in 1920. In 1922, she changed owners twice, first to the Becker Steamship Company and then to the Valley Camp Steamship Company who renamed her c) JOHN W. AILES. In 1926, the vessel was rebuilt and again renamed, this time to d) HARRY T. EWIG, her final title.

In 1935, the vessels of this fleet were incorporated into the Columbia Transportation Company. At the Fairport Machine Shop at Fairport, Ohio, the EWIG was converted into a crane ship in 1939 to be used in carrying scrap steel (3,562 GRT). In 1963, when no longer useful to the Columbia Transportation Company, the EWIG was sold to John Roen of Sturgeon Bay, Wisconsin, who cut down the vessel making two barges out of her hull. The forward end became known as LIGHTER NO. 1 and the stern section, LIGHTER NO. 2.

In 1965, the Bultema Dredge & Dock Company purchased both sections and in turn sold them both to the Asher Marine Rentals Company the same year. While in tow of the tug ROY R. LOVE on October 29, 1965 on Lake Michigan, a violent storm overtook the tow and both barges sank outside Frankfort, Michigan harbor. The tallstacked vessel, once so familiar a feature on the Lakes, had outlived many of the 44 other vessels launched in the 1902 season around the lakes.

a) W. W. Brown
b) Baltic
c) John W. Ailes
d) HARRY T. EWIG

BUILT:	1902
	Chicago Shipbuilding Co.,
	Chicago, Illinois
HULL NUMBER:	52
LENGTH:	352.9
BREADTH:	48.2
DEPTH:	24.0
GRT:	3,582
REGISTRY NUMBER:	US. 81803
ENGINES:	20", 33½", 55" Diameter x 40"
	Stroke
	Triple Expansion
ENGINE BUILDER:	Shipyard

BALTIC downbound in 1920 at Mission Point near the Soo Locks

JOHN W. AILES in the same place a few years later

HARRY T. EWIG as a bulk freighter downbound at Detroit

As a crane-ship upbound in the Fighting Island Channel July 4, 1953

FARRANDOC (2)

The steel diesel canaller STEEL ELECTRICIAN was built in 1926 at Kearney, New Jersey by the Federal Shipbuilding and Dry Dock Company for the Isthmian Lines-U.S. Steel Products Company for service on the Great Lakes and in coastwise trade. (US. 225508; 250.3 x 43.9 x 17.2; 1,694 GRT.) There was a large quantity of iron and steel products to be moved between Great Lakes ports, Montreal, and coastal ports. The STEEL ELECTRICIAN and her sister vessels were equipped to handle steel bars, channels and structural shapes in large sizes. She was equipped with two electric cranes, one amidships and the other aft, to enable the crew to load and unload the steel products.

In 1938, the Tennessee Coal, Iron & Railroad Company took over the vessel to run in their coastwise service. She ran mainly along the coast during World War II. In 1945, she was sold to the Warrior & Gulf Navigation Company. The following year she was registered in Panama by her new owners, the American Eastern Corporation.

In 1947, N.M. Paterson of Fort William, Ontario purchased the vessel and brought her back to the lakes. The vessel's two electric cranes had been replaced in the southern service by two huge derrick masts amidships. Paterson renamed her b) FARRANDOC (2), replacing the FARRANDOC (1) which had been sold and renamed CLAYTON. For about 17 years she worked for Paterson in various capacities. In 1964, Trans-World Chartering Ltd., of Montreal purchased the vessel and renamed her c) QUEBEC TRADER for service in the lower St. Lawrence River. In November the same year, she was purchased by Transportaciones Combinadas, C.A. of Caracas, Venezuela and taken off-lakes to the Caribbean. They renamed her d) SAN TOME. When this firm no longer needed her, the SAN TOME was retired and scrapped in the Orinoco River, Venezuela in 1970.

STEEL ELECTRICIAN downbound in Lake St. Clair

a) **Steel Electrician**   b) **FARRANDOC (2)**   c) **Quebec Trader**   d) **San Tome**

BUILT:	1926	*GRT:*	1,865
	Federal Shipbuilding &	*REGISTRY NUMBER:*	C.173187
	Dry Dock Co.,	*ENGINES:*	15" Diameter x 22" Stroke
	Kearney, New Jersey		Electric Motor 4 cylinder,
HULL NUMBER:	84		S. A. Diesel
LENGTH:	251.5	*ENGINE BUILDER:*	New London S & E. Company
BREADTH:	42.9		New London, Connecticut
DEPTH:	17.0		

FARRANDOC downbound opposite Harsens Island

FARRANDOC downbound opposite St. Clair, Michigan June 14, 1963

QUEBEC TRADER at Montreal July 16, 1964

JOSEPH S. FAY

Among the first Great Lakes freighters built for the iron ore trade was the wooden steamer JOSEPH S. FAY. She was constructed in 1871 by the famous Quayle & Martin shipyard in Cleveland for Captain Alva Bradley and others of Cleveland and H. H. Fay of Boston. The $80,000 craft was especially handsome, with two decks and three tall masts, and the similarly good-looking schooner D. P. RHODES was built to be her consort. Interestingly, the two were paired for more than thirty years.

The FAY and her barge were one-owner boats, operating for the Bradley interests during their entire careers, although a whole list of shareholders were actually involved in the ownership. The Bradley fleet was characterized by hulls of bright green with broad white rails and red stacks. The fleet included some of the finest bulk freight vessels and schooners of the seventies, eighties, and nineties, and were, almost without exception, products of the best Cleveland shipwrights.

The FAY had her engine compounded in 1887, by the Globe Iron Works (24", 44" diameter of cylinder x 38" stroke) and her two firebox boilers were replaced by a new scotch boiler in 1893. The bulwarks were cut down in the eighties, changing her silhouette somewhat, and her top-hamper was also much reduced in her later years, but the ship never had any significant structural changes. She earned a fortune for her owners over the years in the ore and coal businesses.

1905 was a disastrous year for Great Lakes shipping. So many gales caused havoc on ships and sailors during that season that only the year 1913, when eight vessels disappeared with all hands in one storm, surpassed 1905 in tonnage lost.

In a violent gale on Lake Huron on October 19, 1905, JOSEPH S. FAY was downbound with iron ore from Escanaba, Michigan to Ashtabula, Ohio with the schooner D. P. RHODES in tow. While the steamer tried to keep her head to the seas, the strain of the towline to the schooner ripped out the tow bitts, taking part of the FAY's stern with them.

Rather than having his vessel founder in deep water, her captain decided to beach the ship on 40 Mile Point near Rogers City, Michigan. All but one of the crew were rescued. The hapless vessel was pounded to pieces by the huge waves.

JOSEPH S. FAY upbound above the Soo in 1909

BUILT:	1871	GRT:	1,220
	Quayle & Martin,	REGISTRY NUMBER:	US.75315
	Cleveland, Ohio	ENGINES:	28½" Diameter x 36" Stroke
LENGTH:	215.6		High Pressure Non-Condensing
BREADTH:	33.6	ENGINE BUILDER:	Cuyahoga Iron Works
DEPTH:	14.8		Cleveland, Ohio

JAMES E. FERRIS

ONTARIO upbound in the Upper St. Mary's River in 1910

The steamer ONTARIO was one of three almost identical bulk carriers built in 1910 by Great Lakes Engineering Works at Ecorse, Michigan, for the Northern Lakes Steamship Company of Cleveland. This was a small shipping company which was managed by Gustav von den Steinen, junior partner in a Cleveland legal firm. On May 1, 1915, ONTARIO and her sisterships, ST. CLAIR and CHAMPLAIN, were sold to the Pioneer Steamship Company (Hutchinson and Company, managers), Cleveland.

ONTARIO was renamed b) F. R. HAZARD by Pioneer in 1916, and she became c) JAMES E. FERRIS in 1924. She sailed for Pioneer until October, 1961, when she was sold to the Buckeye Steamship Company, Cleveland, which also was managed by Hutchinson. When Pioneer Steamship went into voluntary liquidation in 1962, the Buckeye Steamship Company continued operations independently. Buckeye was a privately held company of John T. Hutchinson and his family, whereas Pioneer stock was traded publicly in the over-the-counter market. Control of Buckeye was acquired during the winter of 1967-68 by the

American Shipbuilding Company and, in 1969, the Buckeye boats were absorbed into the fleet of Kinsman Marine Transit Company, Cleveland.

JAMES E. FERRIS operated until sold in the autumn of 1974 to Marine Salvage Ltd., Port Colborne. She unloaded her last grain cargo at Buffalo and, on October 12, 1974, arrived at Port Colborne under her own power, laying up in the old channel between Dain City and Humberstone. Resold through Poul Christensen, Denmark, she passed down the Welland Canal on April 22, 1975, in tow of SALVAGE MONARCH and HELEN M. McALLISTER.

In tandem tow with KINSMAN VOYAGER behind the tug JANTAR, the FERRIS arrived at Hamburg, Germany, on July 4, 1975. Under the name d) PRAM, she was used there by Lutgens and Reimers as a storage hull. She was towed into Santander, Spain, on April 1, 1979, and there was scrapped by Recuperaciones Submarinas S. A.

JAMES E. FERRIS was a very handsome ship and, at the time of her retirement, was the smallest non-specialty bulk carrier operating on the lakes under U. S. registry.

Ontario, b) F. R. Hazard, c) JAMES E. FERRIS, d) Pram

BUILT:	1910
	Great Lakes Engineering Works,
	Ecorse, Mich.
HULL NUMBER:	71
LENGTH:	444.0
BREADTH:	56.2
DEPTH:	31.0
GRT:	5,494
REGISTRY NUMBER:	US.207283
ENGINES:	22½", 36½", 60¼" Diameter
	x 42" Stroke
	Triple Expansion
ENGINE BUILDER:	Shipyard

F. R. HAZARD downbound at Mission Point in 1922

JAMES E. FERRIS upbound in Lake St. Clair, July 14, 1940

JAMES E. FERRIS downbound in the St. Mary's River, August 5, 1962

Downbound in the St. Mary's River June 30, 1970 in Kinsman colors

114

ERWIN L. FISHER

The steel canal-sized steamer ERWIN L. FISHER, a lumber carrier, was launched June 4, 1910, at Toledo, Ohio by the Toledo Shipbuilding Company for the Argo Steamship Company, managed by Fisher, Wilson & Co. of Cleveland, Ohio. The varied career of this vessel was marred almost immediately when, on her maiden voyage upbound in the Detroit River between Grassy Island and Marmajuda Island, she was in a collision with the heavily laden downbound steamer STEPHEN M. CLEMENT on May 4, 1911 and sunk. She was raised by the Great Lakes Towing Company and taken to dry dock for repairs.

A successive series of owners and incidents ensued a few years later. On March 28, 1916, she was sold to the Lake Transportation Company and almost immediately thereafter to the Bay Steamship Company, a British firm, whose offices were in New York City. At this time she was renamed b) BAYERSHER and operated in overseas trading during World War I. In 1921, the vessel was sold to the French Government which renamed her c) PORT DE CAEN. In 1922, she was sold Canadian to the Interlake Steam Navigation Company and renamed d) BAYERSHER for the second time to facilitate her transfer to Canadian Registry (C.140270). Scott Misener purchased BAYERSHER in 1923, one of his first vessels, renamed her e) CLAREMONT and returned the ship to the lakes.

She served in the Misener fleet until sold early in 1930 to the Kelley Island Lime and Transport Company. At this time the ship was returned to U.S. registry. She was converted to a sand boat at Ecorse, Michigan in 1930 and renamed f) GEORGE J. WHELAN. Her first trip met with tragedy. On July 29, 1930, she capsized and sank in heavy seas on Lake Erie six miles north of Dunkirk, New York. Fifteen crewmen were drowned in the sinking; only six were rescued by the steamer AMASA STONE, which was in the vicinity at the time of the accident. Thus ended the career of the vessel which had 7 owners from 4 nationalities.

ERWIN L. FISHER upbound at the Soo in 1912

CLAREMONT unloading sugar at Toronto

a) **ERWIN L. FISHER**   b) **Bayersher**   c) **Port DeCaen**   d) **Bayersher**
e) **Claremont**   f) **George J. Whelan**

BUILT:	1910	*GRT:*	1,184
	Toledo Shipbuilding Co.,	*REGISTRY NUMBER:*	US. 207617
	Toledo, Ohio	*ENGINES:*	17¼", 27½", 43" Diameter
HULL NUMBER:	117		x 30" Stroke
LENGTH:	220.0		Triple Expansion
BREADTH:	40.0	*ENGINE BUILDER:*	Shipyard
DEPTH:	15.3		

GEORGE J. WHELAN at Cleveland in 1930

116

FONTANA

The fourmasted wooden schooner FONTANA was built by Simon Langell at St. Clair, Michigan in 1888, for Edward Recor's St. Clair Steamship Company, an affiliate of the Cleveland-Cliffs Iron Company.

Perhaps, the greatest claim to fame for this vessel was that she caused so many accidents *after* her own sinking. On the clear night of August 3, 1900, the FONTANA, with a cargo of 2,593 tons of iron ore, was downbound from Presque Isle, (Marquette) Michigan for Cleveland, Ohio, and in tow of the steamer KALIYUGA in lower Lake Huron. Upbound at the same time was the steamer APPOMATTOX towing the schooner SANTIAGO. As the vessels met in the St. Clair Rapids (near where the Blue Water Bridge now spans the river), the FONTANA was struck by the SANTIAGO, staving in her bow. She sank immediately, taking with her one man who was asleep in the forecastle. The rest of the crew, six in all, made their escape before the vessel went down.

Now the headaches began! The stern section of the FONTANA was still above water and the hull presented a terrific hazard to navigation in the narrow confines of the channel. Two buoys were placed on the westerly edge of the channel in the river to mark the 20 foot curve between the wreck and the west bank of the river. Two lights, one above the other, were placed on the wreck.

Traffic up and down the river became snarled. After several vessels had narrow escapes, the schooner KINGFISHER, in tow of the steamer SAMUEL MARSHALL, collided with the wreck and stuck fast doing considerable damage to the KINGFISHER and carrying away the foretop and mainmast of the FONTANA. The tug GEORGE BROCKWAY succeeded in releasing the KINGFISHER, which was then towed to dry dock to be repaired.

Several other close calls later, the U.S. Government awarded a contract to the Harris Baker Company of Detroit, Michigan to begin salvage operations. The consensus of opinion among wrecking firms was that the vessel could not be raised because of the swiftness of the current at that point in the river. Dynamite would have to be used to clear away the wreck.

Before any progress could be made, there occurred another tragic collision involving the wreck. The schooner JOHN MARTIN, in tow of the steamer MAURICE B. GROVER, was downbound with ore from Two Harbors, Minnesota to Lake Erie Ports. The GROVER and MARTIN had hardly bypassed the wreck when the GROVER was passing the straight back steamer YUMA, upbound. Suddenly and without warning, the YUMA veered and hit the MARTIN, sending her to the bottom of the river and taking four of her crew with her. Two other crewmen were rescued by the Marine Reporting boat alongside the YUMA and two were rescued by the YUMA itself.

Now there were two wrecks! The MARTIN lay in 60 feet of water about 225 feet from the American shore, another distinct hazard to navigation. To prevent further mishaps, the tug HAYNES was stationed at the mouth of the river to warn the upbound fleet.

Before both wrecks could be dynamited, the schooner A. J. McBRIER veered out of the way of one wreck knocking a sailor from her crew into the swirling rapids drowning him, and striking the FONTANA which held her fast for several hours. The McBRIER was released and taken to Port Huron for repairs. Approximately ninety boats were detained for days until progress could be made on the wrecks.

The spars and rigging were blasted off the MARTIN. The FONTANA proved to be a harder task. Enough dynamite was used on her to remove most of the vessel so that ships could ride clear over her. Both wrecks are visible to scuba divers today who report that they are still hazardous because of the current and can be visited in the dead of winter when the ice slows down the volume of water coming out of Lake Huron.

FONTANA downbound at the Soo

Steamer FRED PABST passing the wreck of the FONTANA

BUILT:	1888
	Simon Langell,
	St. Clair, Mich.
LENGTH:	231.4
BREADTH:	39.1
DEPTH:	17.0
GRT:	1,163
REGISTRY NUMBER:	US. 120713

The stern of the FONTANA is all that remained above water

GARGANTUA

The wooden ocean-going tug SEAFARER was one of three built by S.C. McLouth at Marine City, Michigan in 1919, for the U.S. Shipping Board but was never completed due to the end of hostilities of World War I. Two of these hulls were made into barges but the SEAFARER, which had no U.S. Registry number, was sold to the Cowles Shipyard Company of Buffalo, New York in 1922. The hull was sold the following year to the Toronto Dry Dock Company and was towed to Chippawa, Ontario where she was completed as b) GARGANTUA (C.138277). A war surplus engine was installed and she was ready for service.

The Lake Superior Paper Company Ltd. of Sault Ste. Marie, Ontario took over the ownership of the tug and in May of 1923, GARGANTUA entered the rafting service of that firm. The rafts, which would consist of as much as 8,000 tons of pulpwood, were loosely enclosed by log booms. These rafts were assembled by smaller tugs along the north shore of Lake Superior between the Michipicoten River and the Puckasaw River, and larger tugs like GARGANTUA hauled them down the lake to the mills at Sault Ste. Marie, where the pulpwood was processed.

On August 7, 1928, the Lake Superior Paper Company Ltd. was acquired by the Abitibi Power and Paper Company and the GARGANTUA had a new owner. Until replaced by more modern steel tugs, GARGANTUA, RELIANCE and G.R. GRAY (2) were the work horses of the fleet.

GARGANTUA last operated for the fleet in 1948 and, in October of that year, was laid up at Sault Ste. Marie and put up for sale. On May 19, 1949, she was purchased by Captain James McColman, who had her taken to Thessalon, Ontario, a small port located along the North Channel of Lake Huron. The tug lay idle at Thessalon until 1952. At that time, Captain McColman made a deal to dispose of GARGANTUA's engine and boiler. He had the tug towed to Collingwood, Ontario. Her pilothouse, cabins and the machinery were removed. She was to be used as a barge to haul hardwood logs to the local lumber mill at Thessalon.

Once the stripping of GARGANTUA was completed, the steam tug MAC began the tow to Thessalon. During the night of December 5-6, 1952, the two vessels encountered a severe storm. They sought shelter behind Cabot Head and ran for safety to Wingfield Basin, a small circular harbor near Tobermory, Ontario. The crew of the MAC realized that the tow was being driven toward the shore and accordingly they opened the seacocks in GARGANTUA to allow her to fill with water and settle to the bottom. The GARGANTUA did settle. The water was not deep, and much of her hull remained above water. It was intended to return for the hull the following spring but this never materialized. Her remains are there to this day. GARGANTUA's registry was closed on December 7, 1967, fifteen years, almost to the day, of her sinking behind Cabot Head.

SEAFARER's launch

GARGANTUA in the Soo locks

a) Seafarer   b) GARGANTUA

BUILT:	1919	*REGISTRY NUMBER:*	C. 138277
	S.C. McLouth,	*ENGINES:*	17", 25", 43" Diameter
	Marine City, Mich.		x 30" Stroke
LENGTH:	130.0		Triple Expansion
BREADTH:	32.1	*ENGINE BUILDER:*	Filer & Stowell
DEPTH:	15.4		Milwaukee, Wisconsin, 1920
GRT:	381		

GARGANTUA and RELIANCE at their dock at the Soo October 10, 1938

GEORGIA

CITY OF LUDINGTON early in her career

For their cross-lake route from Milwaukee to Ludington, Michigan, the Goodrich Transit Company had a new wooden passenger steamer built by Greenleaf S. Rand in Manitowoc, Wisconsin during the spring and summer of 1880. Launched in August, the CITY OF LUDINGTON entered service in November. She made one trip on her assigned route, then joined DE PERE and MENOMINEE on the D. & M. R. R. course between Milwaukee and Grand Haven, Michigan. In 1881, she returned to the Milwaukee-Ludington-Manistee run, carrying freight and passengers for the Flint and Pere Marquette Railroad.

In 1882, the railroad built two boats of their own, the F. & P.M. No. 1 and the F. & P.M. No. 2, and cancelled their contract with Goodrich when the new boats entered service in 1883. Goodrich continued on this route, however, in spite of railroad competition, through the season of 1886. They finally abandoned it in 1887, and put CITY OF LUDINGTON on the run between Chicago and Grand Haven.

Late in the season of 1889, she was shifted to the Chicago-Escanaba run. She ran ashore twice that fall, the second time so hard that lightering and tugs could not get her off. She remained stranded at Shanty Cove, Eagle Harbor (near Ephraim, Wisconsin), all that winter and was finally removed by the use of tugs and jacks the following spring. Towed to Manitowoc, she was dry docked, repaired and generally overhauled and then went on the run between Chicago, Milwaukee and Manistique, Michigan. She stayed on the west shore until the winter of 1897, when she again entered the yards at Manitowoc, to be lengthened and rebuilt and receive a new engine and boiler.

When she came out again, in the spring of 1898, her dimensions were: 195.7 x 34.4 x 12.0; 895 GRT: Engine-

Fore & Aft Compound built in 1898 by the Dry Dock Engine Works, Detroit, Michigan, 21", 44" diameter x 36" stroke. She was renamed b) GEORGIA, and was assigned to cruises between Chicago and the Green Bay ports of the Door County peninsula. In 1899, her route was extended to Mackinac Island, and she ran for the next fifteen years in that service. For a few seasons, starting in 1906, she also made weekend trips carrying resorters between Chicago and White Lake, Michigan.

In 1909, an upper cabin was added, aft. In 1914, she again went into the yards for reboilering and a general overhaul. Still, she was getting old, and finally was replaced on the Mackinac cruises and relegated to mostly freight service between Chicago and Green Bay. In late October, 1920, she was sold to Crosby Transportation Company to replace their sidewheeler MUSKEGON (a) CITY OF MILWAUKEE, destroyed on Muskegon south pier in a severe storm in October of 1919. GEORGIA then went on the regular Crosby run between Milwaukee, Grand Haven and Muskegon. For the season of 1923, she was chartered to Pere Marquette Line Steamers, and ran between Milwaukee and Ludington, ironically, the route for which she was originally built.

In the spring of 1925, all Crosby properties were foreclosed, and GEORGIA came into the hands of the newly organized Wisconsin and Michigan Transportation Co., who used her until November and laid her up at Sturgeon Bay. There she lay, eventually partly submerged, until October, 1932, when it was announced that she would become part of a dock being built by Capt. John Roen at Big Summer Island, Michigan. It is reported that this happened. She is still documented, her final document having never been surrendered.

121

There are still many vessels which remain in official documentation on the records but are no longer extant. The last owners just did not bother to surrender the document or there is litigation still pending for payments never received. So, like the GEORGIA, they remain on the lists of documented vessels even though the ships are at the bottom of some lake, covered over as part of docks or just simply no longer in existence. The last owners may have abandoned them as an expedient to escape the burdensome legalese.

GEORGIA entering the piers at White Lake, Michigan in 1907

GEORGIA upbound at the Soo

a) City of Ludington   b) GEORGIA

BUILT:	1880		
	Greenleaf S. Rand,	GRT:	842
	Manitowoc, Wisc.	REGISTRY NUMBER:	US.125873
LENGTH:	179.9	ENGINES:	24" Diameter x 36" Stroke
BREADTH:	35.4		Reynolds-Corliss High Pressure
DEPTH:	12.0	ENGINE BUILDER:	Edward P. Allis
			Milwaukee, Wisconsin

GODERICH

HOWARD M. HANNA, JR. (1) in the St. Clair River

The steel bulk carrier HOWARD M. HANNA, JR., (US 205260) was launched on April 28, 1908, at Cleveland, Ohio, by the American Ship Building Company for the Hanna Transit Company (W. C. Richardson, Manager).

With a cargo of coal from Lorain, Ohio, destined for Fort William, Ontario, the HANNA, JR. sailed into the teeth of the "Big Storm of 1913." Early on Sunday morning November 9th, the steamers CHARLES S. PRICE, ISAAC M. SCOTT, JOHN A. McGEAN, HOWARD M. HANNA, JR., and ARGUS had entered Lake Huron upbound with coal. What followed will always be known as the "Big Storm." What happened to some of these vessels will never be known as some were lost without a trace.

The HOWARD M. HANNA, JR. was thrown upon a reef at Port Austin, Michigan in the gale and broke in two at #7 hatch. Most of her upper works, including the stack, were carried away by the waves, but her entire crew was rescued by the U.S. Life Saving Service. The HANNA could not keep headway to the sea and was subjected to heavy rolling and pounding in the trough. No lake master, past or present, could recall a storm of such unprecedented violence with such rapid changes in the direction of the wind with gusts of such fearful speed. The incredible punishment the ships must have been subjected to convinced everyone that the storm must have been cyclonic in character.

The aftermath of the storm was incredible. Thousands of pieces of various vessels and their crews were strewn along the shores of Lake Huron. Gradually the clean up was accomplished. The wrecked HANNA, JR. lay broadside to the beach, her after cabins and smoke stack completely torn away from the rest of the vessel. She was abandoned to the underwriters and was later salvaged by the Reid Wrecking Company, then taken to Collingwood, Ontario and put into dry dock. It was determined that the ship could be repaired, though damage was extensive.

James Playfair purchased the vessel, had the repairs made and pressed the ship into service for his Great Lakes Transportation Co., Ltd. in 1915. Playfair intended to name her SIR WILFRED LAURIER, but this name was never registered. Instead, she became b) GLENSHEE.

After recovering from her bout with the "Big Storm," the career of GLENSHEE was rather uneventful. In 1926, GLENSHEE was acquired by Canada Steamship Lines Ltd., Montreal. She was renamed c) MARQUETTE, but apparently carried this name for only one year. In 1927, she was renamed d) GODERICH, which name she held for her remaining years in CSL livery. In 1963, Algoma Central purchased the vessel and sailed her until 1968 as e) AGAWA. She was then retired to serve as a storage barge at Goderich, Ontario for the Goderich Elevator and Transit Company, Ltd. She was renamed f) LIONEL PARSONS for this duty. The end came in mid-1983 when Goderich Elevators, Ltd. sold the PARSONS to Western Metals Corporation of Thunder Bay, Ontario. They towed her to that port and cut her up for scrap.

HOWARD M. HANNA, JR. on the beach after the Big Storm of 1913

After salvage, in Collingwood dry dock in 1914

GLENSHEE with BALL BROTHERS in winter quarters at Midland, Ontario

a) **Howard M. Hanna, Jr. (1),**   b) **Glenshee,**
c) **Marquette,**   d) **GODERICH (1),**   e) **Agawa (2)**

BUILT:	1908	*GRT:*	5,905
	American Shipbuilding Co.,	*REGISTRY NUMBER:*	C. 134511
	Cleveland, Ohio	*ENGINES:*	22½", 36", 60" Diameter
HULL NUMBER:	442		x 42 Stroke
LENGTH:	480.0		Triple Expansion
BREADTH:	54.0	*ENGINE BUILDER:*	Shipyard
DEPTH:	30.0		

GODERICH downbound in the Detroit River August 3, 1952

AGAWA in the St. Clair River October 4, 1963

LIONEL PARSONS with SHELTER BAY in Goderich, August 23, 1972

NISBET GRAMMER

The Eastern Steamship Company Ltd., St. Catharines, Ontario, was formed in 1922 by a number of gentlemen who were associated with the grain business in Buffalo, New York. The fleet, managed by Boland and Cornelius, Buffalo, owned 21 canallers during its 14 years of operation. The first 10 of these boats were built in groups of two each by five British shipyards in 1923. One of the yards involved was that of Cammell, Laird and Company Ltd., Birkenhead, England. It laid the keel for its first Eastern canaller on February 2, 1923. She was launched as NISBET GRAMMER on April 14, 1923, and arrived on the lakes later that spring, bringing with her a cargo of Welsh coal on her delivery voyage.

Unfortunately, NISBET GRAMMER enjoyed only a short life. Downbound with a grain cargo on eastern Lake Ontario during a dense fog on May 31, 1926, NISBET GRAMMER was rammed and sunk by the steamer DAL-WARNIC while off Thirty Mile Point. DALWARNIC, the former CANADIAN HARVESTER, was built in 1921 at Port Arthur for the Canadian Government Merchant Marine. It had just been purchased by the Canada Atlantic Transit Company and was on her delivery voyage into the lakes when the collision occurred.

NISBET GRAMMER sank quickly after the impact. All of her crew members were able to escape and were picked up safely by DALWARNIC. Salvage of NISBET GRAMMER was out of the question because of the depth of water in the area where she foundered.

NESBIT GRAMMER, April 14, 1923, launched at Birkenhead, England

BUILT:	1923
	Cammell, Laird & Co. Ltd.,
	Birkenhead, England
HULL NUMBER:	901
LENGTH:	253.0
BREADTH:	43.1
DEPTH:	17.9
GRT:	1,725
REGISTRY NUMBER:	C. 147208
ENGINES:	16", 27", 44" Diameter
	x 33" Stroke
	Triple Expansion
ENGINE BUILDER:	Shipyard

NISBET GRAMMER in the St. Lawrence River

GRAND ISLAND

The steel bulk freighter EUGENE ZIMMERMAN was built in 1905 at Toledo, Ohio and was launched on January 18, 1906 by the Craig Shipbuilding Company for the fleet managed by L.S. Sullivan of Toledo. On her maiden voyage upbound with coal on April 16, 1906, she was in collision with the steamer SAXONA, downbound with flax in the St. Mary's River at the foot of the dyke. The SAXONA was making the turn and her bow cut through the ZIMMERMAN as far as the windlass. Both ships filled with water, the ZIMMERMAN sinking in 20 feet of water on the Canadian side while the SAXONA continued down river to Little Mud Lake where she sank on the west side of the river. The SAXONA was quickly pumped out and continued her trip to Buffalo, New York, her cargo uninjured. The ZIMMERMAN was not so fortunate. The Donnelly Wrecking Company was hired to raise her. They employed a cofferdam and lightered her cargo which was sold to Algoma Steel. Finally, they succeeded in raising the vessel during the week of May 20, 1906. The ZIMMERMAN was taken to Cleveland, Ohio and repaired. Miraculously, no one was injured in the collision.

Repaired and returned to service, the ZIMMERMAN was a profitable vessel for Sullivan. In 1911, she was purchased by Craig and Adams' Toledo Steamship Company. In 1916, Cleveland-Cliffs took over the vessel and, later that year, renamed her b) GRAND ISLAND. For this fleet the GRAND ISLAND sailed, mostly in the iron ore trade from Marquette, Michigan to lower lake ports for over 40 years. In 1964, the Auxilliary Power Company purchased the vessel to hold storage grain, renaming her c) POWERAUX CHRIS. However, they soon changed their minds and sold the vessel for scrapping overseas. The POWERAUX CHRIS arrived at Hamburg, Germany on September 11, 1964 and was cut up in 1965.

EUGENE ZIMMERMAN downbound in the St. Clair River

Sunk in the St. Mary's River in 1906

a) Eugene Zimmerman   b) GRAND ISLAND   c) Poweraux Chris

BUILT:	1905	*GRT:*	5,630
	Craig Shipbuilding Co.,	*REGISTRY NUMBER:*	US. 202711
	Toledo, Ohio	*ENGINES:*	18", 26", 36", 55" Diameter
HULL NUMBER:	106		x 40" Stroke
LENGTH:	488.6		Quadruple Expansion
BREADTH:	52.0	*ENGINE BUILDER:*	Shipyard
DEPTH:	31.0		

EUGENE ZIMMERMAN in Cleveland Cliffs colors

GRAND ISLAND with tug TEXAS at Cleveland, Ohio in 1956

POWERAUX CHRIS downbound in the Welland Ship Canal on way to scrap August 28, 1964

GREATER BUFFALO

GREATER BUFFALO just after leaving her Detroit dock

The GREATER BUFFALO, like her sistership GREATER DETROIT, was designed by Frank E. Kirby. This steel side-wheel passenger vessel was launched October 29, 1923 at Lorain, Ohio by the American Shipbuilding Company for the D & C Navigation Company of Detroit, Michigan to run between that port and Buffalo, New York. Originally intended to be propelled by steam turbine engines, the power plant design of the two vessels was changed on the drawing board to make them the largest side-wheel passenger boats in the world. The GREATER BUFFALO was towed to Detroit for installation of her machinery.

The GREATER BUFFALO served the D & C well until requisitioned by the U.S. Navy on August 7, 1942. She was taken to Erie, Pennsylvania and converted into a training aircraft carrier by the American Shipbuilding Company. On September 19, 1942, she was renamed b) U.S.S.

SABLE, IX-81. The entire upper works of the vessel were stripped off and a flight deck covered her hull. She was commissioned on May 8, 1943, 6,381 displacement tonnage, for service on Lake Michigan. Along with the U.S.S. WOLVERINE, ex SEEANDBEE, these vessels trained most of the carrier pilots who were to be the vanguard of the U.S. Navy airforce on board the huge, fast carriers of the Pacific Fleet in World War II.

After that conflict, the U.S.S. SABLE was deemed surplus and was decommissioned on November 7, 1945. It was turned over to the U.S. Maritime Commission for disposal. On July 7, 1948, the vessel was sold to H.H. Buncher & Company for scrapping. Towed by the tugs HELENA, LACHINE and GUARDIAN, the once proud vessel was taken to Hamilton, Ontario and reduced to scrap.

GREATER BUFFALO returning to Detroit from Buffalo, July 11, 1935

U.S.S. SABLE on Lake Michigan as a training aircraft carrier

Last voyage on Lake Erie bound for Hamilton in 1948

a) GREATER BUFFALO   b) U.S.S. Sable

BUILT:	1924	GRT:	7,739
	American Shipbuilding Co.,	REGISTRY NUMBER:	US.223663
	Lorain, Ohio	ENGINES:	66", 96", 96" Diameter
HULL NUMBER:	786		x 108" Stroke
LENGTH:	518.7		Inclined Compound
BREADTH:	58.0	ENGINE BUILDER:	Detroit Shipbuilding Company
DEPTH:	21.3		Detroit, Michigan, 1923

U.S.S. SABLE being towed to Hamilton by the tug HELENA

GREYHOUND (2)

The steel day-excursion passenger vessel GREYHOUND was built at Wyandotte, Michigan by the Detroit Shipbuilding Company and launched on February 15, 1902. The engine, built in 1899, was taken out of the former GREYHOUND (1) (ex NORTHWEST) whose original engine had been replaced by this one. The GREYHOUND (1) was dismantled in 1901. Built for the White Star Line of Detroit, Michigan, the GREYHOUND left on her maiden voyage from Wyandotte to Cleveland, Ohio on June 10, 1902.

For most of her years, she sailed out of Toledo, Ohio to Sugar Island and Detroit, with occasional trips to Cedar Point and Put-In-Bay, Ohio plus many wonderful moonlight excursions into Maumee Bay from Toledo. Throughout her career she is said to have never used her anchor. In all her years, she had only one accident. That occurred in 1916 when a sailing yacht ran into her near the Crib Light outside of Toledo harbor.

In 1925, the Red Star Navigation Company of Toledo purchased the vessel. In 1930, the excursion business was severely depressed and the boat was laid up due to the Great Depression. She was sold at auction in 1932 to satisfy a lien, and lay in her birth awaiting a buyer who did not materialize. In 1935, she was taken over by the Toledo Salvage and Sales Company to be scrapped. This was accomplished late in 1935 and into 1936. Her fittings were sold at auction. Her large ensignia, two bronze painted wooden greyhounds in full stride, after decorating the outside of a bar in Toledo for several years, wound up in the museum of the Great Lakes Historical Society at Vermilion, Ohio.

GREYHOUND in the St. Clair River

BUILT:	1902
	Detroit Shipbuilding Co.,
	Wyandotte, Mich.
HULL NUMBER:	146
LENGTH:	276.0
BREADTH:	38.0
DEPTH:	15.0
GRT:	1,392
REGISTRY NUMBER:	US.86621
ENGINES:	60" Diameter x 144" Stroke
	Beam Condensing
ENGINE BUILDER:	S. F. Hodge & Company
	Detroit, Michigan
	Rebuilt in 1902 #263

GREYHOUND leaving her dock on the Maumee River at Toledo

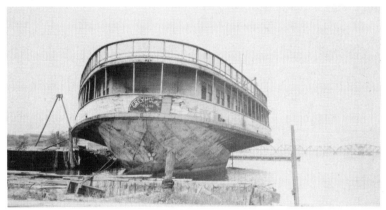
Hull of the GREYHOUND, May 10, 1936

GREYHOUND being scrapped, May 10, 1936

GUNILDA

This steel steam yacht was built in Leith, Scotland in 1897 by Ramage & Ferguson for F.W. Sykes of the port of Leith and Wivenhoe, England. It was designed by Cox & King and was elegantly appointed.

Early in the new century, the palatial yacht was purchased by William L. Harkness of New York City who was the son of Stephen V. Harkness, one of the original investors with John D. Rockefeller in the Standard Oil Company.

Harkness brought the yacht to the lakes to cruise with his family and friends in 1910 and 1911. While cruising the north shore of Lake Superior in August of 1911, tragedy struck. Without the services of modern navigation aids, the GUNILDA stranded on McGarvey's shoal on the Northwest side of Copper Island in Nipigon Bay near Rossport, Ontario, on August 29, 1911. She was high and dry almost to her midships, but no one was injured.

The tug JAMES WHALEN and barge EMPIRE were sent to release her. All the crew and passengers were taken off before the attempt at salvage. The powerful salvage tug, JAMES WHALEN tried to pull the vessel off the rocks. The advice of the salvage master was not heeded and, in the haste to release her, the vessel was not "buttoned up" (the watertight doors not closed). She listed to starboard, took on water and sank backwards into 300 feet of water on August 31, 1911.

Some attempts at salvage were made but soon abandoned due to the depth of water. One skin diver drowned in 1970 in an attempt to reach the vessel. In 1980, divers aboard Jacques Cousteau's research ship CALYPSO photographed the GUNILDA. One of the divers stated that the yacht is in good condition with the masts still up and the rigging is still in good condition because of the cold water. The crew of the CALYPSO considered it one of the most beautiful ships they had ever seen underwater.

GUNILDA anchored near New York

GUNILDA stranded on McGarvey's shoal

BUILT:	1897
	Ramage & Ferguson,
	Leith, Scotland
HULL NUMBER:	Unknown
LENGTH:	166.0
BREADTH:	24.7
DEPTH:	14.2
GRT:	385
REGISTRY NUMBER:	Br. 104928
ENGINES:	15", 24", 39" Diameter
	x 27" Stroke
	Triple Expansion
ENGINE BUILDER:	Shipyard

August 30, 1911, the day before she sank

ERIE L. HACKLEY

The wooden steamer ERIE L. HACKLEY was named for the adopted daughter of the Muskegon, Michigan lumberman, Charles H. Hackley. The boat was built in 1882 at the Arnold Boat Yard, Muskegon, for Capt. Seth Lee. For 10 years she ran with CENTENNIAL and MARY E. MENTON, in Capt. Lee's "Muskegon Lake Ferry Line." In 1891, Lee sent her north, under Capt. Peter Pillow, to run on Pine Lake (Lake Charlevoix) between Charlevoix and East Jordan, Michigan. She was back to Muskegon Lake in 1892 because of insufficient business on Pine Lake.

At the end of that season, she was sold to Capt. P. D. (Pete) Campbell of Whitehall who fitted her cabin with 16 folding berths for excursions to the World's Fair in Chicago, Illinois. Various attempts to run these excursions from Whitehall, Michigan or Muskegon and, finally, from Michigan City, Indiana did not pay, and the HACKLEY ended the season of 1893 running local excursions out of Chicago.

The next two years were spent in ferry service between White Lake and Muskegon, connecting that resort community with the trans-lake steamers out of Muskegon. In 1896, the boat was moved to Charlevoix where, for the next seven years, she ran tri-weekly trips, early in the morning and late in the afternoon between Charlevoix and St. James, Beaver Island, Michigan. On her "off" days, she made frequent trips to other points on Pine Lake, with some stops on Little Traverse Bay, and ports including Cross Village on Sturgeon Bay on the Michigan shore.

In 1902, the Harbor Springs steamer OVAL AGITATOR was bought to replace the HACKLEY on the Beaver Island route, and was promptly renamed BEAVER. The HACKLEY, put up for sale, soon passed to Capt. Sam Rose of Charlevoix, who used her that one summer on a route between Frankfort, Michigan and the Manitou Islands, with stops at Glen Haven and Glen Arbor, Michigan. The vessel was plagued with a broken tail shaft in April and a broken crankshaft in August. It was not a happy summer for the new owner.

In March 1903, the HACKLEY was sold to Capt. Joseph Vorous of Fish Creek, Wisconsin. Capt. Rose delivered her to Fish Creek in May, and brought home, as part payment, the fish tug LILLIE CHAMBERS. Captain Vorous put the HACKLEY on a route between Sturgeon Bay, Wisconsin, Menominee, Michigan and Detroit Harbor, Washington Island, Wisconsin. She had less than a full season on Green Bay. At five p.m. October 3, 1903, she left Menominee for Egg Harbor and, an hour after leaving port, was caught in a furious storm and foundered, with a loss of twelve passengers and three of her crewmen, including Captain Vorous.

The HACKLEY was built as a typical single-decked inland lakes ferry, and went through many structural changes during her lifetime. It is not known exactly when she was first "housed in" for operation in open water, but odds are it was at some point before she began her years of service to Beaver Island. The enclosed bulwarks forward and the upper cabin were added in 1901 to give her more space below for cargo.

In the past few years attempts have been made to raise the vessel to make a museum out of it. Work is still in progress at this time.

ERIE L. HACKLEY prior to 1893 at Lee's Ferry dock, Muskegon

ERIE L. HACKLEY in later years

BUILT:	1882
	J. A. Arnold,
	Muskegon, Mich.
LENGTH:	79.0
BREADTH:	17.4
DEPTH:	5.2
GRT:	54
REGISTRY NUMBER:	US.135615
ENGINES:	14" Diameter x 18" Stroke
	High Pressure Non-Condensing
ENGINE BUILDER:	Wilson & Hendrie
	Montague, Michigan, 1888

D. B. HANNA

The steel canaller D.B. HANNA was built in 1925 by the Furness Shipbuilding Company at Haverton-Hill-on-Tees, England for the Toronto Insurance and Vessel Agency, Ltd., better known as Captain Foote's Union Transit Company. Her routes were the usual canaller trade between the Upper Lakes and ports on the St. Lawrence River, carrying mainly grain and coal.

In 1939, she was purchased by the Paterson Steamships Ltd., and renamed b) COLLINGDOC (1). Among the cargoes she carried were pulpwood and grain from the Lakehead to Lake Ontario ports but she was in this service just a short while before being requisitioned for war service in 1940 by the British Government. The rare photo of her shows her being readied for war service. Her name and the huge letter "P" on the stack have been painted out.

On July 13, 1941, she struck a mine 200°, 4 cables from Southend Pier, Southend, England and sank. No loss of life was reported. Later that same year, she was salvaged and became a "special service vessel" and was sunk at Brest, France in March of 1942 as a blockship. What happened to her after this is not known. Presumably, she was scrapped or abandoned in place.

a) **D.B. HANNA**   b) **Collingdoc (1)**

BUILT:	1925
	Furness Shipbuilding Co.,
	Haverton-Hill-on-Tees, England
HULL NUMBER:	91
LENGTH:	252.5
BREADTH:	43.2
DEPTH:	17.8
GRT:	1,780
REGISTRY NUMBER:	C.147780
ENGINES:	16", 27", 44" Diameter
	x 33" Stroke
	Triple Expansion
ENGINE BUILDER:	Earles Shipbuilding &
	Engineering Company Ltd.
	Hull, England

D.B. HANNA upbound at Mission Point in 1930

COLLINGDOC downbound in the Detroit River for the last time

HERMAN H. HETTLER

WALTER VAIL downbound with lumber

HERMAN H. HETTLER at the Soo in 1913

a) Walter Vail   b) HERMAN H. HETTLER

BUILT:	1890	*GRT:*	726
	James Davidson,	*REGISTRY NUMBER:*	US.81263
	W. Bay City, Mich.	*ENGINES:*	22", 42" Diameter x
HULL NUMBER:	34		40" Stroke
LENGTH:	200.0		Fore and Aft Compound
BREADTH:	35.0	*ENGINE BUILDER:*	Frontier Iron Works
DEPTH:	13.3		Buffalo, New York

The wooden steam barge WALTER VAIL was built in 1890 at West Bay City, Michigan by James Davidson for H. D. Campbell and H. W. Cook of Michigan City, Indiana. In 1897, she was bought by Henry J. Pauly of Milwaukee, Wisconsin.

In 1906, the VAIL was owned by James F. Rose of Duluth, Minnesota and rebuilt by him to 210.0 x 34.7 x 13.2; 789 GRT. The J. O. Calbick Lumber Company of Chicago, Illinois managed the vessel in 1906 for W. H. Wood. W. E. Holmes & Co. of Chicago took her over in 1912. The H. H. Hettler Lumber Company of Chicago bought the VAIL in 1913 and renamed her b) HERMAN H. HETTLER. Cargoes were mainly the firm's lumber products to various ports on the lakes. The HETTLER served in this fleet for more than 12 years.

In 1924, she was operated by O. W. Blodgett of Bay City, Wenonah Transportation Co., owners. During the heavy gale of November 5-6 on Lake Superior, the wooden lumber barge JOHN L. CRANE broke away without warning from the steamer HERMAN H. HETTLER, which was towing her, and plunged to the bottom off Crisp Point, where many other lumber carriers have met their fate. The entire crew of six seamen and one woman perished. The HETTLER survived after assistance from the U. S. Coast Guard at Crisp Point.

The year 1926 was not so fortunate for the HETTLER. During another of the "Gales of November", the HERMAN H. HETTLER, while trying to seek shelter behind Grand Island on Lake Superior, slammed into the rocky reef off Trout Point at the Northeast end of the East Channel, stranded on the island north of Munising, Michigan and started breaking up on November 23, 1926. She was carrying a load of 1,100 tons of bulk table salt. The captain and crew managed to escape in lifeboats to Munising the next day. On Friday the 26th, another storm came up and completely demolished the vessel. The old wooden lumber vessels were rapidly disappearing from the Lakes in the 1920's, and the loss of this ship depleted the number further. By the time another decade passed, hardly any wooden vessels of this vintage remained on the Great Lakes.

HERMAN H. HETTLER at Montreal in 1916

ELIZABETH HINDMAN

The steel canaller GLENCLOVA was launched on November 21, 1920 from the yard of the Midland Shipbuilding Company at Midland, Ontario for James Playfair's Great Lakes Transportation Company Ltd. The vessel was equipped with the engine of the old wooden steamer MAJOR, ex JOHN MITCHELL, built in 1889. The GLENCOVA was intended for the grain trade, and sailed many waters under various names and owners in its lifetime. In 1922, Playfair and A. E. Mathews, Toronto, combined in a partnership. The GLENCLOVA and others were operated as the Glen Line.

The partnership was dissolved in 1925. The George Hall Coal Company purchased the vessel in March, 1926. After a partial season, they sold her to Canada Steamship Lines Ltd., in October, 1926. She was renamed b) ANTICOSTI in 1927. She served C.S.L. until 1940, when the vessel was chartered to the British Ministry of War Transport for service overseas. Of interest in her travels and experiences during World War II was the fact that she was a part of the Normandy Invasion fleet from June 6 to July 4, 1944.

After hostilities had ended, the ANTICOSTI was sold to William Cory & Son of Liverpool, England and registered British on February 19, 1946. In 1949, she was sold to Cia. Maritima Panamana (Panamanian registry #1792) and renamed c) RISACUA. In April 1953, she was again sold, this time to the Hindman Transportation Company of Owen Sound, Ontario, and registered Canadian again. Captain George Hindman purchased her at Genoa, Italy in April and brought her back to the lakes as d) GEORGE HINDMAN (2).

In 1955, the old steam engine was replaced by a modern diesel (16 cyl. 242 mm x 305 mm) built in 1942 by General Motors, Cleveland Engine Division, Cleveland, Ohio. In order to name another boat GEORGE HINDMAN, the vessel was renamed e) ELIZABETH HINDMAN in 1962. During her career she was painted in various colors but none were as unique as the yellow-grey-purple colors she carried for a while in the Hindman Fleet.

Even after the opening of the St. Lawrence Seaway in 1959, when most of the canallers were retired from service, the ELIZABETH HINDMAN continued hauling various bulk cargoes around the lakes. Finally, on October 23, 1970 her register was closed. The veteran was scrapped at Duluth, Minnesota by the Hyman-Michaels Company in 1970-71.

GLENCOVA in Matthews colors in 1922

GLENCOVA in Great Lakes Transportation Co. Ltd. colors

ANTICOSTI unloading coal at Toronto

a) **Glenclova** b) **Anticosti** c) **Risacua**
d) **George Hindman (2)** e) **ELIZABETH HINDMAN**

BUILT:	1920
	Midland Shipbuilding Co.,
	Midland, Ontario
HULL NUMBER:	9
LENGTH:	246.0
BREADTH:	42.5
DEPTH:	18.5
GRT:	1,925
REGISTRY NUMBER:	C. 150232
ENGINES:	18", 30", 50" Diameter
	x 42" Stroke
	Triple Expansion
ENGINE BUILDER:	Frontier Iron Works
	Detroit, Michigan, 1889

GEORGE HINDMAN in her early Hindman colors

GEORGE HINDMAN after being Dieselized, August 5, 1961

ELIZABETH HINDMAN, September 5, 1962

DOUGLASS HOUGHTON

DOUGLASS HOUGHTON with twin stacks

The DOUGLASS HOUGHTON was a steel bulk freighter built in 1899 at Cleveland, Ohio by the Globe Iron Works for the Bessemer Steamship Company of Cleveland. She was launched on June 3, 1899.

On September 5, 1899, while downbound with the consort barge JOHN FRITZ in tow, DOUGLASS HOUGHTON suffered a steering failure in the Middle Neebish Channel of the St. Mary's River, just above the turn at Sailors' Encampment. Her master reduced speed to dead-slow so she could be anchored and her steering gear repaired. The barge FRITZ could not be stopped and she rammed the HOUGHTON, sinking her on the spot.

The sunken HOUGHTON blocked the river for five days and over 100 ships found their passage impeded by the wreck. The incident came to be known as "The Houghton Blockade", and resulted in the construction of the West Neebish (Rock Cut) Channel a few years later as an alternate route. Thereafter, the Middle Neebish Channel was used for upbound traffic, while the Rock Cut was used by downbound vessels, except during the late 1950's when the Rock Cut temporarily was closed for deepening.

In 1901, the HOUGHTON was purchased by the Pittsburgh Steamship Company. In 1910, she was reboilered and one of her two stacks was removed. Because of her powerful engine, she towed a barge most of her life. Around 1928, her Gross Registered Tonnage was changed to 4,515.

The HOUGHTON was sold in July, 1945 to the Upper Lakes and St. Lawrence Transportation Company, Ltd., Toronto (C.174976) and served that fleet for 23 years, often towing her nemesis, the barge JOHN FRITZ, which had joined the same fleet. She was finally laid up at Toronto in 1967.

After having been stripped of her superstructure, the hull of DOUGLASS HOUGHTON was filled with stone and sunk in 1969 as part of the breakwater around the Ontario Government's park, Ontario Place, located just west of the western entrance to Toronto Harbor. An observation platform now stands atop her forecastle and her name is still proudly displayed on her side, a reminder of her many years of service.

BUILT:	1899
	Globe Iron Works,
	Cleveland, Ohio
HULL NUMBER:	78
LENGTH:	456.0
BREADTH:	50.0
DEPTH:	24.2
GRT:	5,332
REGISTRY NUMBER:	US.157552
ENGINES:	26½", 37", 51½", 80" Diameter
	x 42" Stroke
	Quadruple Expansion
ENGINE BUILDER:	Shipyard

Upbound off Belle Isle in the Detroit River

DOUGLASS HOUGHTON in the ice in the upper St. Mary's River

HURON (LIGHTSHIP #103)

The steel lightship #103 was built in 1920 at Morris Heights, New York by the Consolidated Shipbuilding Company for the United States Lighthouse Service. She was immediately brought to the lakes and painted a brilliant red with huge white letters denoting her station. #103 arrived at Milwaukee, Wisconsin and assumed the position of RELIEF through the 1923 season. From 1924 to 1929 she was stationed at GRAY's Reef and then again from 1929 to 1932 as RELIEF. During the seasons of 1933 and 1934, she was at MANITOU Shoals in Lake Michigan.

In 1934, the #103 assumed a position on Corsica Shoals in lower Lake Huron as HURON. Her paint job was now black with white letters, because she marked the port side of the upbound channel. It was the only lightship to be painted black, all the others were painted red.

The U.S. Coast Guard took over the Lighthouse Service in 1939. Its designation for the HURON lightship was WAL-526 by which she was known until decommissioning ceremonies on August 25, 1970. The small steam boiler was replaced by a diesel engine in 1959.

On August 29, 1972 the former lightship was eased from her mooring in the Black River at Port Huron, Michigan and moved to a permanent final berth just below the Blue Water Bridge in Pine Grove Park, where it has become a permanent fixture and tourist attraction. One of the last lightships of the U.S., and the last one of the lakes, now rests peacefully and serves as a reminder of the days she rode the waves of Lake Huron to guide ships to safety around the shoals and into the safe channels of the St. Clair River.

Lightships, with their relatively costly operational expenses for manpower and upkeep, have become a thing of the past. They are gone, but not forgotten. HURON is still a reminder of safety, a signal never to be forgotten; a sign of hope for lost sailors. She is still a beacon and visitors are welcome.

#103 as RELIEF at Milwaukee

BUILT:	1920
	Consolidated Shipbuilding Co.,
	Morris Heights, New York
HULL NUMBER:	Unknown
LENGTH:	69.5 — Lengthened in 1936 to 96.5
BREADTH:	24.0
DEPTH:	11.9
	Displacement Tonnage 320

#103 as MANITOU at Charlevoix. Tug JAMES E. SANFORD at left

#103 as HURON before World War II

#103 Dieselized. On station, June 26, 1960

HYACINTH

The steel buoy and lighthouse tender HYACINTH was launched July 26, 1902 at Port Huron, Michigan by the Jenks Shipbuilding Company for the United States Lighthouse Service. She was stationed on Lake Michigan for most of her life and serviced the various ports and harbors up and down both sides of the lake. Normal duties included placing buoys in the spring and removing them each fall at the approach of winter. She serviced the lighthouses and lightships bringing needed supplies and removing the keepers whenever necessary.

The Lighthouse Service was merged with the U.S. Coast Guard in 1939 but the HYACINTH's duties remained the same. After World War II, newer tenders, built during the war, replaced aging vessels like the HYACINTH and she was sold to Lyons Construction Company in 1946. This firm intended to document her and rename her NORTHWIND but this never transpired. Captain John Roen of Sturgeon Bay, Wisconsin purchased the vessel in 1956, after it had been laid up for 10 years, and scrapped it in January 1957 at Sturgeon Bay, Wisconsin.

BUILT:	1902
	Jenks Shipbuilding Co.,
	Port Huron, Mich.
HULL NUMBER:	22
LENGTH:	150.7
BREADTH:	28.0
DEPTH:	14.0
GRT:	738
ENGINES:	22", 42" Diameter x 36" Stroke
	Horizontal Compound
ENGINE BUILDER:	Shipyard

HYACINTH placing buoys in Lake Michigan

At her dock

IDLEWILD

GRACE McMILLAN in the Detroit River

The iron steamer GRACE McMILLAN was built at Wyandotte, Michigan by the Detroit Dry Dock Company and launched on June 6, 1879 for the Detroit Steam Navigation Company which was controlled by the McMillan family of Detroit, Michigan. The steamer's cabin was finished in mahogany and trimmed with gold leaf. Her engine had been in the wrecking tug MAGNET (US.16819) of 1858 and was rebuilt by Fletcher & Co. of Hoboken, New Jersey.

The ship was named for Senator James McMillan's daughter, Grace. The reasons for its being renamed b) IDLE-WILD on April 18, 1881 have come down in history as rather interesting. When the GRACE McMILLAN was dry-docked, a Detroit newspaper came out with the comment that Grace McMillan was having her bottom scraped. This did not go well with the prominent Senator and he promptly had the steamer's name changed.

IDLEWILD was chartered to the Wabash Railroad and started running from Toledo, Ohio to the Lake Erie Islands and Lakeside, Ohio on Wednesday July 2, 1879. The following year she ran from Detroit to the St. Clair Flats and Port Huron, Michigan. In 1887, she ran from Toledo to Detroit and was operated by the White Star Line. In 1889, the IDLEWILD was modified at Cleveland, Ohio by the Cleveland Shipbuilding Company. Her new dimensions were: 186.0 x 26.0 x 7.4: 363 GRT. On July 19, 1889 the Red Star Line, controlled by Darius Cole of Detroit, purchased the vessel. This company became the Star-Cole Line in 1898. The vessel spent the rest of her days on the Detroit to Port Huron run except the season of 1905 when she was chartered to run from Buffalo to Dunkirk, New York.

In the fall of 1913, she was laid up at Windsor, Ontario and never ran again. Her cabins were dismantled at Detroit in 1914, she was sold and the hull made into a barge (229 GRT). It was used in the molasses trade from Oswego, New York to Port Hope. In May of 1919 the barge went ashore at Peekskill, New York in the Hudson River. She was abandoned there March 3, 1923 and her document surrendered, her owners still being the White Star Line; but of New York City at that time.

IDLEWILD under full steam with a good crowd aboard

a) Grace McMillan   b) IDLEWILD

BUILT:	1879	*DEPTH:*	7.9
	Detroit Dry Dock Co.,	*GRT:*	312
	Wyandotte, Mich.	*REGISTRY NUMBER:*	US. 85595
HULL NUMBER:	33	*ENGINES:*	42" Diameter x 120" Stroke
LENGTH:	160.9		Beam Condensing
BREADTH:	26.0	*ENGINE BUILDER:*	Detroit Locomotive Works
			Detroit, Michigan, 1864

Laid up at Windsor, Ontario

INDIA

The wooden steam barge INDIA was built in 1899 at Garden Island, Ontario by the Calvin Company for their own fleet of lumber steamers. It was the fourth steam barge built by the Calvins who also built and installed their own engines. Like other Calvin steamers, the INDIA was painted a bright green with white trim and cabins and a black funnel. On one of her early trips while towing the barge AUGUSTUS and carrying a load of iron ore, she went ashore 8 miles above Port Colborne, Ontario on Lake Erie on Sunday, August 20, 1899 in heavy smoke and little visibility. She was released the next day and proceeded to her destination.

In 1914, the vessel was sold to Montreal Transportation Company. This firm was absorbed in 1920 into Canada Steamship Lines. After sinking in the Welland Canal in 1922, INDIA was abandoned to the underwriters who engaged the Reid Wrecking Company, salvors, to raise the vessel. Crawford & Company of Montreal became the owners in 1923 and sailed her as a part of their India Navigation Company until 1926. That year she was sold to Ramsey Brothers of Sault Ste. Marie, Ontario.

On September 4, 1928, in the North Channel behind Manitoulin Island, Lake Huron, 8 miles east of Little Current, Ontario, she caught fire and burned to the water's edge. No one was injured and all managed to escape the inferno. INDIA was completely destroyed and her last remains are today marked by a buoy in the channel.

BUILT:	1899
	Calvin Company,
	Garden Island, Ontario
LENGTH:	215.9
BREADTH:	36.4
DEPTH:	15.0

GRT:	976
REGISTRY NUMBER:	C. 107735
ENGINES:	18", 30", 48" Diameter
	x 30" Stroke
	Triple Expansion
ENGINE BUILDER:	Shipyard

INDIA upbound with coal in 1919

INDIA in C.S.L. colors unloading grain at Montreal

Afire near Manitoulin Island September 5, 1928

IOCOMA

The steel tanker IOCOMA was built in 1912 at Dundee, Scotland by the Caledon Shipbuilding & Engineering Company for Imperial Oil Ltd., of Sarnia, Ontario to service their burgeoning oil products trade on the Great Lakes and ports along the St. Lawrence River. IOCOMA saw service in both World Wars both on the lakes and on the coast. She spent most of the Second War in bunkering service at Halifax, and subsequently served in the same capacity at Montreal. In 1947, all the vessels of the Imperial Oil fleet were renamed. Each name was prefixed by the word "Imperial". The IOCOMA became b) IMPERIAL WHITBY.

In 1949, after close to 40 years of service, the IMPERIAL WHITBY was retired and purchased by Port Weller Dry Docks Ltd. The IMPERIAL WHITBY was converted to a self-unloading bulk carrier by St. Lawrence Drydocks, Montreal, in 1951 for Bayswater Shipping Ltd., who purchased the vessel and renamed it c) GEORGE S. CLEET.

Her dimensions now were: 248.2 x 42.6 x 23.1; 2,174 GRT. Now her cargoes became more varied. She carried coal, grain and stone for this Brockville, Ontario-based company.

In 1961, the vessel's stern was removed and replaced with a cruiser stern by Kingston Shipyards Ltd., at Kingston, Ontario. Her new GRT was 2,184 and Bayswater renamed her d) BAYGEORGE. In 1965, she was lengthened 76.5 feet to 324.7. The new GRT was 3,172. For the next few years the BAYGEORGE was operated in the coal, stone and gravel trade, but her days were numbered. In late 1967, Bayswater Shipping went into voluntary liquidation. BAYGEORGE was seized by the Industrial Development Bank of Ottawa and in 1968 was sold to Transworld Shipping Ltd., of Montreal. She never again operated. In 1969, the ex-tanker was sold to United Metal and Refining Company Ltd., of Hamilton, Ontario and was scrapped in 1971 at Strathearne Terminals, Hamilton.

IOCOMA at the Soo in 1916

a) IOCOMA	b) Imperial Whitby	c) George S. Cleet	d) Baygeorge

BUILT:	1912
	Caledon Shipbuilding &
	Engineering Co.,
	Dundee, Scotland
HULL NUMBER:	226
LENGTH:	248.2
BREADTH:	42.6

DEPTH:	15.6
GRT:	1,669
REGISTRY NUMBER:	C. 132745
ENGINES:	18", 24", 41" Diameter
	x 36" Stroke
	Triple Expansion
ENGINE BUILDER:	Shipyard

IMPERIAL WHITBY downbound on Lake St. Clair, August 21, 1948

GEORGE S. CLEET leaving Toronto

BAYGEORGE unloading a cargo of sand

IRONWOOD

a) Charles Beatty   b) Usona   c) Bayusona   d) Port De St. Malo
e) Bayusona   f) Roslyn   g) Usona   h) IRONWOOD

BUILT:	1902
	Craig Shipbuilding Co.,
	Toledo, Ohio
HULL NUMBER:	88
LENGTH:	211.5
BREADTH:	40.5
DEPTH:	13.4
GRT:	986
REGISTRY NUMBER:	US.127641
ENGINES:	15¼", 25", 42" Diameter
	x 36" Stroke
	Triple Expansion
ENGINE BUILDER:	Shipyard

CHARLES BEATTY upbound in the St. Clair River

The steel canal-sized freighter CHARLES BEATTY was launched on April 16, 1902, at Toledo, Ohio by the Craig Shipbuilding Company for the Volunteer Transportation Company. In the beginning, this vessel was employed in the general bulk cargo trades to transport lumber, iron ore, coal and grain on the lakes. The adventures of this little vessel began during World War I.

In 1916, the BEATTY was sold to Atlantic coast operators, Bay Steamship Company of New York, to be engaged in the carrying of war-time necessities. Concurrent with the change in ownership she was renamed b) USONA. The following year she was sold to Bay Steamship Company Ltd., a British firm, and renamed c) BAYUSONA, (BR 140405).

On December 10, 1917, while traversing the English Channel, she was attacked with gunfire from a German "U" Boat. However, the Captain of the "U"-Boat was forced to reconsider his obviously rash action when the fire was returned from the small deck gun which had been installed on the BAYUSONA. Not one casualty was incurred on the

BAYUSONA during this exchange. Following three years of active service, she was sold in 1920 to French interests and renamed d) PORT DE ST. MALO, but only for a brief period of time.

Many canallers taken to the ocean during the War were returned to the lakes shortly after the fighting. The PORT DE ST. MALO was sold Canadian, (C.140405) to the Interlake Steam Navigation Company in 1922. They promptly gave her back the name e) BAYUSONA. In that same year her name was changed yet again; this time to f) ROSLYN. In 1923, she was sold to White, Gratwick & Mitchell (Mitchell Associated Lumber Companies). That same year these gentlemen too decided to rename her. For the second time she was given the name g) USONA. This was her seventh name change!

Needing a small vessel to do dredging work in the rivers, the Gleason Coal Co., of Detroit purchased the multinamed vessel in 1926 and converted her to a sand dredge at the Great Lakes Engineering Works in Ecorse. Her dimensions were slightly altered to 212.6 x 40.2 x 13.2; 1,300 gross registered tons. Amazingly she was not renamed!

For ten years she continued to operate under this name. In 1936, USONA was once again sold. Her new owners, Nicholson Transit Company, renamed her h) IRONWOOD. She served Nicholson as a sand dredge until 1942 when they re-converted her to a bulk carrier at River Rouge. Following this, she once again returned to salt water and yet another World War, this time under the ownership of the British War Ministry of Transport. No record of her war activities is noted this time.

In late 1945, the IRONWOOD returned to the lakes. Her old triple expansion steam engine was removed in 1951 and replaced by a diesel engine (4 cyl., 10½ x 13½, Cooper Bessemer built in 1942, recovered from a naval vessel). The forward cabins were placed astern, making her a smart little stem-winder and she was once again placed in the bulk trade, primarily finished steel. She served for Nicholson until 1961, when she was sold to Toth Transportation Co., of Toledo, Ohio.

By now, too small for any other trade, the vessel was reduced to a barge in 1963. She was sold again and again. The other names involved in her ownership were: The King Construction Company of Holland, Michigan (1968) who contemplated her purchase; Lucas County State Bank (July 1968-Aug. 1970); Walter Kolbe of Pt. Clinton, Ohio (1970) and Capital Dredge & Dock Co., of Lorain, Ohio (1974). Her history was confusing, but she served well for fifteen different companies, under eight names, flying the colors of four nations, in two world wars, and as three different types of carrier. The IRONWOOD was scrapped at Hamilton, Ontario in 1974.

PORT DE ST. MALO at Montreal in 1921

USONA in Mitchell Associated Lumber Companies' colors

159

USONA at Detroit

IRONWOOD at Alpena

IRONWOOD in World War II colors, May 2, 1943

160

IRONWOOD, cabins astern, downbound in the Detroit River, June 13, 1953

IRONWOOD as a barge at Lorain, April 14, 1971

ISLAND QUEEN

The wooden side-wheel steamer ISLAND QUEEN was launched on December 12, 1854 at Kelley's Island, Ohio by Daniel Dibble for D., A., A.S., & W.D. Kelley et al. It was designed by Thomas Bates of Milan, Ohio and was constructed of native white oak and red cedar. The ISLAND QUEEN was towed to Sandusky, Ohio on January 6, 1855 by the steamer ARIEL, where the engine and boiler were installed. She ran to the Lake Erie Islands with side trips to Toledo, Ohio and occasionally ran as far east as Cleveland, Ohio.

At the beginning of the Civil War she was placed on a daily schedule from Sandusky to the Islands with an occasional excursion to Huron and Black River (Lorain), Ohio.

On the 19th of September, 1864, she left Sandusky at 2:30 PM on her regular run. Stopping at Kelley's Island, she picked up part of Company "K", 130th Ohio Volunteer Infantry, island men who were to be mustered out at Toledo the following day.

Arriving off Middle Bass dock, they found the Detroit and Sandusky steamer PHILO PARSONS at the dock so the ISLAND QUEEN made fast alongside. The lines were no more than put out when she was boarded by a party of armed men under the orders of one Lt. Beall of the Confederacy, who a few hours previously had taken possession of the PARSONS in the name of Jefferson Davis, President of the Confederate States of America. This was all a part of a plot to liberate the Confederate prisoners at Johnson's Island in Sandusky Bay. After seizing the ISLAND QUEEN, the crew and men of Company K were arrested. In the excitement, the engineer of the ISLAND QUEEN was shot in the face and a private was struck over the head with a musket.

After an hour, the passengers and crew were allowed to go ashore, as well as the soldiers, who were put on 24 hour parole. About 7:30 PM, the PARSONS got underway with the ISLAND QUEEN alongside. When about a mile away from Ballast Island, the suction pipe of the ISLAND QUEEN was broken and she was cut loose. During the night she drifted eastward past Middle Island, grounding on Chickenolee Reef where she settled in ten feet of water. The rebels on the PARSONS took off toward Detroit. On September 22, a wrecking crew rescued the ISLAND QUEEN and she was back on her route by September 25. (The failure of the Rebel plot is related in the story of the PHILO PARSONS later in this volume).

The ISLAND QUEEN was sold in 1866 to A. D. Dickerson of Detroit. Her owners were many after the Rebel incident and are as follows: William Dana of Algonac, Michigan 1868-1869; River & Lake Shore Steamboat Company of Detroit-1869-70; S.B. Grummond of Detroit-1870-1873; R.J. Hackett et al of Detroit-1873-1874; Engleman Interests of Milwaukee, Wisconsin-June 28, 1876; and Squires et al of Grand Haven, Michigan - July 8, 1876.

The engine of the ISLAND QUEEN was removed early in 1875 and her hull was converted to a barge and towed to Lake Michigan on June 11, 1875. Her engine was placed into the steambarge J.S. RUBY in 1877.

The barge ISLAND QUEEN was wrecked at Grand Haven late in the fall of 1876 and her document was surrendered at Grand Haven on December 31, 1876. Thus ended quite a saga for the little passenger boat.

ISLAND QUEEN at Put-In-Bay

BUILT:	1854	*GRT:*	168
	Daniel Dibble,	*REGISTRY NUMBER:*	US.12097
	Kelley's Island, Ohio	*ENGINES:*	22" Diameter x 60" Stroke
LENGTH:	122.6		Crosshead
BREADTH:	20.6	*ENGINE BUILDER:*	N.G. Old
DEPTH:	7.1		Sandusky, Ohio

JASMINE

The small, wooden-hulled, passenger and freight propeller WILLIAM M. ALDERSON was built in 1884 at Port Burwell, Ontario for William M. Alderson, the gentleman for whom she was named. She was intended for service on Lake Erie but, by the spring of 1886, she was operating between Meaford and Tobermory, on Georgian Bay. In 1888, she ran from Owen Sound to Wiarton and various Manitoulin Island ports. It is believed that she was on this same route when she rammed and sank the tug ANNIE WATT near Barrie Island on August 16, 1890.

On August 4, 1891 WILLIAM M. ALDERSON's upperworks were destroyed by fire at Port Dover, Ontario. The hull was sold to A.J. Tymon and Company, of Toronto, and it was towed to Toronto where it was lengthened and rebuilt at the George Dickson yard, which was located at the foot of Berkeley Street. A new steeple compound engine was built for the vessel by the Polson Iron Works, and Polson's took back a mortgage on the steamer in the amount of their account. Remeasured at Toronto on July 7, 1892, as 130.5 x 21.6 x 8.7, 194 GRT, she was renamed b) A.J. TYMON (C.100038).

Andy Tymon operated ferries across Toronto Bay from the city to Centre Island. He placed A.J. TYMON on a route from Toronto to Long Branch, Lorne Park, Grimsby and Jordan Harbour. By 1894, she was operating on weekends to Alderman Thomas Davies' Victoria Park, which was located just east of Toronto. She also ran excursions across Lake Ontario to Wilson, New York, at a fare of 25 cents return.

By 1903, A.J. TYMON's owner had encountered financial difficulties, and the vessel was turned over by the Admiralty Court to George Gooderham, of Toronto. He sold her on May 18, 1903 to George Thomas Marks, of Port Arthur, Ontario. She was renamed c) OJIBWAY at Sault Ste. Marie on June 15, 1903, and operated on the "Hiawatha Route" from the Soo to the North Channel ports of Bruce Mines, Thessalon, and Blind River, Ontario.

OJIBWAY was not successful on this run and she was sold on May 7, 1906 to Capt. Benjamin V. Naylor. He took her to Sorel, Quebec, in July 1906, and there she was rebuilt by Telesphore Miseau. In this reconstruction, OJIBWAY was shortened to 112.4 feet. Her tonnage became 298 GRT.

In March, 1908, OJIBWAY was purchased by the Toronto Ferry Company Ltd., which renamed her d) JASMINE. It was the custom of "Lol" Solman, the proprietor of the Ferry Company and amusement park at Hanlan's Point, on Toronto Island, to name his ferry steamers for various flowers. JASMINE was placed on the Island ferry route, and operated on Toronto Bay for some twenty years.

During 1926, the Toronto Ferry Company Ltd. was acquired by the City of Toronto and, prior to the opening of service in 1927, the ferries were turned over to the Toronto Transportation Commission, which operated the city's public transit system. JASMINE operated for the T.T.C. in 1927 but, after fitting out in June, 1928, she failed to pass inspection.

JASMINE was laid up at Hanlan's Point, and she remained there until August 2, 1929, when she was burned as a spectacle as part of the Civic Holiday celebrations at Toronto's Sunnyside Park. This was a popular way to dispose of old wooden hulls at that time.

OJIBWAY at her dock at the Soo

JASMINE on trials at Oakville, Ontario

a) **William M. Alderson**   b) **A.J. Tymon**   c) **Ojibway**   d) **JASMINE**

BUILT:	1884
	Port Burwell, Ontario
	Ship Builder: Unknown
LENGTH:	98.0
BREADTH:	21.0
DEPTH:	8.0
GRT:	122
REGISTRY NUMBER:	C.73920
ENGINES:	12-1/20" Diameter x
	22" Stroke
	Steeple Compound
ENGINE BUILDER:	Polson Iron Works
	Toronto, Ontario, 1892

JASMINE at one of the Islands in Toronto Harbour

B.F. JONES

B. F. JONES leaving Lime Island fuel dock in 1917

The steel bulk freighter B. F. JONES was completed in 1906. It was launched on December 31, 1905 by the Great Lakes Engineering Works at Ecorse, Michigan for the Interstate Steamship Company (Jones & Laughlin Steel). She was equipped with a triple expansion steam engine and was designed mainly to carry iron ore.

In 1952, Wilson Transit Company bought the entire Interstate fleet. Among these was the B. F. JONES. She was badly damaged in a collision in dense fog on August 21, 1955. The steamer CASON J. CALLAWAY, downbound with a load of iron ore, and the JONES, upbound light, collided below Lime Island in the St. Mary's River near DeTour, Michigan. The JONES was towed to Superior,

Wisconsin, while the CALLAWAY proceeded down to Lake Erie. The JONES was considered a constructive total loss and laid up. She was warped her entire length. The damage to the CALLAWAY was also severe. The pilothouse of the JONES, along with the hatch covers and her Texas deck, were transferred to the SPARKMAN D. FOSTER in 1956. Furthermore, her funnel was transferred to the LYMAN C. SMITH. Finally, a large part of her hull was saved by the salvagers and became a crane lighter known as SSC-1.

The JONES' final days came in 1956 at Superior, Wisconsin where she was dismantled by Fraser-Nelson Shipyards.

Downbound in the St. Mary's River near the Rock Cut

B. F. JONES being towed out of Cleveland Harbor. Tug IOWA at the bow

Just after the collision. Tug LAWRENCE C. TURNER assisting

B. F. JONES — extent of the damage — after arrival at Superior

BUILT:	1906	*GRT:*	6,939
	Great Lakes Engineering Works,	*REGISTRY NUMBER:*	US.202839
	Ecorse, Michigan	*ENGINES:*	23", 37", 63" Diameter x
HULL NUMBER:	15		42" Stroke
LENGTH:	530.0		Triple Expansion
BREADTH:	56.2	*ENGINE BUILDER:*	Shipyard
DEPTH:	32.0		

Another view of the damage

HARVEY J. KENDALL

The wooden steam barge HARVEY J. KENDALL was launched on April 10, 1892 by the master shipbuilder Alex Anderson of Marine City, Michigan for Captain Harvey J. Kendall and John E. Mills of Port Huron, Michigan. In 1912, she was purchased by Mitchell & Company of Cleveland and operated by J.E. Mills of Marysville, Michigan. In 1914 she was back in the ownership of Harvey J. Kendall of Marysville. Used mostly in the lumber and coal trades, the KENDALL was a familiar sight in the St. Clair River.

In 1917, the George Hall Coal & Transportation Company of Ogdensburg, New York bought her and she was converted to a self-unloader at Ogdensburg by the St. Lawrence Marine Railway Company. Her role for the "Wishbone Fleet" (from the insignia on the stacks) was in the coal and stone trades. During her career the aging vessel ran into its share of difficulties. On May 8, 1920, she ran aground on Sunken Rock Reef near the lighthouse at Alexandria Bay, New York but was released without damage after her cargo was lightered. On October 5, 1922, she was aground 3 miles west of Fair Haven, New York and again released but with stern damage. On November 4, she was ashore 9 miles west of Oswego, New York and retrieved without damage.

Captain Augustus R. Hinckley of Oswego, New York, purchased the KENDALL in 1928. In December, 1930, the aging steamer holed herself in the ice near Cardinal, Ontario, while upbound in the St. Lawrence River after picking up buoys. The KENDALL was able to reach a dock at Cardinal before she sank and the crew reached shore safely.

In the spring of 1931, HARVEY J. KENDALL was raised, beached and repaired. She was taken to Cape Vincent, New York, but the steamboat inspectors denied her permission to operate on Lake Ontario, permitting her only to run on the sheltered waters of the St. Lawrence River. Accordingly, she was of no further use to Capt. Hinckley. After being stripped, the hull of the KENDALL was laid up in the marsh at Button Bay, near Oswego. In early 1932, the hull floated free and drifted down to Perch Cove, where it sank. The remains of the little steamer lie there to this day.

HARVEY J. KENDALL upbound in the St. Clair River

HARVEY J. KENDALL as a self-unloader

BUILT:	1892
	Alex Anderson,
	Marine City, Michigan
LENGTH:	141.7
BREADTH:	30.9
DEPTH:	9.2
GRT:	398
REGISTRY NUMBER:	US. 96166
ENGINES:	15", 30" Diameter x
	28" Stroke
	Steeple Compound
ENGINE BUILDER:	H. G. Trout
	Buffalo, New York

D.G. KERR (2)

D. G. KERR leaving Two Harbors with her loading record cargo, September 7, 1921

The steel bulk freighter D.G. KERR was built for the Pittsburgh Steamship Company by the American Shipbuilding Company at Lorain, Ohio. She was launched on May 6 and made her maiden voyage on June 29, 1916. Five years into her career, the KERR set a record by loading 12,508 gross tons of iron ore in 16½ minutes at Two Harbors, Minnesota on September 7, 1921. Even though this record has never been broken because of the danger to the stability of a vessel, the 1,000-footers of today can load many times that much in a few hours.

The life of the KERR in the Pittsburgh S.S. Co. had never been very eventful but her final five years were somewhat the opposite. She was laid up in Duluth, Minnesota in late 1975 and was shifted around the harbor for the following five years.

In 1980, the Pittsburgh S.S. Co. sold her and five other ships for scrap. She was to be towed out of Duluth that summer. The other vessels involved were the THOMAS F. COLE, ALVA C. DINKEY, EUGENE J. BUFFINGTON, D.M. CLEMSON and the GOVERNOR MILLER. The COLE and CLEMSON were scrapped at Thunder Bay,

Ontario, while the KERR, DINKEY, BUFFINGTON and MILLER were all sold for dismantling in European scrap yards.

On the tow out of Duluth, on September 22, 1980, the KERR struck the north pier at the Duluth entrance, hitting the cement hard, but receiving no damage to her bow. Later on in her final voyage, the KERR, now in tow of the tug TUSKER, grounded during a severe northeast gale in Sydney Harbor, Nova Scotia on November 19, 1980 but again received no appreciable damage.

On December 12, 1980, the D.G. KERR, while in tow of the tug FEDERAL 6, sank in the North Atlantic 8 miles east of Santa Maria Island, Azores on her way to the scrap yard. She became the twelfth lake steamer to sink on her way overseas for scrapping. It is not beyond the realm of possibility that the strain placed upon her hull during the 1921 loading feat, together with the earlier incidents in 1980, caused structural problems which eventually led to her foundering in the unfamiliar waters of the North Atlantic Ocean.

BUILT:	1916	*GRT:*	7,756
	American Shipbuilding Co.,	*REGISTRY NUMBER:*	US. 214147
	Lorain, Ohio	*ENGINES:*	24½", 41", 65" Diameter x
HULL NUMBER:	714		42" Stroke
LENGTH:	580.0		Triple Expansion
BREADTH:	60.0	*ENGINE BUILDER:*	Shipyard
DEPTH:	32.0		

D. G. KERR downbound in the St. Mary's River July 26, 1964

Aground in Sydney Harbor, November 19, 1980

S.R. KIRBY

The composite bulk freighter S.R. KIRBY was launched on May 24, 1890 at Wyandotte, Michigan by the Detroit Dry Dock Company for the North Western Transportation Company. The KIRBY was one of only a few ships which was constructed with a combination wood and iron hull and it was the 100th vessel built by Detroit Dry Dock Co.

In 1916 the British load line, called the Plimsoll mark, had not yet been adopted for use by American vessels on the Great Lakes and the loading of a vessel was left up to the discretion of the master. Many vessels, therefore, were often loaded beyond their safe limits because of usual calmness on the lake waters. The Plimsoll line was invented by Mr. Samuel Plimsoll as a means of assigning safe freeboards for different seasons of the year. It was accepted by the maritime insurance community and the hull classification societies.

When the S.R. KIRBY left Ashland, Wisconsin on the evening of May 7, 1916 with the barge GEORGE E. HARTNELL in tow, and both loaded with iron ore, the weather was fine. The next day, a storm of hurricane proportions drove down Lake Superior with such force that waves of 40 to 50 feet were reported. The captain of the steamer E.H. UTLEY passed the downbound KIRBY and tow around ten o'clock in the morning and asked the captain of the KIRBY by whistle signal if he needed assistance. The KIRBY was laboring under the stress of the seas and its limited freeboard. The captain received no visible answer but decided to keep the struggling vessels in view. About two hours later, when the UTLEY was two miles to east of the KIRBY, the master and some of the crew saw the KIRBY hit two successive huge waves and, when she was on the crest of the second, they saw the KIRBY crack at number one hatch and disappear below the cold waters of Lake Superior. The UTLEY rushed back, picked up one survivor and then went to the aid of the HARTNELL in order to grasp her from the rocks near Eagle Harbor, Michigan on the Keweenaw Peninsula. The steamers HARRY A. BERWIND and JOSEPH BLOCK were also in the vicinity but only the BLOCK managed to rescue one more man. Twenty perished in the icy lake.

This unfortunate sinking led members of the lake fraternity to investigate the accident and the Plimsoll mark was finally adopted for lakes use shortly thereafter.

As in many instances of shipwrecks where a member of the crew was saved from tragedy by "missing the boat", the same was true in this case. Five men from Marine City, Michigan lost their lives on this vessel, but one regular member of the crew was on leave at home at the time when the KIRBY went down.

S.R. KIRBY leaving the Soo locks

BUILT:	1890	*GRT:*	2,338
	Detroit Dry Dock Co.,	*REGISTRY NUMBER:*	US. 116325
	Wyandotte, Michigan	*ENGINES:*	21", 33", 56" Diameter
HULL NUMBER:	100		x 42" Stroke
LENGTH:	294.0		Triple Expansion
BREADTH:	42.0	*ENGINE BUILDER:*	Dry Dock Engine Works
DEPTH:	21.0		Detroit, Michigan

S.R. KIRBY downbound in the St. Mary's River

In her later years with a box-like top pilothouse (1912)

LAFAYETTE

The steel bulk freighter LAFAYETTE was built in 1900 at Lorain, Ohio by the American Shipbuilding Company, and launched on May 31 for Carnegie's Pittsburgh Steamship Company, forerunner of the United States Steel fleet. U.S. Steel took over the company in 1901 and amalgamated it with various fleets to form their Pittsburgh Steamship Company with 101 vessels.

The most severe storm ever to hit Lake Superior, to that time, struck with fury on November 28, 1905. It caught many vessels in its grip and sank some while destroying others on the rocky shorelines. The LAFAYETTE was towing the barge MANILA enroute to West Superior, Wisconsin when the Nor'easter struck them. The LAFAYETTE was driven off her course and then smashed broadside against large rocks 50 feet off shore opposite the north end of Encampment Island, six miles northeast of Two Harbors, Minnesota.

The barge MANILA came right along, ramming into the stern of the steamer. Four men scrambled onto the deck of the barge as the barge came to rest closer to the shore. In three minutes the LAFAYETTE broke in two. The crew of the barge rushed ashore and went to the aid of the steamer's crewmen. All the crews of both vessels, with the exception of one man who did not make it across a line thrown ashore from the steamer, were safe on shore. They suffered terribly. The following day they managed to get back on the barge for better comfort when the seas subsided. The warmth renewed their vigor. They found a fisherman who returned the six miles back to Two Harbors to get help. The tug EDNA G., towing a few dories, returned to the scene of the accident and brought the crews back to safety.

The barge MANILA was not in bad shape and was retrieved but only 150 feet of the stern and the engine of the LAFAYETTE were salvaged. On August 31, 1906 the stern section was brought into Duluth, Minnesota harbor. The rest of the steamer was just so much scrap metal which was later salvaged from the rocks. The engine was placed in a new vessel, the J.S. ASHLEY, which was built in 1909 at Lorain and served for many years thereafter.

As a memorial to this shipping accident, the high sheer cliff above the scene of this wreck was named Lafayette Bluff shortly after 1905.

LAFAYETTE in Carnegie steamship colors

LAFAYETTE at the Soo early in 1905

BUILT:	1900	*GRT:*	5,113
	American Shipbuilding Co.,	*REGISTRY NUMBER:*	US. 141657
	Lorain, Ohio	*ENGINES:*	18", 26¾", 41", 63" Diameter
HULL NUMBER:	301		x 42" Stroke
LENGTH:	454.0		Quadruple Expansion
BREADTH:	50.0	*ENGINE BUILDER:*	Shipyard
DEPTH:	28.5		

LAFAYETTE on the rocks November 29, 1905

Another view of the severe damage to her bow

The stern section at Howard's Pocket, Superior, Wisconsin May 5, 1908

LAKESIDE

LAKESIDE in the ice

The passenger and freight steel steamer LAKESIDE was built in 1901 at Toledo, Ohio by the Craig Shipbuilding Company and launched on May 7th for Eugene McFall of Sandusky, Ohio. He was the owner of the Sandusky and Peninsula Steamboat Company and would operate this vessel from that port to Marblehead, Lakeside, Catawba Island and Put-In-Bay during the summer season. During spring, fall and part of the winter months, she ran from Sandusky to Marblehead, Kelley's Island and North Bass and Put-In-Bay. She also made many other trips to Lake Erie ports such as Toledo and Cleveland. The ship was built for this dual purpose as a summer excursion steamer and an ice breaker in winter and early spring when the channels were barricaded with ice fields.

In 1905, the LAKESIDE was lengthened to 148.5 x 28.0 x 9.5; 337 GRT. In 1911, she was renamed b) OLCOTT, having been chartered to the Buffalo, Rochester, Syracuse and Eastern Railway, and ran two daily trips from Toronto, Ontario to Olcott, N.Y. The summer seasons of 1913 and 1914, she operated a daily round trip from Oswego, New York to the Thousand Islands, stopping at Cape Vincent, Clayton and Alexandria Bay. The summer seasons of 1915 and 1916 found her running a daily round trip from Detroit, Michigan to Wallaceburg, Ontario and she then returned to island service.

December, 1916 was the last she ran on the Lake Erie Island Route. She was purchased by the French Government in June of 1917 and left Sandusky for New York on the 29th. After a few mishaps on the outbound journey, she arrived at Stapleton, Staten Island, New York at the Staten Island Shipbuilding Company. All her houses and upper works were stripped off and she was converted into an ocean-going tug. The French renamed her c) HURON and the tug left for Brest, France the latter part of August towing a coal barge.

After World War I, the tug was engaged in towing on the west coast of France. In 1924, she was converted to a survey steamer for Bureau Veritas and renamed d) ZELEE. Later, she received her last name change, e) CHIMERE. The survey vessel was taken off the French Naval list at Toulon and the hulk was acquired by the German Navy early in 1943. The proposal to put her into service as SG.30 never materialized and the ship was scrapped.

a) **LAKESIDE**
b) **Olcott (I)**
c) **Huron**
d) **Zelee**
e) **Chimere**

BUILT:	1901 Craig Shipbuilding Co., Toledo, Ohio
HULL NUMBER:	84
LENGTH:	128.5
BREADTH:	28.0
DEPTH:	9.5
GRT:	285
REGISTRY NUMBER:	US.141738
ENGINES:	20", 42" Diameter x 24" Stroke Fore & Aft Compound
ENGINE BUILDER:	Shipyard

OLCOTT at Port Dover

176

LAKESIDE with 583 passengers, Saturday August 20, 1910

OLCOTT stuck in the ice

HURON in 1917

LAKETON

The steel bulk freighter SAXONA was launched on June 6, 1903 by the American Shipbuilding Company at Cleveland, Ohio for the Zenith Steamship Company, an affiliate of the Tomlinson fleet.

On April 16, 1906, she collided with the steamer EUGENE ZIMMERMAN just below Neebish Island in the St. Mary's River. The SAXONA was downbound with flaxseed and the ZIMMERMAN upbound with coal on her maiden voyage. The SAXONA struck the ZIMMERMAN about 20 feet back from the bow, causing her to flood and sink almost immediately. The SAXONA was also holed and taking on water but went a few miles before she also sank. Both vessels were raised and repaired. No one was lost in the collision.

On May 14, 1917, the SAXONA was in another collision, this time with the steamer PENTECOST MITCHELL, again in the St. Mary's River. The SAXONA upbound with coal struck the MITCHELL head-on in the Pipe Island Channel. Again, both vessels sank but they were locked together in 45 feet of water. The salvagers would have a hard time. Until the raising of the GEORGE M. HUMPHREY in 1944, this proved to be the most notable recovery of a large vessel from a considerable depth of water. The MITCHELL was raised first and sent to a repair yard but the salvagers had a harder time with the SAXONA. She was abandoned to the underwriters who engaged the Reid Wrecking Company of Sarnia, Ontario to raise the vessel. It was raised and taken to Collingwood. R.M. Wolvin, Capt. J.W. Norcross and H.W. Smith purchased the SAXONA "as is, where is", had her repaired and sold her in 1918 to the Mathews Steamship Company of Toronto who renamed her b) LAKETON (C.137906).

When the Mathews Steamship Company went bankrupt in 1933, during the Great Depression, Colonial Steamships Ltd. of Port Colborne, Ontario took over the ship. Capt. R. Scott Misener, owner of the fleet, retained the stack insignia, and names of the former Mathews vessels, all ending with the suffix "ton."

Most of this ship's cargoes were grain and the LAKETON served the fleet well. In 1946, her engine and boilers were removed and replaced by those of the former R.C.N. corvette PORT ARTHUR. The new engine dimensions were: 18½"-31"-38½"-38½" diameter of the cylinders x a 30" stroke. This was a 4 cylinder triple expansion engine built in 1942 by the John Inglis Engine Company.

In 1959, the Misener fleets were consolidated into Scott Misener Steamships Ltd. In 1965, LAKETON was sold to Crosbie Shipping Ltd., to be used as a storage barge. In 1966, the vessel was owned by Lundrigan & Lundrigan of Newfoundland and in 1967 was sold for scrap to Steel Factors Ltd. In January of 1968, she was towed from St. Johns, Newfoundland to Vado, Italy by the tug KORAL in tandem tow with the Canadian Coast Guard cutter SAUREL which had been renamed G.S.S. No. 2. When 200 miles northwest of the Azores, the LAKETON foundered in heavy seas in a position 39°, 42' N/30°, 36' W on January 13, 1968.

SAXONA upbound at Mission Point in 1916

Wrecks of SAXONA and PENTECOST MITCHELL, May 14, 1917

178

LAKETON in Mathews colors in 1928

	a) **Saxona**	b) **LAKETON**
BUILT:		1903
		American Shipbuilding Co.,
		Cleveland, Ohio
HULL NUMBER:		416
LENGTH:		416.0
BREADTH:		50.0
DEPTH:		28.0
GRT:		4,716
REGISTRY NUMBER:		US.200036
ENGINES:		20", 33½", 55" Diameter x
		42" Stroke
		Triple Expansion
ENGINE BUILDER:		Shipyard

LAKETON upbound in the St. Mary's River July 27, 1962

179

LA SALLE

J. H. SHEADLE leaving the locks at the Soo in 1907

a) **J. H. Sheadle (1)**   b) **F. A. Bailey**   c) **LA SALLE (2)**   d) **Meaford (3)**
e) **Pierson Independent**   f) **Company**

BUILT:	1906
	Great Lakes Engineering Works,
	Ecorse, Mich.
HULL NUMBER:	22
LENGTH:	530.0
BREADTH:	56.2
DEPTH:	32.0
GRT:	6,924
REGISTRY NUMBER:	US.203628
ENGINES:	23", 37", 63" Diameter x
	42" Stroke
	Triple Expansion
ENGINE BUILDER:	Shipyard

J. H. SHEADLE upbound at Mission Point

The saga of the steel bulk freighter J. H. SHEADLE (1) is interesting and unusual. The vessel was built in 1906 at Ecorse, Michigan by the Great Lakes Engineering Works for the Cleveland-Cliffs Iron Company. The SHEADLE was one of the lucky ones in 1913. She survived the "Big Storm" of November of that year, sailing down Lake Huron while being tormented by the cyclonic winds and towering seas which claimed many ships and their crews in the most destructive storm ever to hit the Great Lakes. Excellent seamanship and pure luck helped this vessel survive.

In 1924, the SHEADLE was sold to the Forest City Steamship Company of Cleveland, Ohio and renamed b) F. A. BAILEY. This venture was shortlived because of the oncoming depression. In 1928, Cleveland-Cliffs repossessed the vessel and renamed it c) LA SALLE (2). From that time until 1965, the LA SALLE worked diligently in Cliffs' colors. In 1951, the vessel was given a new engine, a two-cylinder DeLaval steam turbine, at the Toledo, Ohio yard of American Shipbuilding Co. It was installed during the Winter of 1951-52 and the gross tonnage was changed to 7,236.

Upper Lakes Shipping Ltd. purchased the vessel in 1966, renaming it d) MEAFORD (3) (C. 203628). For this fleet,

the vessel carried many cargoes of grain. In 1979, Robert S. Pierson, the owner of the Soo River Company, purchased the MEAFORD, had her refurbished at Toronto, Ontario, and renamed her e) PIERSON INDEPENDENT. The ship's good fortune, however, was not with her in these colors. After many years of service for four other owners, on October 28, 1979 at 1:15 a.m., her luck ran out when she struck a shoal in the Brockville Narrows of the St. Lawrence River near Kingston, Ontario and was subsequently beached. The steamer was taken to the dry dock at Port Weller, Ontario on November 14, 1979 and declared unfit for further service as a result of the extensive damage she had suffered in the accident. Repairs would prove too costly, so the ship was sold for scrap. When she was being readied for overseas towing, the vessel was renamed f) COMPANY, the strangest rename ever given a lakes vessel. What was done was that all the names on the ship were painted out except the word, "Company," a portion of the words, "Soo River Company" that were painted on her bow. The COMPANY was towed across the Atlantic and arrived at Santander, Spain on June 11, 1980 and was dismantled there.

F. A. BAILEY in 1927 in Forest City Steamship colors

LA SALLE downbound in the Detroit River, July 4, 1953

MEAFORD downbound in the St. Mary's River, July 1, 1966

PIERSON INDEPENDENT upbound in the St. Clair River at Port Huron

COMPANY on her way to European Shipbreakers, May 4, 1980

LAWRENCE

The wooden passenger and freight propellor LAWRENCE was built in 1868 at Cleveland, Ohio by W. H. Radcliffe & Co. (Ira Lafranier) as one of a large fleet of similar boats for the Northern Transportation Company. Because the company had both long and short trade routes extending from Ogdensburg, New York to Chicago, Illinois, the fleet was built to dimensions for the second Welland canal. The LAWRENCE sailed on the various N.T. Co. routes until May of 1883 when she, as the last of the fleet, was sold to Burke, Klein and Seymour, founders of the Northern Michigan Line.

For the next eleven years, she went on a route from Chicago to Mackinac, stopping at various way ports. When the Northern Michigan Line merged with Seymour Transportation Co. in 1894, the LAWRENCE became surplus and was put on a route between Milwaukee, Wisconsin, Manistee and Frankfort, Michigan. For the next few years, she operated on a series of charters, sailing from Benton Harbor, Michigan to Milwaukee for Graham & Morton in 1895, Milwaukee to Muskegon for Milwaukee, Grand Rapids and Indiana Line in 1897 and St. Joseph, Michigan to Chicago for O'Connor Transportation Co. in 1898.

In the spring of 1899, the ship was sold by Burke and Klein to the newly formed Peoples' Transit Co. of Chicago, and again went on the route between Milwaukee and St. Joseph. After two seasons there, she went into the Burger yards at Manitowoc, Wisconsin for an extensive rebuild, including being lengthened to 169.4 x 26.5 x 10.3; 626 GRT and having her engine replaced by a 18", 38" x 36" stroke steeple compound engine built by the Atlantic Iron Works of Boston, Massachusetts. She came out in the spring of 1901 as b) FRONTENAC and went on a summer-resort route between Chicago, White Lake and Pentwater, Michigan. In her third and last season on this route, she ran opposite ARGO, chartered from Graham & Morton. In the spring of 1905, ownership was transferred to Henry B.

Burger, probably for debt arising from her 1901 rebuild. Within a month, Mr. Burger had sold her to N. C. Burrell of Lorain, Ohio, but FRONTENAC did not immediately leave Lake Michigan. For the season of 1906, she was chartered to Nessen Transportation Co., of Manistee, Michigan and sailed opposite their steamer MANISTEE, (a LORA of 1882) between Manistee, Ludington and Milwaukee.

In 1907, FRONTENAC went to Lake Erie and entered a none-too-successful excursion trade out of Lorain, Ohio under management of her owner. At 8:15, July 17, 1908, she caught fire while moored at the docks of the American Shipbuilding Co. at Lorain, Ohio, destroying all but the hull to just above the water line. The remains of the hull were towed to the south side of the Nickel Plate bridge at Lorain.

In the spring of 1909, H.N. Jex, a Toledo, Ohio contractor, became a part owner of the hulk, which was towed to Toledo and rebuilt as a steam barge, the c) H. N. JEX (420 GRT). These owners kept her for less than a year and sold her in June of 1910 to Theobald Emig, of St. Clair, Michigan. Mr. Emig kept the boat for six seasons, using her principally in the coal and lumber trades, towing the barge IDA KEITH and at times the barge THREE BROTHERS as well. Principal ports of call were Goderich, Ontario, Alpena, Michigan, Point Edward, Ontario, Cleveland and Toledo.

In June of 1910, the JEX (C.137982) was sold to John F. Sowards, a well-known coal dealer of Kingston, Ontario, and was then used in the coal trade between the New York shore and Kingston, across the eastern end of Lake Ontario. At 11:45 on the morning of August 16, 1921, she departed Sodus, N.Y. with coal for Kingston. She encountered a heavy storm, and foundered about 15 miles southeast of Long Point, Lake Ontario. Her crew was picked up by the steamer LEHIGH of the George Hall Coal Co., Ogdensburg, N.Y. and there was no loss of life. At the time of her loss, the boat was in her fifty-fourth season on the lakes.

LAWRENCE at Rose Dock, Petoskey about 1890

LAWRENCE with a nice crowd, leaving her dock on her way to Chicago

FRONTENAC in the St. Clair River

H. N. JEX upbound in the St. Clair River with a load of coal

a) **LAWRENCE**   b) Frontenac   c) **H. N. Jex**

BUILT:	1868
	W. H. Radcliffe & Co.
	(Ira Lafranier),
	Cleveland, Ohio
LENGTH:	135.5
BREADTH:	25.8
DEPTH:	11.0
GRT:	447
REGISTRY NUMBER:	US.15450
ENGINES:	26" Diameter x 36" Stroke
	High Pressure Non-Condensing
	Direct Acting
ENGINE BUILDER:	Cuyahoga Steam Furnace Company
	Cleveland, Ohio

LEMOYNE

When the Midland Shipbuilding Company Ltd. laid the keel for its Hull 16, which was under construction for James Playfair's Great Lakes Transportation Company Ltd., of Midland, Ontario, the steamer was named GLENMHOR. By the time of her launching on June 23, 1926, the spelling of the name had been changed to GLENMOHR, and it was under this name that she was enrolled on the Canadian register. Before she entered service, however, she was renamed b) LEMOYNE, because the fleet of the Great Lakes Transportation Company Ltd. had just then been absorbed by Canada Steamship Lines Ltd., Montreal.

LEMOYNE was the largest ship on the Great Lakes at the time of her commissioning, and the first with a beam of 70 feet. Her first cargo was 15,415 net tons of coal which she loaded at Sandusky, Ohio, on August 19, 1926. Thereafter she distinguished herself by setting many different cargo records. As a result, it was LEMOYNE that was chosen to participate in the ceremonies which were held on August 6, 1932 to mark the official opening of the Fourth Welland Canal.

Reboilered in 1961, LEMOYNE spent her entire life in C.S.L. colors. She was retired in 1968 and was laid up at Kingston. Sold to Steel Factors Ltd., Montreal, and resold to Spanish breakers, she cleared Quebec City on June 9, 1969, along with GOUDREAU, in tow of the tug KORAL. She arrived at Santander, Spain, on June 27, 1969, and was soon dismantled.

As LEMOYNE set records during her years of service, so did she also when she was broken up. She was the first laker of more than 600 feet in length to be scrapped. As well, she was the largest laker to be scrapped up until that time.

GLENMOHR just prior to launch

The launch, June 23, 1926

LEMOYNE at the official opening of the Welland Canal

	a) Glenmohr	b) **LEMOYNE**
BUILT:		1926
		Midland Shipbuilding Company Ltd.,
		Midland, Ontario
HULL NUMBER:		16
LENGTH:		621.1
BREADTH:		70.2
DEPTH:		25.4
GRT:		10,480
REGISTRY NUMBER:		C.152647
ENGINES:		25½", 41½", 72" Diameter x
		48" Stroke
		Triple Expansion
ENGINE BUILDER:		Hooven, Owens, Rentschler Co.
		Hamilton, Ontario

Upbound in the St. Clair River, May 17, 1964

LEVIATHAN

Along with the sidewheel tug MAGNET and the two propellors named FAVORITE, the LEVIATHAN was among the most famous wreckers ever to serve the Great Lakes. The big, twin-screw wooden craft was built in 1857 at Buffalo, New York by B. B. Jones for the Lake Navigation Company of Buffalo, which at that time operated approximately one hundred sailing craft. Considering the susceptibility of schooners to accidents in that era, it was expedient for the owners to operate their own salvage vessel, and the LEVIATHAN was designed and constructed to serve that purpose. She was stationed in Chicago, Illinois.

The Lake Navigation Company failed in the Panic of 1857, and the LEVIATHAN was sold at a liquidation sale in July, 1858 to Buffalo vessel-owner Asa Hart. Operating her under the name of the "Columbian Coast Wrecking Company", Hart personally commanded the ship for the next several years. She was stationed at Mackinac Island, Michigan where she remained for the rest of her long career. Her name is associated with many of the most exciting and the most technically difficult salvage efforts in lakes annals.

Hart sold the big tug to Capt. Lemuel Ellsworth and other parties of Milwaukee, Wisconsin in 1868. The ship was rebuilt in 1880 at Milwaukee, and "housed-in" or double-decked. In 1887, she was sold to Capt. Stephen B. Grummond of Detroit, who operated a whole fleet of powerful tugs, including the wreckers CHAMPION and MARTIN SWAIN.

Leviathan's proud career came to an end when she burned at a dock in Cheboygan, Michigan on November 12, 1891. Her documents were surrendered on February 15, 1892, after careful examinations had proven her beyond repair.

LEVIATHAN at her dock

BUILT:	1857
	Benjamin Buhl Jones,
	Buffalo, N.Y.
LENGTH:	126.0
BREADTH:	25.0
DEPTH:	9.0
GRT:	232
REGISTRY NUMBER:	US. 14612
TWIN ENGINES:	24" Diameter x 26" Stroke
	Simple High-Pressure
ENGINE BUILDER:	Unknown

EDWARD E. LOOMIS

WILKESBARRE in the Upper St. Mary's River in 1917

The steel package freighter WILKESBARRE was launched on December 1, 1900 at Buffalo, New York by the Union Dry Dock Company for the Lehigh Valley Transportation Company, to carry package freight between Buffalo, Duluth, Minnesota and Chicago, Illinois. She ran for this railroad-owned company until the U.S. Congress passed legislation requiring railroads to divest themselves of any shipping fleet subsidiaries. The Lehigh Valley fought the legislation, and it was not until 1919 that the ship was purchased by the Great Lakes Transit Corporation who, after renaming her b) EDWARD E. LOOMIS in 1920, ran the vessel on just about the same route.

On November 21, 1934, shortly after 3 o'clock in the morning, the steamers EDWARD E. LOOMIS, downbound with package freight, and the Canadian W.C. FRANZ, upbound light for grain, collided at a point about 30 miles southeast of Thunder Bay Island on Lake Huron, culminating in the sinking of the FRANZ in deep water. The

collision occurred during a period of low visibility caused by fog and funnel smoke. During the tumult immediately following the accident, four members of the crew of the W.C. FRANZ were thrown into the icy water and were drowned. The steamer REISS BROTHERS reached the scene soon after and stood by. The crew of the LOOMIS took aboard the remaining 16 members of the FRANZ's crew. The FRANZ remained afloat for about two hours before she went down by the bow. It is probable that the loss of life would have been averted but for the unfortunate haste on the part of some of the FRANZ's crew.

The LOOMIS returned to Buffalo and was laid up. Because of her severe damage and the depressed economy, the LOOMIS never ran again. After deteriorating in Buffalo harbor, the vessel was finally sold for scrap in 1940. She was towed by the tugs PROGRESSO and PATRICIA McQUEEN to Hamilton, Ontario in May 1940 and scrapped at the Stelco Plant there.

a) Willkesbarre   b) EDWARD E. LOOMIS

BUILT:	1901
	Union Dry Dock Co.,
	Buffalo, N.Y.
HULL NUMBER:	92
LENGTH:	381.7
BREADTH:	50.5
DEPTH:	28.0
GRT:	4,153
REGISTRY NUMBER:	US. 81733
TWIN ENGINES:	20½", 30", 43½", 63" Diameter
	x 42" Stroke
	Quadruple Expansion
ENGINE BUILDER:	Detroit Shipbuilding Company
	Detroit, Michigan, 1900

EDWARD E. LOOMIS on her regular route

EDWARD E. LOOMIS and MILWAUKEE laid up at Buffalo

B. B. McCOLL

The tanker B. B. McCOLL had the distinction of beginning her life as the Royal Fleet Auxiliary tanker SERVITOR, which was built in 1914 in England at the Chatham Naval Dockyard. She served in that capacity during World War I, but became excess tonnage to the British fleet following the cessation of hostilities. She was renamed b) PULOE BRANI in 1923.

In 1926, the vessel was sold by C. S. Brady, London, to McColl Bros. Ltd., Toronto, for service between Buffalo, New York and their new refinery at Toronto. After two unsuccessful attempts at crossing the North Atlantic under her own power, the PULOE BRANI was towed to Montreal and, under her own power, arrived at Toronto in November, 1926. She was refitted at Toronto during the winter of 1926-27, and repowered by the installation of twin four-cycle diesel engines. She was rechristened in 1927 as c) B. B. McCOLL.

On September 12, 1928, the McCOLL was docked at Buffalo, loading a cargo of crude oil for Toronto. Nearby, the wooden canal barge JAMES F. CAHILL was also loading crude for the McColl refinery at Toronto when she caught fire. The blaze soon spread to the McCOLL. The barge was completely destroyed and the McCOLL was so heavily damaged that she was abandoned to the underwriters.

In 1929, B. B. McCOLL was sold by the insurers to Capt. C. D. Secord, of Cleveland, an associate of John E. Russell, Toronto. Towed to Ogdensburg, N.Y., the hull was completely rebuilt by the St. Lawrence Marine Railway Company. Her twin diesels were removed and the two tailshafts and propellers left in place. The hull was surveyed at Ogdensburg on September 21, 1929, and was returned to service as the tank barge d) A.J. PATMORE (946 GRT). Her new owner was Ohio Tankers Corp., Cleveland, Ohio, of which Capt. Secord was the manager.

In 1930, Ohio Tankers had two new, six-cylinder 350 h.p. Nelesco diesels built for the ship by the Electric Boat Works, Groton, Connecticut. Following inspection of the diesels at Cleveland on August 16, 1930, the vessel's Gross Registered Tonnage was measured 858. New deck fittings permitted her to operate on the New York State Barge Canal. The following year, while unloading gasoline at the Sun Oil Company dock at Toronto, she suffered considerable damage from an explosion in one of her tanks. She was once again rebuilt and returned to service.

In 1940, her ownership was transferred to the R.T.C. No. Eleven Corp., of Lyndhurst, New Jersey. She was placed in service on the east coast and, in 1942, was sold to Kimball Transportation Company. She was requisitioned for the U.S. Navy on November 13, 1942, and renamed e) U.S.S. ROTARY (YO-148). She was commissioned by the Navy on February 23, 1943 at Brooklyn, N.Y. From then until December 1945, she was used to fuel destroyers at Casco Bay, Maine.

U.S.S. ROTARY was removed from the Navy list on May 21, 1946, and was transferred to the U.S. Maritime Commission on July 30, 1946. She was then given her old name, f) A.J. PATMORE. Later in 1946, she was acquired by Reinauer Oil Transport, Inc., and renamed g) PEGGY REINAUER. The tanker returned to lake trade in 1953, when she was sold to Michigan Tankers, Inc., Detroit, a wholly owned subsidiary of Marathon Oil Company. In 1955, she was renamed h) DETROIT. In 1959, she was lengthened to 249.5 feet by Manitowoc Shipbuilding Inc., Manitowoc, WI., and given her fourth set of engines — twin Caterpillar diesels.

In 1962, the DETROIT was owned directly by the Marathon Oil Company, Detroit, a company which later was based at Park Ridge, Illinois, and, still later, at Findlay, Ohio. Latterly operated on Lake Michigan, she was sold in 1975 to the Hannah Inland Waterways Navigation Corp., of Lamont, Illinois, for non-transportation purposes. Reportedly, in late 1982, the vessel was being scrapped at South Chicago, Illinois.

PULOE BRANI at Port Colborne, Ontario

a) R.F.A. Servitor   b) Puloe Brani   c) B. B. McCOLL   d) A. J. Patmore
e) U.S.S. Rotary   f) A. J. Patmore   g) Peggy Reinauer   h) Detroit

BUILT:	1914
	Chatham Naval Dockyard,
	Chatham, England
LENGTH:	200.0
BREADTH:	34.2
DEPTH:	16.2
GRT:	1,023
REGISTRY NUMBER:	Br. 136820, US. 229053
ENGINES:	11-3/4" Diameter x
	17-2/3" Stroke
	4 cylinder 2 cycle Diesel
ENGINE BUILDER:	Scott, Still,
	Greenock, Scotland

At Buffalo after the collision and fire, July 27, 1928

B. B. McCOLL entering the Welland Canal

A. J. PATMORE in Lake St. Clair

PEGGY REINAUER upbound light

DETROIT downbound in the St. Clair River in 1960

WILLIAM HENRY MACK

The steel bulk freighter WILLIAM HENRY MACK was launched on February 7, 1903 at Cleveland, Ohio by the American Shipbuilding Company for the Mack Steamship Company of Cleveland. In 1906, this fleet became known as the Jenkins Steamship Company.

The MACK had a number of collisions that were unfortunate in their results. On July 10, 1911, she rammed and sank the steamer JOHN MITCHELL off Vermilion Point in Whitefish Bay on Lake Superior near Crisp Point. The MACK, which was downbound light, struck the MITCHELL, which was upbound with a cargo of coal, on the starboard side during thick weather. Within seven minutes thereafter, the MITCHELL had disappeared, rolling completely over as she went down. Three lives were lost. The MACK's bow was badly crushed and about 30 plates were damaged. She was taken to Lorain, Ohio to be repaired. In 1914, the MACK was sold to Lake Commerce, Ltd., of Toronto, Ontario and renamed b) VALCARTIER (C. 116573); her Canadian dimensions were: 361.0 x 48.2 x 24.0; 3,755 GRT.

In heavy fog, abreast Corsica Shoal Lightship on lower Lake Huron on May 13, 1915, the VALCARTIER collided with the steamer A.W. OSBORNE. Both ships sustained severe damages, the VALCARTIER suffering $35,000 to her hull and $25,000 to her grain cargo.

On December 5, 1916, the Sault Shipping Company, Ltd. of Sault Ste. Marie, Ontario purchased the vessel. In 1920, she went to the Montreal Transportation Company, Ltd. and, later in 1920, to Canada Steamship Lines Ltd.

After many years of service, the VALCARTIER was sold for scrap to the Frankel Brothers who scrapped her in 1937 at Midland, Ontario.

WILLIAM HENRY MACK after the collision which sank the JOHN MITCHELL in 1911

Repaired and back in service in 1912

VALCARTIER upbound at Mission Point in 1918

a) WILLIAM HENRY MACK   b) Valcartier

BUILT:	1903
	American Shipbuilding Co.,
	Cleveland, Ohio
HULL NUMBER:	414
LENGTH:	354.0
BREADTH:	48.0
DEPTH:	28.0
GRT:	3,781
REGISTRY NUMBER:	US. 81857
ENGINES:	20", 33½", 55" Diameter x
	40" Stroke
	Triple Expansion
ENGINE BUILDER:	Shipyard

VALCARTIER in C.S.L. colors

MACKINAW CITY

In 1919, the steel ferry COLONEL CARD was built in Milwaukee, Wisconsin for the Quartermaster Corps of the U.S. Army by the Fabricated Shipbuilding Company and taken to the East Coast to serve in transporting supplies and troops to various ports.

In 1923, the newly formed Michigan State Ferry Service, Michigan Highway Department, purchased the vessel and brought her back to the lakes with the COLONEL POND to transport automobiles between the Lower Peninsula port of Mackinaw City and St. Ignace in the Upper Peninsula of Michigan. The COLONEL CARD was lengthened in 1923 to 172.5 x 28.0 x 10.7; 429 GRT at the Great Lakes Engineering Works at Ecorse, Michigan, who widened the vessel in 1926 to 172.5 x 44.0 x 10.7; GRT 518. She was completely remodeled, converted to carry automobiles across the Straits of Mackinac and renamed b) MACKINAW CITY.

The floating link between the peninsulas lasted until the Mackinaw Bridge was opened in 1957. Eight fine ships were purchased or built for the ferry service in its history and the MACKINAW CITY saw many years of service. During the hunting season automobiles were lined up for five or more miles waiting to be ferried across the Straits and a wait of several hours was common. Even at the peak of summer tourist travel, a wait in line for ferry service was usual.

In 1940, the MACKINAW CITY was replaced by a larger boat and sold back to the U.S. Army Transportation Corps. She went back to the coast and was renamed c) BRIG. GEN. WILLIAM E. HORTON in 1942. In 1947 she was renamed d) MACKINAW CITY again and taken over by the U.S. Maritime Commission (Keansburg Steamboat Line out of Keansburg, New Jersey, Mgrs.). The vessel was sold for scrap in June, 1952 at Keyport, New Jersey and dropped from the American Bureau of Shipping *Record* in 1954.

COLONEL CARD at the builder's yard at Milwaukee

MACKINAW CITY crossing the Straits of Mackinac

a) **Colonel Card**   b) **MACKINAW CITY**   c) **Brig. Gen. William E. Horton**   d) **Mackinaw City**

BUILT:	1919
	Fabricated Shipbuilding Co.,
	Milwaukee, Wisc.
LENGTH:	123.0
BREADTH:	28.0
DEPTH:	12.0
GRT:	535
REGISTRY NUMBER:	US. 223692
TWIN ENGINES:	13", 26" Diameter x
	18" Stroke
	2 cylinder Compound
ENGINE BUILDER:	Plains Engineering Company
	General Ordinance Company
	Denver, Colorado

BRIG. GEN. WILLIAM E. HORTON laid up after World War II

MAGNA

MAGNA upbound at the Soo in 1914

The steel bulk freight barge MAGNA was launched on August 15, 1896 by the Chicago Shipbuilding Company at Chicago, Illinois for the Minnesota Steamship Company. This fleet became part of the Pittsburgh Steamship Company in 1901 upon that company's organization by a merger of several other vessel lines.

October 9, 1903 was the day of her first wreck. The MAGNA sank the wooden steamer JOHN N. GLIDDEN in the St. Clair Flats Canal. At 9 A.M., upbound light, the EMPIRE CITY swung well out into the channel to avoid a pile driver doing repair work. Because of a heavy wind, the EMPIRE CITY sped up and the suction drew the downbound GLIDDEN closer. The MAGNA, being towed behind the EMPIRE CITY, veered out of control and its steel bow plowed into the GLIDDEN, cutting its bow cleanly like a knife as far back as the front of the pilot house. The GLIDDEN, with its cargo of iron ore, sank immediately in 20 feet of water, the anchors of the MAGNA sticking to her as she went down.

The impact snapped the MAGNA's tow line and the barge drifted downstream with the current. A dredge tug succeeded in getting a line aboard her and towing her back to the EMPIRE CITY. The GLIDDEN had sunk diagonally across the channel, effectively blocking it almost completely. To add to the general confusion at the time, the steamer W.R. STAFFORD towing the schooner barge ED McWILLIAMS was coming down the canal right behind the GLIDDEN and couldn't stop. The McWILLIAMS' tow line broke and she bounced off the MAGNA, almost hitting the GLIDDEN. The MAGNA was taken in tow by the EMPIRE CITY and later repaired. The poor GLIDDEN, after being hit by no less than seven other ships the next day, was pulled out of the way and left there until dynamited out of existence the following spring.

On July 20, 1912, the MAGNA was in collision with the steamer R.L. AGASSIZ in the Detroit River. While in tow of the steamer ALEXANDER McDOUGALL, the MAGNA veered into the AGASSIZ. A big hole was torn in MAGNA's side and she had to be taken to Detroit for repairs.

John T. Hutchinson purchased the MAGNA for his Buckeye Steamship Company on July 8, 1936 for the pulpwood trade. She served well in this and other bulk trades such as iron ore, coal and grain. After a 20-year career with Buckeye, the barge was sold to Merritt, Chapman & Scott Company for use as a breakwater for construction of a water intake off Bay Village, Ohio in 1956 and 1957. The MAGNA and her sister, MAIA, were sold to Inland Ship Salvage Company, raised from their resting place, and taken in tow to Ashtabula, Ohio in 1962. The pair arrived there in November and were reduced to scrap the following spring.

BUILT:	1896
	Chicago Shipbuilding Co.,
	Chicago, Illinois
HULL NUMBER:	22
LENGTH:	352.0
BREADTH:	44.2
DEPTH:	22.3
GRT:	3,259
REGISTRY NUMBER:	US. 92740

MAGNA downbound at Mission Point

Leaving the Soo Locks, April 18, 1949

MAKAWELI

The steel cabins-aft "Laker" COWEE was launched on February 1, 1919 at Ashtabula, Ohio by the Great Lakes Engineering Works for the United States Shipping Board. Too late for her intended purpose of carrying war supplies overseas during World War I, which had ended, the COWEE was sold in 1922 to F.A. Gauntlet who in turn sold her to the Matson Navigation Company of San Francisco, California. She was renamed b) MAKAWELI in 1922 and converted to an oil burner. She carried West Coast lumber to Hawaii and returned with cargoes of sugar.

In 1937, she was converted to a tanker at the Bethleham Shipbuilding Company yard in San Francisco (2,665 GRT). MAKAWELI then carried a variety of liquids including molasses, petroleum and even water. It just so happened that the ship was in Pearl Harbor that fateful day, December 7, 1941, when Japanese bombers sank many U.S. ships but MAKAWELI was a bit more fortunate. She was damaged but without loss of life. The vessel was repaired, requisitioned in 1942 by the U.S. War Shipping Administration, and survived the Pacific war making many trips in convoy to hasten the end of hostilities. When peace came she was sold to Lakeland Tankers, Ltd. of Toronto, Ontario.

That year she was brought back to the lakes, cleaned and refitted extensively at Port Weller, Ontario and returned to service under the Canadian flag (C. 177814). She carried petroleum products all over the lakes and as far east as Newfoundland and north into Hudson's Bay. She was nick-named "The Deep One" because when she was empty she rode very high out of the water showing almost all of her 25 foot depth.

The MAKAWELI was retired in 1966 and sold to Steel Factors Ltd., of Montreal in 1967 to be towed overseas for scrap. Along with the old lake steamer MOHAWK DEER, she left Quebec towed by the tug JUNAK. Enroute the MOHAWK DEER sank but the tug and the "Deep One" arrived at La Spezia, Italy on November 5, 1967. The MAKAWELI had reached her last port, still as lucky as had been her career.

COWEE at the fit-out dock at Ashtabula, Ohio, February 20, 1919

MAKAWELI as a Matson "Liner" leaving Honolulu harbor

a) Cowee   b) MAKAWELI

BUILT:	1919	*GRT:*	2,507
	Great Lakes Engineering Works,	*REGISTRY NUMBER:*	US. 217844
	Ashtabula, Ohio	*ENGINES:*	21", 34½", 57" Diameter x
HULL NUMBER:	503		42" Stroke
LENGTH:	253.4		Triple Expansion
BREADTH:	43.6	*ENGINE BUILDER:*	Shipyard
DEPTH:	25.1		

"The Deep One" showing why she was so nicknamed, July 25, 1965

MAPLEDAWN

MANOLA in Minnesota Steamship Co. colors

a) Manola   b) MAPLEDAWN

BUILT:	1890		*GRT:*	2,325
	Globe Iron Works,		*REGISTRY NUMBER:*	US. 92170
	Cleveland, Ohio		*ENGINES:*	24", 38", 61" Diameter x
HULL NUMBER:	30			42" Stroke
LENGTH:	282.4			Triple Expansion
BREADTH:	40.3		*ENGINE BUILDER:*	Shipyard
DEPTH:	21.2			

MANOLA upbound in the St. Clair River — Pittsburgh Steamship colors

MANOLA, November 12, 1918, being converted for ocean service

On January 21, 1890, the steel bulk freighter MANOLA was launched from the Globe Iron Works shipyard at Cleveland, Ohio for the Minnesota Steamship Company for the iron ore trade. In 1901, along with all the other units of the Minnesota fleet, the MANOLA was sold to the Pittsburgh Steamship Company, U.S. Steel Corporation.

On January 25, 1918 she was sold to the Emergency Fleet Corporation of the U.S. Government for war service. She was cut in two at Buffalo, New York by the Buffalo Dry Dock Company to be towed through the canals to the coast. On December 3, 1918 at 1 a.m., her forward end foundered near Duck Island in Lake Ontario and all 12 of her crew perished. They had no warning of impending danger. The after-end reached Quebec City safely and lay there for a year because only half the ship remained and because World War I was over.

Canada Steamship Lines purchased the stern section in 1920 and a new forward end was built by Davie Shipbuilding Company at Lauzon, Quebec (C. 141836). The dimensions of the new hull were: 248.6 x 40.0 x 24.6; 2,404 gross tons

for the St. Lawrence canal trade. Later, the MANOLA was renamed b) MAPLEDAWN by CSL, and was involved in a collision with the wooden schooner barge BROOKDALE (the former MORAVIA) on June 1, 1923 off Alexandria Pier, Montreal. The BROOKDALE was a total loss, but the MAPLEDAWN was not seriously damaged. She was taken to Collingwood, Ontario later in 1923 and lengthened to 350.0 feet by the Collingwood Shipbuilding Company (3,100 gross tons).

While downbound with a cargo of barley on November 30, 1924, the MAPLEDAWN was wrecked on the northwest side of Christian Island in Georgian Bay just outside of Midland, Ontario. There were no casualties and the vessel was abandoned for the winter as a constructive total loss. The storms of the winter of 1924-25 reduced her to rubble. The underwriters sold what remained of the hull to Reid Towing & Wrecking Co. on June 1, 1925. They salvaged parts but left the balance of the wreck as it lay. Today, the wreck of MAPLEDAWN is frequently explored by scuba divers.

MANOLA at Montreal in CSL colors prior to her being lengthened

MAPLEDAWN downbound at Mission Point in 1924

MAPLEHURST

The steel bulk freighter CADILLAC (1) (US. 126876) was launched on May 24, 1892 at South Chicago, Illinois by the Chicago Shipbuilding Company for the Cleveland-Cliffs Iron Company. In 1912, Roy M. Wolvin bought her for his Canadian Interlake Line and, in 1913, she became the property of Canada Steamship Lines.

In 1919, there was a reorganization of CSL. The CADILLAC was renamed b) MAPLEHURST in 1920. The miserable night of November 30, 1922 was a tragic one for the MAPLEHURST. A 60 MPH gale with wet slushy snow hit Lake Superior. Southeast of Isle Royale the coal laden vessel was enroute to the Canadian lakehead when it became impossible to go further. The captain decided he'd take his chances and tried to seek shelter along the Keweenaw Peninsula. The vessel was three miles off the piers of the Portage Ship Canal shortly after midnight.

The little ship was starting to break up and distress flares were lighted. The Coast Guard crew at the Portage Ship Canal station saw the flares and started out in their motor lifeboat. The MAPLEHURST was buffeted by the waves and was now about 4 miles west of the canal and 2 miles off shore. Ten men jumped for the lifeboat when it arrived. One man drowned in the attempt. When a giant comber disabled her power plant, the MAPLEHURST was at the mercy of the seas which drove her into the shoals west of the Ship Canal and battered her to pieces. She sank in 35 feet of water, only her upper works above water. Eleven men including her captain perished.

The Reid Wrecking Company arrived at the disaster after the lake had calmed down but the poor old MAPLEHURST was beyond salvage. The men rescued by the Coast Guard got home safely.

CADILLAC at the Soo in 1911

In CSL colors at Buffalo, September 13, 1918

MAPLEHURST laid up for the winter

a) Cadillac (1)	b) MAPLEHURST	
BUILT:	1892	GRT:	1,263
	Chicago Shipbuilding Co.,	REGISTRY NUMBER:	C. 138230
	Chicago, Illinois	ENGINES:	15", 25", 42" Diameter x
HULL NUMBER:	5		30" Stroke
LENGTH:	230.0		Triple Expansion
BREADTH:	37.2	ENGINE BUILDER:	Cleveland Shipbuilding Company
DEPTH:	15.3		Cleveland, Ohio

The wreck

MARTHA

MARTHA downbound at Mission Point in 1913

This "one of a series" of steel barges was launched on March 7, 1896 for the Minnesota Steamship Company at Chicago, Illinois by the Chicago Shipbuilding Company for the iron ore trade. The MARTHA was one of many vessels involved in the large merger that formed the Pittsburgh Steamship Company in 1901. Steel freight barges were an accepted practice at the turn of the century and this one contributed its share to the growing steel industry along with the others.

In 1937, John P. Geistman of Duluth, Minnesota bought this vessel for his Pigeon River Timber Company. It was to be used in the pulpwood trade and he renamed it b) FLORENCE. The next year he renamed her c) MAUREEN H. Later the same year she was transferred to the Lakehead Transportation Company based at the Canadian Lakehead (C. 170554). The barge was renamed d) FLORENCE J. in 1939. In 1942, the corporate name was changed to the Great Lakes Lumber & Shipping Company Ltd.

In 1949, the barge was sold to Paterson Steamships Ltd., and again renamed, becoming e) OWENDOC. For many years thereafter she was towed by the steamer QUEDOC (1) in the grain trade to Georgian Bay, Lake Huron and Lake Erie ports. In 1962, the barge was sold to the Goderich Elevator and Transit Company Ltd. for use as a grain storage hull at Goderich, Ontario. She was renamed f) C.S. BAND by this firm the same year. The barge was loaded each fall with grain and unloaded when needed. During the summer months, she rested quietly in Goderich harbor.

McNamara Construction Company purchased the vessel early in 1976, intending to use her in their marine construction business. The barge was used in connection with the construction of the Ontario Hydro nuclear generating plant at Douglas Point, Lake Huron that summer, then towed to their marine yard at Whitby, Ontario late in September and from there to Toronto, Ontario on October 30. She had proved to be too old and the next day workers of the C.D. Metal Company began dismantling the vessel. Work was completed in February 1977.

a) **MARTHA**   b) Florence   c) Maureen H.
d) **Florence J.**   e) Owendoc   f) C. S. Band

BUILT:	1896
	Chicago Shipbuilding Co.,
	Chicago, Illinois
HULL NUMBER:	18
LENGTH:	352.0
BREADTH:	44.2
DEPTH:	22.3
GRT:	3,256
REGISTRY NUMBER:	US. 92697

MAUREEN H. downbound with pulpwood

FLORENCE J. upbound at the Soo, April 19, 1949

OWENDOC downbound at the entrance to the Rock Cut

C. S. BAND listing to starboard to receive bottom repairs at Goderich November 11, 1962

Being towed to the scrap yard, September 19, 1976. Tugs SOULANGES and PRINCESS NO. 1

MARY

The wooden passenger and freight steamer MARY was built at Marine City, Michigan by Morley & Hill and launched on August 24, 1882 for C. & F. McElroy's River line. She ran from Port Huron, Michigan to Algonac, Michigan with stops in between and was an extremely popular vessel. In 1887, another cabin was added and her dimensions were altered slightly: 126.0 x 20.9 x 9.9; 170 GRT. She ran as long as conditions permitted each year and was usually the first boat out and the last one in each season on her run up and down the St. Clair River.

Late in 1894, S. H. Burnham took over the vessel when Crockett McElroy decided to build a new vessel. This new giant was named the UNIQUE and proved to be the most unreliable vessel ever to ply the waters of the St. Clair River. The MARY ran in generally the same routes and was just as popular as she was before. Competition on the river routes proved to be too much for the MARY and she was sold to Graham & Morton Transportation Company of Benton

Harbor, Michigan on November 18, 1899. She sailed for Lake Michigan that fall and was laid up for the winter at St. Joseph, across the river from Benton Harbor.

On December 9, 1899, she burned and sank at the dock. Cause of the fire was undetermined. The remains were raised and the hull completely rebuilt at St. Joseph by W. A. Prestock. It was relaunched on May 5, 1900. Completely refurbished, her new dimensions were: 124.0 x 26.2 x 11.0; 360 GRT. The following year, on March 23, 1901, Graham & Morton sold her to the Indiana Transportation Company of Michigan City, Indiana to run between that port and Chicago, Illinois. She proved too small for the Lake Michigan trade, was sold to East Coast parties in 1905, and sailed towards the ocean with S. Sorenson of Boston, Massachusetts as her new owner. The MARY sailed in the Boston vicinity until April 12, 1908 when she was completely destroyed by fire at Chelsea, Massachusetts.

MARY in the St. Clair River

In Michigan City & Chicago Line colors

BUILT:	1882
	Morley & Hill,
	Marine City, Michigan
LENGTH:	126.0
BREADTH:	20.0
DEPTH:	9.4
GRT:	116
REGISTRY NUMBER:	US. 91493
ENGINES:	14", 24" Diameter x 24" Stroke
	Fore & Aft Compound
ENGINE BUILDER:	Herreschoff & Company
	Rhode Island

MATAAFA

PENNSYLVANIA in Minnesota Steamship colors

MATAAFA with an all white stack

The steel bulk freighter PENNSYLVANIA was launched on February 25, 1899 at Lorain, Ohio by the Cleveland Shipbuilding Company for the Minnesota Steamship Company (Federal Steel Company) which purchased the vessel on the ways. After a few trips in 1899, the ship was renamed b) MATAAFA to correspond to the system used by the Minnesota fleet for naming their vessels — all beginning with the prefix MA and ending with an A. In 1901, this fleet was absorbed by the Pittsburgh Steamship Company in the giant merger that shook the Great Lakes shipping world as a result of the formation of the United States Steel Corporation.

The storm of November 28, 1905 on Lake Superior etched the name of the MATAAFA in Great Lakes history. With the barge JAMES NASMYTH in tow, the MATAAFA had left the Duluth, Minnesota piers about 3:30 P.M., on November 27 with a cargo of iron ore bound for a Lake Erie port. Despite the ominous forecast, the vessels departed the shelter of the harbor. When the steamer and barge were abreast Two Harbors, Minnesota about 7:30 P.M., the fury of the storm struck. The captain of the MATAAFA succeeded in turning the ship and barge around in the maelstrom and headed back to Duluth. This was accomplished at about 8:30 A.M., on the 28th. Just as they were approaching the piers, the NASMYTH was ordered to drop her anchors to ride out the storm. She did just that. The MATAAFA, meanwhile, tried to run for safety by entering the piers. Just as she approached the entrance at 2:15 P.M., a huge comber struck the stern of the vessel, forcing her bow against the north pierhead. The engine died and the ship was dashed onto the north beach, breaking her in two. In view of many onlookers on shore, the plight of the men in the vessel was intense. Twelve men were in the forward end of the ship and these were supplemented by three more who made a dash from the stern section across the open and split deck despite the huge waves and freezing winds to find safety in the forward cabins. The men from the U.S. Life Saving Service finally were successful in rescuing these beleaguered sailors by making two trips in the surf boat to take them to shelter. Nine others perished in the stern section of the vessel.

The remains of the MATAAFA were salvaged by Captain Reid of Sarnia, Ontario. His job was another painstaking and tedious undertaking, but he succeeded. The MATAAFA was raised and rebuilt in 1906. Another accident occurred on October 14, 1908, when MATAAFA rammed and sank the steamer SACRAMENTO in the Rice's Point Channel between Duluth and Superior.

The MATAAFA collided with the steamer G. WATSON FRENCH off Grosse Pointe, Michigan on Lake St. Clair on July 27, 1912. The MATAAFA was heavily damaged and almost sank while being towed to Detroit for temporary repairs. When she was on the dry dock at Toledo, it was found that her portside was broken and bent for a distance of 100 feet and the deck was severely buckled. It took three weeks to repair her.

In 1926, she was remodeled, so that her depth became 24.8 feet (4,319 GRT).

In 1946, the Ecorse Transit Company, a division of the Nicholson Transit fleet, purchased the vessel and converted her to an auto carrier (4,775 GRT). A flight deck for carrying autos was installed in 1950 along with oil burners to comply with City of Detroit smoke abatement regulations. From 1958 to 1964, she was chartered to the T. J. McCarthy Steamship Company to carry autos to Cleveland, Ohio and Buffalo, New York from Detroit. The MATAAFA lay in ordinary in 1964, until sold for scrapping. Along with the tanker L.S. WESCOAT, the MATAAFA arrived in Hamburg, Germany on July 19, 1965 to be cut up.

MATAAFA being smashed by the surging waves, November 28, 1905

The aftermath of the 1905 storm. The barge NASMYTH still rides at anchor at right

Another view of the ill-fated MATAAFA

In the Rock Cut in 1923

213

	a) Pennsylvania	b) MATAAFA

BUILT: 1899
Cleveland Shipbuilding Co.,
Lorain, Ohio
HULL NUMBER: 33
LENGTH: 429.6
BREADTH: 50.0
DEPTH: 25.0

GRT: 4,840
REGISTRY NUMBER: US. 150810
ENGINES: 15¾", 23¾", 36½", 56"
Diameter x 40" Stroke
Quadruple Expansion
ENGINE BUILDER: Shipyard

MATAAFA downbound in the Detroit River

First boat into Cleveland, March 2, 1951

In McCarthy colors leaving Detroit

214

E. G. MATHIOTT (1)

S. S. CURRY with engines amidship in 1900

On the 27th of April, 1893, the steel bulk freighter S. S. CURRY was launched at West Bay City, Michigan by F. W. Wheeler & Company for H. A. Hawgood of Cleveland, Ohio for the ore trade. This vessel was different than the usual Great Lakes freighter of the day in so far as her engine was placed amidships instead of in the usual aft position. However, most ocean freighters were built with their engines amidships. The CURRY was the largest vessel ever built on the lakes up to that time.

In 1904, the owners decided to lengthen the carrier and move the engine room to the normal lakes' position. This was accomplished during the winter of 1904-05 at Cleveland, Ohio by the American Shipbuilding Company. New dimensions were: 432.0 x 45.0 x 25.0; 3,931 GRT. In 1916, Jones & Laughlin Steel Corporation took over the

vessel for their Interstate Steamship Company. In 1920, they renamed her b) ELMORE.

In 1922, the ELMORE was sold to the Valley Camp Steamship Company and renamed c) P. W. SHERMAN. The vessel lasted only four years under this name. In 1926, it was renamed d) E. G. MATHIOTT (1). The ship's main cargoes were coal upbound and iron ore downbound but she did carry other bulk cargoes as well. The MATHIOTT was laid up in 1932 and never saw service again. The Great Depression had hit the country hard and most lake vessels were laid up. Even though this vessel was purchased in 1935 by the Columbia Transportation Company along with the other Valley Camp steamers, she never left the dock in their service. In the winter of 1936-37, the E. G. MATHIOTT was reduced to scrap at Fairport, Ohio due mainly to her age and condition.

a) S. S. Curry   b) Elmore   c) P. W. Sherman   d) E. G. MATHIOTT (I)

BUILT:	1893
	F. W. Wheeler & Co.,
	W. Bay City, Mich.
HULL NUMBER:	94
LENGTH:	360.0
BREADTH:	45.0
DEPTH:	20.8
GRT:	3,260
REGISTRY NUMBER:	US. 116558
ENGINES:	20", 37½", 53" Diameter
	x 42" Stroke
	Triple Expansion
ENGINE BUILDER:	Shipyard

S. S. CURRY in 1919

ELMORE in 1921

F. W. SHERMAN downbound at Mission Point

E. G. MATHIOTT in 1928

THOMAS MAYTHAM

The steel bulk freighter THOMAS MAYTHAM was launched on October 8, 1892 at South Chicago, Illinois by the Chicago Shipbuilding Company for John Kelderhouse et al, M.M. Drake manager, for various bulk trades. In 1897, Gilchrist Transportation Company took over the steamer. In 1913, the vessel was purchased by the General Transit Company. So far, this vessel had done her job routinely for three firms and was not involved in any serious mishaps. Her fortunes were soon to change.

Because of the Great Depression, the MAYTHAM was laid up for lack of work from 1929 until when, in 1933, she was sold in bankruptcy to the Maytham Steamship Company, C.W. Bryson, manager. Times were still bad, however, and cargoes were scarce. In 1934, the Dolomite Marine Corporation took over the MAYTHAM. She was left in ordinary until 1937 when the ship was partially dismantled at Fairport, Ohio. In 1938, she was taken to Rochester, New York and was completely rebuilt as a canal tanker. A new diesel engine was installed. Her new dimensions were: 286 x 41.2 x 18.8; 1,958 GRT. The engine was built by the American Locomotive Company / twin-8 cylinder, 12½" x 13" diesels. The ship was renamed b) DOLOMITE 2 and was now owned by the Rochester Shipbuilding Company. She was to operate in the New York State Barge Canal system to various ports throughout that system.

When the Second World War broke out in 1939, matters changed. After the United States entry into the war in 1941, the DOLOMITE 2 was sold to the Seaboard Transportation Company and renamed c) MOTOREX in 1942. Later the same year, the MOTOREX was purchased by the British Ministry of Transport but saw service only on the east coast of the U.S. and the Caribbean as far south as Venezuela. MOTOREX was attacked at 0200 hours on June 18, 1942 by U-172, Captain Emmerman, by gunfire. With nowhere to go and under enemy attack, the MOTOREX succumbed at 0400 hours, 10°, 10' N, 81° 30' W near the Panama Canal and dipped below the surface. Her job was finished. The crew was later rescued and lived to tell of her demise.

THOMAS MAYTHAM in 1907

a) THOMAS MAYTHAM   b) Dolomite 2   c) Motorex

BUILT:	1892	*GRT:*	2,329
	Chicago Shipbuilding Co.,	*REGISTRY NUMBER:*	US. 145631
	Chicago, Illinois	*ENGINES:*	19", 32", 52" Diameter x
HULL NUMBER:	6		45" Stroke
LENGTH:	286.0		Triple Expansion
BREADTH:	41.3	*ENGINE BUILDER:*	King Iron Works
DEPTH:	21.3		Buffalo, New York

THOMAS MAYTHAM towing a barge

DOLOMITE 2 at the Soo Locks

MOTOREX in War gray, March 4, 1942

METEOR

The steel whaleback steamer FRANK ROCKEFELLER was launched on the 25th of April 1896 at West Superior, Wisconsin by the American Steel Barge Company for its own fleet. In 1900, she became a part of the Bessemer Steamship Company and, the following year, entered the Pittsburgh Steamship Company on its establishment.

During the terrible wind and snow storm of November 2, 1905 on Lake Superior, the ROCKEFELLER was downbound with a cargo of iron ore and towing the barge MAIDA. In the maelstrom and fury of the storm the ROCKEFELLER plowed full speed into the rocks of Rainbow Cove on the western side of Isle Royale and the barge crashed headlong into her stern. Because of the exposed position and the deteriorating weather, the crews of both vessels sought refuge immediately. They found little refuge but managed to survive without injury until salvage vessels could arrive at the scene. The wrecker FAVORITE and the tugs S.C. SCHENCK and RESCUE began salvage operations. The iron ore cargo of the ROCKEFELLER was lightered into the steamer MARITANA which had been diverted to the site. The MAIDA was damaged only slightly and was easily removed. The wreckers released the ROCKEFELLER one week later. She was towed to Two Harbors, Minnesota by the MARITANA for survey of damages. They were severe but the ship was deemed repairable. She was subsequently dry docked, repaired and returned to service.

In 1927, the ROCKEFELLER was purchased by the Central Dredging Company and the following year was renamed b) SOUTH PARK. She was used in the sand and gravel trade. The Great Depression hit the shipping industry hard and this vessel was laid up. A series of owners ensued. In 1934, the vessel belonged to the Customs Office and Maurice H. Sobel, and in 1936 to the Erie Steamship Company and sailed in the grain and automobile trades following conversion for that purpose. Nicholson Universal Steamship Company took over the SOUTH PARK and used her after another conversion back to a bulk carrier until 1943. She was then purchased by Cleveland Tankers Inc.

The vessel was converted into a bulk tanker in 1943 at Manitowoc, Wisconsin by the Manitowoc Shipbuilding Company and renamed c) METEOR (3,383 GRT). The revitalized vessel carried a variety of petroleum products all over the lakes for this firm for many years. In late 1969, after running aground near Marquette, Michigan, the METEOR was laid up at Manitowoc.

In 1972, various civic minded citizens of Superior, Wisconsin purchased the vessel and had it towed to that city. She entered Superior harbor on September 11, 1972 in tow of the tug JOHN ROEN V to begin a new career as a museum ship for the Barker's Island Museum. After permanently mooring the vessel, the area around her was filled in. Maritime displays have been set up and a bookstore is open. The vessel was painted and refurbished. It is the last of the whalebacks and is open to visitors. Hopefully it will be there for posterity.

FRANK ROCKEFELLER in 1914

a) Frank Rockefeller	
b) South Park	
c) METEOR	

BUILT:	1896 American Steel Barge Co., W. Superior, Wisc.
HULL NUMBER:	136
LENGTH:	366.5
BREADTH:	45.0
DEPTH:	26.0
GRT	2,759
REGISTRY NUMBER:	US. 121015
ENGINES:	23", 38", 63" Diameter x 40" Stroke Triple Expansion
ENGINE BUILDER:	Cleveland Shipbuilding Company Cleveland, Ohio

SOUTH PARK with a load of new cars

At Detroit, June 10, 1941

SOUTH PARK downbound in Lake St. Clair

METEOR upbound in the St. Mary's River, August 3, 1969 during her last season of operation

MIDLAND QUEEN

MIDLAND QUEEN upbound in the St. Clair River

The steel canaller MIDLAND QUEEN was built in 1901 at Dundee, Scotland by the Caledon Shipbuilding & Engineering Company for James Playfair's Midland Navigation Company, Ltd. She was his first vessel and had a varied career. After builder's trials, the MIDLAND QUEEN left for Manchester, England, loaded coal for Chicago, Illinois and set out on July 27th to cross the Atlantic on her maiden voyage to the lakes. Her regular cargoes would be in the grain and coal trades.

In 1910, the Midland Navigation Company, the Empress Transportation Company and the Inland Navigation Company merged into a fleet named the Inland Lines Ltd. Canada Steamship Lines took over this company in 1913.

Because of the shortage of ocean vessels during World War I, the MIDLAND QUEEN and other canallers not engaged in vital shipping duties on the lakes were pressed into service on the high seas. German submarines had wreaked havoc among shipping to England and these vessels were sorely needed. In 1915, the MIDLAND QUEEN was chartered to the Nova Scotia Steel & Coal Company and to the Dominion Iron & Steel Company for various trips. On July 21, 1915, she sailed from Sydney, N.S. for Newport, Monmouthshire, England loaded with war material. Early in the morning of August 4th, the MIDLAND QUEEN was captured and boarded by men of the German submarine U-28 (Capt. Frhr. Van Forstner). The vessel was 70 miles southwest of Fastnet Rock Lighthouse on the southern tip of Ireland. After placing the crew of 24 and two passengers in two lifeboats, the U-23 sank the MIDLAND QUEEN by gunfire. A Norwegian vessel rescued the people in both lifeboats on August 5th and brought them to shore safely. MIDLAND QUEEN's register was closed on October 1, 1915. It was the first lake ship lost to enemy action in World War I.

MIDLAND QUEEN at dock in Owen Sound

BUILT:	1901	*DEPTH:*	20.5
	Caledon Shipbuilding & Engineering Co.,	*GRT:*	1,993
	Dundee, Scotland	*REGISTRY NUMBER:*	Br. 110991
HULL NUMBER:	160	*ENGINES:*	18", 30", 50"
LENGTH:	249.0		Diameter x 36" Stroke
BREADTH:	42.7		Triple Expansion
		ENGINE BUILDER:	Shipyard

MINNESOTA

In the spring of 1888, the Detroit Dry Dock yard at Wyandotte, Michigan built two beautiful iron package freighters, the HUDSON and HARLEM. The latter vessel was launched on July 3rd. Both were built to the order of the Western Transit Company, the marine affiliate of the New York Central and Hudson River Railroad. They were painted with light brown hull, white cabins and had two buff stacks in line. These were placed well aft, each with a broad red band below a black top. They were fine, fast carriers and made 27 round trips each between Buffalo, New York and Chicago, Illinois in 1890.

On November 26, 1898, the HARLEM stranded on a reef off Menagerie Island, entrance to Siskiwit Bay, on the south shore of Isle Royale, Lake Superior, her bow in 12 feet of water and her stern in 20 feet. By spring of 1899, she had shifted 100 feet. She was abandoned to the underwriters June 1, and the wreck was sold to Thompson Towing & Wrecking Company of Port Huron, Michigan. Salvage work went on all that summer and it was not until September 27th that the vessel was pulled off and into the bay for further shoring and patching. She finally arrived at Port Huron on November 26th. It was first drydocked at Port Huron, then towed to Toledo, Ohio, where John Craig replaced her entire bottom and rebuilt her as a bulk freighter. The HARLEM then came into the hands of the Jenks Shipbuilding Company of Port Huron, who sold her in the spring of 1905 to ship broker Henry J. Pauly at Milwaukee, Wisconsin.

On February 11, 1911, the HARLEM entered the dry-dock at Manitowoc, Wisconsin to be rebuilt as a passenger steamer by the Manitowoc Shipbuilding & Dry Dock Company. Her new owner was the Chicago & Duluth Transportation Company which renamed the vessel b) MINNESOTA (3,320 GRT). This company operated the ship for George B. Caldwell of Chicago and L. W. Larson of Michigan City, Indiana. On October 23, 1913, the MINNESOTA was purchased by the Lake Michigan Steamship Company and, on May 20, 1915, went to the Chicago, Racine and Milwaukee Line, a division of the Northern Michigan Transportation Company.

On November 24, 1917, the MINNESOTA was sold to the United States Shipping Board for service as a hospital ship in World War I. She was taken to Cleveland, Ohio where she was cut in half for the trip through the canals to the Coast. The sections were joined at Lauzon, Quebec by Davie Shipbuilding Company and the vessel proceeded to New York.

After the war, the MINNESOTA was purchased by George S. Bennett of New Bern, North Carolina on January 21, 1921 and, on December 31, 1925, by Emmett E. Robinson, who used her under various titles such as: The SS Minnesota, Inc., St. John's Attraction Company, and the Latin American Amusement Company — all out of Jacksonville, Florida. The vessel was used as a floating hotel and in various other schemes, none of which prospered. She was renamed c) FELICIANA in 1928. The forlorn vessel was "abandoned" and her certificate surrendered at Jacksonville on December 9, 1930. Presumably she was cut up for scrap the following year.

HARLEM as a package freighter with auxiliary sales up

HARLEM in 1908

a) Harlem	b) MINNESOTA	c) Feliciana		
			DEPTH:	22'7"
			GRT:	2,299
	BUILT:	1888	*REGISTRY NUMBER:*	US. 95972
		Detroit Dry Dock Co.,	*ENGINES:*	23¼", 36¼", 62" Diameter
		Wyandotte, Mich.		x 48" Stroke
HULL NUMBER:		84		Triple Expansion
LENGTH:		288.0	*ENGINE BUILDER:*	Dry Dock Engine Works
BREADTH:		41.0		Detroit, Michigan

MINNESOTA in the St. Clair River

MINNESOTA in Chicago & Duluth colors

In Northern Michigan Line colors in 1915

FELICIANA in Florida

MINNIE M.

The little wooden passenger and freight steamer MINNIE M. was built in 1884 at Detroit, Michigan by John Oades for Ira H. Owen and others of St. Clair, Michigan and Chicago, Illinois. They in turn sold her to the Delta Transportation Company of Escanaba, Michigan after one month of ownership. Her route was between Cheboygan, Michigan and Sault Ste. Marie, Michigan until 1891. In 1892, MINNIE M. was chartered to the St. Joseph and Lake Michigan Transportation Company (the popular Vandalia Line) to run between St. Joseph, Michigan and Milwaukee, Wisconsin. On November 3, 1892, she was sold to the Arnold Line of Mackinac Island, Michigan, and the following season resumed her former route to the Soo. Late in 1899, the vessel was chartered by the Crosby interests to run on a trip on Lake Michigan between Muskegon and Grand Haven, Michigan to Sheboygan and Manitowoc, Wisconsin.

On October 17, 1899, the MINNIE M. was purchased by the Algoma Central Railway to run between Sault Ste. Marie and Michipicoten, Ontario to supply the Helen Mine near Wawa, Ontario. The vessel also brought supplies for the building of the railroad from the Soo to that point and to supply the needs of the local paper company. Her Canadian registry number was C. 107889.

On May 4, 1909, MINNIE M. came back to U.S. registry when John J. Hickler of Sault Ste. Marie purchased the vessel. On May 1, 1913, MINNIE M. was purchased by the House of David who ran her in their Great Waters Transportation Company out of Benton Harbor and St. Joseph, Michigan to High Island. On June 27, 1913, the vessel was renamed b) RISING SUN.

While carrying a cargo of lumber and vegetables on October 29, 1917, she stranded off Pyramid Point, 7 miles southeast of Sleeping Bear Point on Lake Michigan in thick weather. All 18 on board were rescued but the vessel pounded itself to pieces in the surf and was destroyed. Her final document was surrendered on April 29, 1918.

MINNIE M. in the Canadian Lock at the Soo

a) **MINNIE M.**   b) **Rising Sun**

BUILT:	1884	*REGISTRY NUMBER:*	US. 91647
	John Oades,	*ENGINES:*	15½", 30" Diameter x
	Detroit, Mich.		36" Stroke
LENGTH:	133.3		Steeple Compound
BREADTH:	26.0	*ENGINE BUILDER:*	Samuel F. Hodge
DEPTH:	10.8		Detroit, Michigan
GRT:	447		

MINNIE M. in U.S. Registry

In Algoma Central colors

RISING SUN — In the service of the House of David

MONKSHAVEN

MONKSHAVEN being unloaded at her dock at the Soo

The iron-hulled canal-sized freighter MONKSHAVEN was built in 1882 at South Shields, England by J. Redhead & Sons for R. Harrowing of Whitby, England to be used in the general package freight business. In 1900, Francis Clergue brought her to the lakes for his Algoma Central Railway.

Despite being built for ocean use and able to withstand much stress, this strong little freighter met her match in the big storm of 1905 and became its first victim. On the night of November 27, the MONKSHAVEN was overwhelmed by the huge seas less than 15 miles from a safe haven and dashed onto Pie Island in Lake Superior. Her crew managed to reach safety on shore but had to withstand the severity of the icy winds and blasts of snow that night and the next day. They were rescued but the fate of the vessel was still in doubt.

The MONKSHAVEN lay on the rocks all that winter. When spring came the Reid Wrecking Company of Sarnia, Ontario attempted to make a salvage. Captain Reid had made himself a name in the past for salvaging the seemingly unsalvagable. His crew succeeded in refloating the vessel in August of 1906, but again fate interfered. After all the work, the MONKSHAVEN broke away from her moorings on October 18th and stranded again, this time on Angus Island. She was smashed beyond repair and was abandoned in place. What was left of her remains there to this day.

BUILT:	1882
	J. Redhead & Sons,
	South Shields, England
HULL NUMBER:	183
LENGTH:	249.0
BREADTH:	36.1
DEPTH:	17.5
GRT:	1,415
REGISTRY NUMBER:	Br. 86632
ENGINES:	29", 54" Diameter x
	36" Stroke
	Compound
ENGINE BUILDER:	Shipyard

228

The first stranding on Pie Island

MONKSHAVEN stranded on Angus Island, October 18, 1906

MONTROSE

MONTROSE upbound in the St. Mary's River, July 3, 1961

This particular salt water vessel is included in this volume because of its unusual sinking in the Detroit River on July 30, 1962. Other salt water ships have been lost on the lakes and still lie beneath their waters but this ship seemed to be special, perhaps because of her beautiful design and perhaps because she left a part of herself here in the Detroit area.

This steel freighter was built at Sunderland, England by C. Bartram & Sons Ltd., and launched on September 23, 1960 for Montship Lines Ltd. (Buries Marks Ltd., managers). She was built for service into the Great Lakes and made her maiden voyage to the lakes early in 1961.

Just as MONTROSE was leaving the Detroit Harbor Terminals dock on July 30, 1962, upbound with general cargo, the vessel was struck by the downbound cement clinker carrying barge ABL-502 being pushed by the tug B. H. BECKER. The collision occurred in darkness and neither vessel saw the other. The barge knifed a hole in the MONTROSE which immediately filled up and finally capsized, lying on her side just underneath the Ambassador Bridge on the American side of the river. There were no casualties.

When salvage operations began in late August, the vessel was lying on its side in about 45 feet of water, approximately 400 feet from the Detroit shore, and at about a 20 degree angle with the shore, with its bow pointed upstream. The ship was listed at 85 degrees to port and the starboard side projected above the water. Divers reported that a hull rupture of about 34 feet in length and varying up to 3 feet in width extended into holds #1 and #2. To bring the vessel to the surface, offshore anchors and pulling tackle had to be used. The process which was used in righting the vessel required much patience and an adept concept of marine salvage. The hulk was gradually dragged shoreward by means of beach gear and pumping. The hole in the side of the ship was patched up with 73 cubic yards of cement. Righting booms were used on the starboard side to help keep the vessel from sliding back. The work went on day and night and gradually the MONTROSE was righted.

After 101 days underwater, the Merritt-Chapman & Scott salvage vessels succeeded in raising the ship on November 9th. The vessel was taken to the Lorain, Ohio shipyard of American Shipbuilding Company for repairs. While there, the vessel was sold to Skibs A/S Hilda Knudsen, Chr. Haaland, manager, of Haugesund, Norway and renamed b) CONCORDIA LAGO (5,005 GRT). She sailed out of the lakes in 1963.

In 1979, the CONCORDIA LAGO was sold to Triton Maritime Ltd., Armada Marine, Inc., managers, of Piraeus, Greece. She was renamed c) LAGO early in 1982 and, later the same year, was sold for scrapping to Pakistani breakers.

a) MONTROSE   b) Concordia Lago   c) Lago

BUILT:	1961
	C. Bartram & Sons Ltd.,
	Sunderland, England
HULL NUMBER:	386
LENGTH:	421.6
BREADTH:	58.6
DEPTH:	35.9
GRT:	4,993
REGISTRY NUMBER:	Br. 302620
2 ENGINES:	760 mm Diameter x 1500 mm Stroke
	SA 5 cylinder Diesel
ENGINE BUILDER:	Götaverken Angteknik Gavle, Sweden

MONTROSE on her side in the Detroit River, August 22, 1962

CONCORDIA LAGO ready to leave the lakes in 1963

R. E. MOODY

The Miller Steamship Company, J. E. Ball manager, had the steel bulk freighter P.P. MILLER built at Buffalo, New York by the Buffalo Shipbuilding Company in 1903. She was launched on September 12th and began operations in November. In 1911, the MILLER was transferred to the ownership of Donaldson of Buffalo and, in December 1915, back to the Miller Steamship Company (Brown & Company) which in turn sold her to the Interstate Steamship Company (Jones & Laughlin Steel Corp.). The ship was renamed b) COLLIER in 1920. Later that same year, the Becker Steamship Company took over her management.

In 1922, the Valley Camp Steamship Company became the owner and promptly renamed the vessel c) JOHN McCARTNEY KENNEDY. In 1926, they had the vessel rebuilt into a self-unloader at Sturgeon Bay, Wisconsin by the Leatham D. Smith Dock Company. The new dimensions were: 361.5 x 48.6 x 23.9; 3,663 GRT. The KENNEDY became the first upper lakes freighter to transit the new Welland Canal. Downbound in ballast, the steamer passed through the yet uncompleted waterway on October 29, 1930, and proceeded to Sodus Point where she took on a cargo of 4,000 tons of coal. On October 31, she descended the St. Lawrence River to Prescott, Ontario to unload. Wherever possible along the route, the KENNEDY was welcomed by shrieking whistles from Lake Ontario and river craft.

The Columbia Transportation Company took over the Valley Camp boats in 1935. The KENNEDY was renamed d) R.E. MOODY in 1937. A familiar sight all over the lakes, the MOODY carried various bulk cargoes but mainly it was the movement of coal and gravel products, to almost all the ports on the Great Lakes, that brought her into view to so many. The ship's size could be accommodated at many dying ports in the final years of their viability.

Due to her age and condition, the R.E. MOODY was retired from service and sold in October 1958 to the Marine Iron & Shipbuilding Company in Duluth, Minnesota. Resold, the vessel was dismantled at Superior, Wisconsin by the Fraser-Nielson Shipyard in 1959-60.

P.P. MILLER downbound light in the St. Clair River

COLLIER in the locks at the Soo with PIONEER astern in 1920

a) P.P. Miller   b) Collier   c) John McCartney Kennedy   d) R.E. MOODY

BUILT:	1903
	Buffalo Shipbuilding Co.,
	Buffalo, N.Y.
HULL NUMBER:	205
LENGTH:	354.0
BREADTH:	48.0
DEPTH:	28.0
GRT:	3,845
REGISTRY NUMBER:	US. 200346
ENGINES:	20", 33½", 55" Diameter
	x 40" Stroke
	Triple Expansion
ENGINE BUILDER:	American Shipbuilding Company
	Cleveland, Ohio

JOHN McCARTNEY KENNEDY downbound light in the Detroit River

R. E. MOODY upbound loaded in Lake St. Clair, July 9, 1950

234

MOONLIGHT

MOONLIGHT under full sail

BUILT:	1874
	Wolf & Davidson,
	Milwaukee, Wisc.
LENGTH:	205.9
BREADTH:	33.6
DEPTH:	14.2
GRT:	777
REGISTRY NUMBER:	US. 90719

When lakes connecting channels were deepened to 16 feet in 1871, a large number of new vessels were built for the grain and ore trades. Between 1870 and 1874, almost two hundred big schooners were constructed, most of them roughly 200 feet in length and capable of carrying some 60,000 bushels of wheat or 1,400 tons of other cargo. MOONLIGHT, built at Milwaukee, Wisconsin by Wolf & Davidson in 1874, was one of the proudest of the new 200-footers. Built for the firm of Hibbard & Vance of Milwaukee, the ship, with a 105 foot tall mainmast, spread an immense footage of canvas. Under the command of Capt. Dennis Sullivan, she gained an immediate reputation for fast passages, and newspapers referred to her as the "Queen of the Lakes." In a much-publicized race in 1879, however, she lost her title to the PORTER, although the results were long contested.

In 1888, the MOONLIGHT was sold to William S. Mack and others of Cleveland, Ohio and from that time on she spent increasing amounts of her time at the end of a tow line, usually as a consort to the bulk freighter CHARLES J. KERSHAW. The Mack interests owned several steamers and barges.

On September 29, 1895, the KERSHAW was towing the MOONLIGHT and the barge HENRY A. KENT up Lake Superior to Marquette, Michigan when they met a Northwest gale. Working hard to breast the heavy seas, the KERSHAW burst a steam pipe and became helpless, and all three vessels were blown ashore near Chocolay Reef, just east of Marquette. The steamer stranded on the boulder-strewn reef, and both barges went high and dry on a sandy beach. The KERSHAW went to pieces, but both the MOONLIGHT and the KENT were pulled off the beach in the Spring of 1896 after several costly salvage attempts. After the salvage, the MOONLIGHT was awarded by the underwriters to Jay Hursley of Sault Ste. Marie in consideration of wrecking bills, and he sold the ship to J.C. Gilchrist & Company, one of the largest operators on the lakes at the time.

Gilchrist removed most of the schooner's rig and employed her from then on strictly as a barge, towed behind various steamers. During 1898, she was chartered out to the Atlantic Transportation Company for the East Coast coal trade, but she returned to the lakes in 1901.

The MOONLIGHT was loading iron ore at Ashland, Wisconsin on September 16, 1903. The following day a violent storm came up but the captain of the steamer VOLUNTEER, the towing steamer, decided to venture out into Lake Superior in spite of the weather. They did not get very far. Just off Michigan Island, the MOONLIGHT started taking on water quickly. The crew of the VOLUNTEER succeeded in removing the men aboard the MOONLIGHT and the 29-year-old former "Queen of the Lakes" slid beneath the waves.

On the beach: MOONLIGHT at left, HENRY A. KENT center, tugs at work on wreck of KERSHAW

MOONLIGHT as a tow barge

236

WILLIAM C. MORELAND

One of the most unusual stories of the Great Lakes is the saga of the WILLIAM C. MORELAND. This steel bulk freighter was launched on July 27, 1910 at Lorain, Ohio by the American Shipbuilding Company for Jones & Laughlin Steel Corporation's Interstate Steamship Company. On her fifth trip, with a cargo of 10,700 tons of iron ore, the MORELAND stranded on the rocks at Eagle Harbor, Lake Superior on October 18, 1910. The site of the wreck is one of the most dangerous on the lakes owing to its exposed position. Wreckers were immediately dispatched to the vessel's assistance but heavy weather prevented work. When they did arrive, they succeeded in removing only part of the cargo. More severe weather set in and the ship was abandoned by her owner as a constructive total loss on November 2. The MORELAND lay on Sawtooth Reef rocks, broken into three parts. The center section of the ship was hard on the rocks and the bow was over deep water. Breaks in the hull were at numbers 12 and 24 hatches. The crew was removed and winter set in.

The tremendous job of trying to salvage the vessel was left up to the Reid Wrecking Company of Sarnia, Ontario. Nothing much could be done until the very severe winter loosened its icy grip. In the spring of 1911, Reid began work on the vessel. More bad storms ensued and gradually the forward end of the vessel sank deeper. After one particularly heavy gale, the entire forward section sank into deep water and was lost. The center section was also beyond salvage and the stern was all that was left. It was bulkheaded with a cofferdam and floated off the reef on August 8th. It was then towed to Portage Harbor in September, boarded up and left in the protection of the harbor for the winter.

Unable to get a ready purchaser for the 254 foot stern section, Captain Reid started shopping around. In September 1912, he towed the after end to Port Huron, Michigan then to Ecorse, Michigan and across the river to Windsor, Ontario in November. Again towing it to Port Huron in October 1913, Reid finally decided to scuttle it in shallow water to await a bid. His patience was rewarded in early

1916. Due to the increase of steel prices with consequently higher costs for new ships caused by the enormous demand for tonnage in World War I, Reid found a buyer. Roy M. Wolvin of Duluth, Minnesota purchased the stern section. It was raised, towed back to Detroit and put on the drydock. American Shipbuilding Company was the successful bidder for the work of rebuilding the vessel.

The MORELAND was towed to the yard of the Superior Shipbuilding Company at Superior, Wisconsin in May 1916. A new forward section was built and the old stern section repaired. On September 9, 1916, the new bow section (346 feet long) was launched (Hull #524). Both sections were floated into the drydock and joined.

A brand new freighter, the SIR TREVOR DAWSON (US. 214499) was christened later that fall and it entered service for the American Interlake Line, a Wolvin subsidiary of Canada Steamship Lines. The new GRT was 7,215. (It had been the intention to rename the vessel after Mr. R.M. Wolvin but he demurred.)

In 1920, the vessel was sold to Pioneer Steamship Company, Hutchinson & Co., managers and renamed b) CHARLES L. HUTCHINSON (1) in 1921. For this company she served over 40 years. In 1951, because another, newer vessel was to receive the name, the CHARLES L. HUTCHINSON was renamed, c) GENE C. HUTCHINSON.

When Hutchinson & Company went out of the shipping business in 1963, the vessel was sold Canadian to Redwood Enterprises, Ltd., (Capt. Norman Reoch, manager) and renamed d) PARKDALE (2) (C. 316355). She was used mainly in the grain and coal trades until 1970, when sold for overseas scrapping.

The PARKDALE, along with the ALEXANDER LESLIE in tandem tow behind the tug SALVONIA, left Quebec City on May 12, 1970 and arrived safely at Cartagena, Spain on June 8th, to be cut up. The stern of the former MORELAND, after 60 years of existence, ended up far away from her sunken original bow section which still lies beneath the cold waters of Lake Superior.

WILLIAM C. MORELAND at Ashtabula harbor

Working on the wreck late in 1910

MANISTIQUE with the salvaged stern of the MORELAND nearing the Soo downbound

238

SIR TREVOR DAWSON upbound at Mission Point in 1919

a) **WILLIAM C. MORELAND**   b) **Sir Trevor Dawson**   c) **Charles L. Hutchinson (1)**
d) **Gene C. Hutchinson**   e) **Parkdale (2)**

BUILT:	1910
	American Shipbuilding Co.,
	Lorain, Ohio
HULL NUMBER:	387
LENGTH:	580.0
BREADTH:	58.0
DEPTH:	32.0
GRT:	5,714
REGISTRY NUMBER:	US. 207851
ENGINES:	24", 39", 65" Diameter x
	42" Stroke
ENGINE BUILDER:	Shipyard

CHARLES L. HUTCHINSON downbound at the Soo

GENE C. HUTCHINSON downbound in Lake Huron in 1960

PARKDALE downbound at the Soo, May 31, 1964

JOE S. MORROW

An early photo of JOE S. MORROW under the unloading rig

In 1906, the American Shipbuilding Company of Lorain, Ohio was commissioned to build a steel bulk freighter for Joseph Sellwood of Duluth, Minnesota. This vessel was launched on December 15, 1906 and completed in 1907. She was christened JOE S. MORROW and began a long career as a favorite among boat-watchers who admired her lines. Many vessels on the Great Lakes have been renamed at one or another period of their existence. The MORROW retained her original name even though six different owners possessed the vessel in the course of its life.

In 1908, Joseph Sellwood sold the MORROW to John Mitchell of Cleveland, Ohio and Mr. Mitchell sold it to Masaba Steamship Company in 1912. After 25 years under this company flag, the MORROW was sold to the Red Arrow Steamship Company, an affiliate of the C. Reiss Coal Company of Sheboygan, Wisconsin. For the Reiss fleet, the MORROW carried primarily grain downbound to Buffalo, New York and coal upbound to Duluth/Superior. The Red Arrow Steamship Company was a privately held company owned by some senior members of the parent C. Reiss Coal

Company. All Reiss associated boats were sold in 1969 to the American Steamship Company of Buffalo, New York. The arrangement was that all stock in the companies was purchased by the new parent firm although the vessels retained their former corporate names.

American Steamship Company had to sell some of the boats because of an anti-trust ruling against them for too much concentration of tonnage and trade routes after the purchase of the Reiss and Gartland Steamship Companies. They were required to divest themselves of some freighters and the JOE S. MORROW was one of them. In 1972, Kinsman Marine Transit Company became her owner. It, too, kept the name of this venerable vessel. Thus, the MORROW underwent 6 changes in ownership or management, but not a single rename. The final voyage of this ship began on April 19, 1974 from Quebec City with the HENRY LA LIBERTE in tandem tow behind the tug JANTAR. The trio arrived at Santander, Spain on May 8, 1974. The JOE S. MORROW was dismantled there along with the HENRY LA LIBERTE.

JOE S. MORROW in 1918

241

JOE S. MORROW downbound at Port Huron, December 6, 1963

Downbound at the Soo, August 4, 1969

JOE S. MORROW in Kinsman colors, August 9, 1973

BUILT:	1907
	American Shipbuilding Co.,
	Lorain, Ohio
HULL NUMBER:	350
LENGTH:	420.0
BREADTH:	52.0
DEPTH:	28.0
GRT:	4,760
REGISTRY NUMBER:	US. 203908
ENGINES:	22", 35", 58" Diameter x
	40" Stroke
	Triple Expansion
ENGINE BUILDER:	Shipyard

CHARLES S. NEFF

The steel lumber hooker CHARLES S. NEFF was launched on June 5, 1901, at Port Huron, Michigan by the Jenks Shipbuilding Company for the Sidney Neff Lumber Company of Milwaukee, Wisconsin to be used in the lumber trade. She sailed successfully until the lumber trade diminished. Then the vessel was put up for sale.

On March 15, 1917, A. B. MacKay of Hamilton, Ontario, a ship broker and purchaser of lake vessels for overseas use, bought the ship and sold her a year and ten days later to James Donald of New York City. He in turn sold it the same day to the Argonne Steamship Company, a French firm. The ship was renamed b) SERPENTINE in 1918 after being rebuilt for ocean service at Buffalo, New York by the Buffalo Dry Dock Company (1,069 GRT).

In 1921, the ship was renamed c) GABINO while owned by G. Hermanos, Bilboa, Spain. In 1923, along with 14 other ships, she carried a cargo of grain out of Fort William, Ontario for foreign ports, thus marking the first overseas clearance ever made from the Canadian head of the lakes. The Niagara Sand Corporation purchased the vessel and brought her back to the lakes in 1925, renaming her d) WESTON M. CARROLL. In 1925, the vessel was also converted to a sand dredge, in which capacity she served the rest of her life. In 1926, she was owned by the Buffalo Gravel Corporation and worked in eastern Lake Erie until the Second World War. She was taken to the coast again in 1944, now owned by the R. C. Huffman Construction Company and, in 1949, sold to the Overseas Dredge & Dock Company who renamed her e) SAN PEDRO the same year.

The vessel was chartered to Brazilian parties, who took her down to the southern hemisphere. In 1953, the SAN PEDRO capsized and sank in the harbor of Fortaleza, Brazil and remained there until the mid 1960's, when she was finally reduced to scrap to clear the harbor. She is still listed in the U.S. Merchant Vessel list in 1979.

CHARLES S. NEFF outbound after delivering a load of lumber

a) **CHARLES S. NEFF**   b) **Serpentine**   c) **Gabino**
d) **Weston M. Carroll**   e) **San Pedro**

BUILT:	1901	*GRT:*	992
	Jenks Shipbuilding Co.,	*REGISTRY NUMBER:*	US. 127547
	Port Huron, Mich.	*ENGINES:*	22", 44" Diameter x
HULL NUMBER:	16		30" Stroke
LENGTH:	200.0		Fore & Aft Compound
BREADTH:	38.0	*ENGINE BUILDER:*	Shipyard
DEPTH:	11.6		

CHARLES S. NEFF being prepared for ocean service, July 10, 1918

WESTON M. CARROLL

SAN PEDRO at Norfolk, Virginia before leaving for Brazil

BENJAMIN NOBLE

Designed especially to carry railroad steel, the steel canaller BENJAMIN NOBLE was launched from the yards of the Detroit Shipbuilding Company, at Wyandotte, Michigan on April 28, 1909 for the Capitol Transportation Company, J.A. Francombe, Manager. She quite frequently carried cargoes of coal as well as the steel products she was designed to carry and was a financial success.

In April 1914, she left Conneaut, Ohio destined for Duluth, Minnesota with a cargo of railroad steel. Many people who saw her later reported that she was overloaded. Apparently, she almost made the Duluth piers on April 27, 1914, but the south pier light was extinguished during a severe gale and blinding snowstorm, and the captain decided to turn about and head for Two Harbors, Minnesota. She foundered somewhere near Knife Island that night and her crew of twenty went down with her.

Lifebelts, hatch covers and other wreckage bearing her name came ashore on April 29th on Minnesota Point in Duluth, but no bodies were ever found. To date, skin divers have not located the wreck of the NOBLE beneath the icy waters of Lake Superior.

BUILT:	1909
	Detroit Shipbuilding Co.,
	Wyandotte, Mich.
HULL NUMBER:	178
LENGTH:	239.2
BREADTH:	42.2
DEPTH:	18.8
GRT:	1,481
REGISTRY NUMBER:	US. 206240
ENGINES:	17", 27½", 46" Diameter x
	36" Stroke
	Triple Expansion
ENGINE BUILDER:	Shipyard

BENJAMIN NOBLE upbound at the Soo in 1909

246

NORMAC

The steel fireboat JAMES R. ELLIOTT was launched on November 29, 1902 at Port Huron, Michigan by the Jenks Shipbuilding Company for the Detroit Fire Department. She helped quell many a fire on the Detroit riverfront and always was in reserve in the event of a major conflagration. Her engine had been in the fireboat DETROITER of 1883 and was later placed in the tug SARNIA CITY.

In 1930, the City of Detroit sold the vessel to the Owen Sound Transportation Company, which took out the steam engine and installed a 5 cylinder 12" x 15" diesel engine built by Fairbanks Morse & Co., Beloit, Wisconsin. The Canadian registry number awarded her was C. 154621. She was renamed b) NORMAC for service between Tobermory and South Baymouth, Ontario on Manitoulin Island. The NORMAC made many trips between these ports and later was used on the North Shore route between Owen Sound and Sault Ste. Marie, Ontario with stops at ports in the pretty channels of northern Lake Huron. Her last voyages were between Meldrum Bay on Manitoulin Island and Blind River, Ontario.

There were a few anxious moments in her life. Among them was a capsizing off Owen Sound in Georgian Bay in 1936 when seven crewmen, including the captain, were lost.

There were a few groundings in the treacherous waters off Cove Island, the entrance to Georgian Bay from Lake Huron. In each case, the NORMAC was refloated, refitted and put back into service.

In 1968, the NORMAC was sold to a Port Lambton, Ontario man, Don Lee, and moved to Wallaceburg, Ontario. In 1969, John Letnik bought the vessel and converted it into a floating restaurant at Toronto, Ontario. His problems were many, but he succeeded. The NORMAC was berthed at the foot of Yonge Street and named "CAPTAIN JOHN'S HARBOUR BOAT RESTAURANT," even though she was officially still NORMAC. Two entire decks in the hull of the ship were turned into dining rooms, the kitchen was in the bow and she was later given a new aluminum and wood superstructure. The vessel was popular with tourists but some complained about cramped space and high prices.

On June 6, 1981, the restored and refurbished sidewheel ferry TRILIUM had a power failure and struck the NORMAC broadside. Two weeks later, after temporary patches failed, the NORMAC sank at the dock. The superstructure was stripped from the vessel early in 1982, but the hull still rests at the bottom.

JAMES R. ELLIOTT at her Detroit dock

NORMAC at Owen Sound, MANITOULIN is astern

James R. Elliott,   b) NORMAC

BUILT:	1902	*REGISTRY NUMBER:*	US. 77566
	Jenks Shipbuilding Co.,	*ENGINES:*	18" Diameter x 20" Stroke
	Port Huron, Mich.		Double High Pressure
LENGTH:	110.0		Non-Condensing
BREADTH:	25.0	*ENGINE BUILDER:*	Cowles Engine Company
DEPTH:	12.0		Brooklyn, N.Y. - 1893
GRT:	210		

NORMAC upbound in the St. Mary's River, August 17, 1961

CAPTAIN JOHN'S RESTAURANT at Toronto, August 3, 1977

On the bottom, August 17, 1981, JADRAN at right

NORTHWESTERN

The steel canaller NORTHWESTERN, launched on December 29, 1900 at Chicago, Illinois by the Chicago Shipbuilding Company, was the first of four vessels which were to provide express service from Chicago to Liverpool, England in the package freight trade for the Northwestern Steamship Company, known as the Counselman Line after the Chicago financier. Service was to be provided monthly between the two cities. On its first trip outbound, the NORTHWESTERN was disabled by ice in the St. Clair River and was rescued by one of the Detroit River ferry boats. Her propeller was replaced and she made the round trip safely. Three other nearly identical sisterships were built: NORTHTOWN, NORTHEASTERN and NORTHMAN.

The proposed service was not a success and all four boats were sold in 1905. (There had been a tonnage change in 1903 to 2,207 GRT.) The NORTHWESTERN went to the Texas Company of Port Arthur, Texas and was converted to carry case oil (oil in barrels). On February 11, 1920, the vessel was partially burned at Port Neches, Texas and was sold in 1921 to the American Petroleum Company of Texas. She was converted to a regular bulk tanker, lengthened to 303.2 x 42.2 x 23.2; 2,881 gross tons and renamed b) FEDERAL. In 1926, she belonged to the Petroleum Navigation Company and served this fleet the rest of her life.

During the World War II years, all vessels were pressed into service for the war effort and FEDERAL was included. Unfortunately, her war service was short lived. On April 30, 1942, while on a voyage in the Caribbean from Tampa, Florida to Banes, five miles north of Gibara, Santiago, she was sunk by gunfire from an enemy submarine. Her position was 21°.30' N/76°.05' W. Five out of 33 on board at the time were lost with the FEDERAL.

NORTHWESTERN just after her trials

NORTHWESTERN,	**b) Federal**

BUILT:	1901
	Chicago Shipbuilding Co.,
	Chicago, Ill.
HULL NUMBER:	43
LENGTH:	242.0
BREADTH:	42.2
DEPTH:	23.2
GRT:	2,157
REGISTRY NUMBER:	US. 130908
ENGINES:	20", 33", 54" Diameter of Cylinders x 40" Stroke Triple Expansion
ENGINE BUILDER:	Shipyard

NORTHWESTERN in the ice on Lake St. Clair

FEDERAL, July 10, 1941

E. W. OGLEBAY

Launched on May 16, 1896 at West Bay City, Michigan by F. W. Wheeler & Company, the steel bulk freighter E. W. OGLEBAY was built for D. C. Whitney of Detroit, Michigan for service in his fleet. In 1902, the vessel was purchased by the Gilchrist Transportation Company. With the breakup of the Gilchrist fleet in 1913, the OGLEBAY went to the General Transit Company of Cleveland, Ohio, C. W. Bryson, Manager.

While sailing in ballast for Fort William, Ontario, in a severe gale whose winds reached more than 50 mph in velocity, the E. W. OGLEBAY stranded at 5:30 p.m. on Wednesday, December 8, 1927, 600 feet from shore off Shot Point, about 10 miles from Marquette, Michigan in Lake Superior. She caught fire and the crew was in double peril. Fortunately, the U.S. Coast Guard was able to get a boat out to the stricken vessel. The fish tug COLUMBIA also raced to the scene as best it could in the rough water. The entire crew was removed by the Coast Guard, transferred to the tug and taken to Marquette and safety.

The hull was later stripped and left where it was for the winter. She was purchased by the T. L. Durocher Towing & Wrecking Company of DeTour, Michigan. The salvagers succeeded in getting her off the rocks on May 11, 1929, one year and four months after she had struck. The vessel was released, patched up and taken to Drummond Island in the lower St. Mary's River. In 1930, the cabins and upper works were removed and the vessel was sunk to be made a part of a dock for the Drummond Island Dolomite Company. There she remains, as today's vessels tie up to load stone at the plant.

E. W. OGLEBAY downbound in the St. Clair River

BUILT:	1896
	F. W. Wheeler & Co.,
	W. Bay City, Mich.
HULL NUMBER:	114
LENGTH:	375.6
BREADTH:	45.8
DEPTH:	23.2
GRT:	3,666
REGISTRY NUMBER:	US. 136547
ENGINES:	23", 37", 63" Diameter x
	44" Stroke
	Triple Expansion
ENGINE BUILDER:	Shipyard

E. W. OGLEBAY upbound just below Mission Point in 1916

Stranded at Shot Point, Lake Superior December, 1927

253

ONOKO

The largest vessel then on the lakes and one of the proto-types of the modern Great Lakes bulk freighter, the iron bulk carrier ONOKO was launched on February 16, 1882 at Cleveland, Ohio by the Globe Iron Works for the Minch Transportation Company (Kinsman Steamship Company); also known as the Nicholas Transportation Company. For a while, the vessels in the fleet had no letter on the smoke stack, then a "K," and later an "S." The ONOKO served her entire life under one flag and one name. She earned her original price tag many times over.

The vessel did not have many accidents in her career, but she did manage to sink one ship. Off Racine, Wisconsin on May 16, 1896, the ONOKO hit the schooner MARY D. AYER. The weather had "socked in" and visibility in the fog was almost nil. The AYER went to the bottom in short order. Five of the schooner's crew were lost.

The ONOKO's own demise, on September 14, 1915, was not due to gales, fire, fog or collision but simply to hull failure. After leaving Duluth, Minnesota with a cargo of grain destined for Toledo, Ohio, under charter to the Tomlinson fleet of Duluth, the ONOKO was about 17 miles northeast of Duluth, off Knife Island, when the engineer noticed water coming up through the grates. He immediately notified the skipper and started the pumps. This did not help and "abandon ship" was sounded. The lake was calm and the 16 crewmen and one passenger got into the lifeboats. The Standard Oil Company tanker RENOWN was nearby and picked up all the survivors. The old vessel sank stern first in view of all on board the RENOWN. Some even took pictures as the forerunner of bulk freighters on the lakes took her final plunge. Apparently a plate had loosened and fallen off her hull.

Sprague painting of ONOKO with auxiliary sails

BUILT:	1882
	Globe Iron Works,
	Cleveland, Ohio
HULL NUMBER:	4
LENGTH:	287.3
BREADTH:	38.8
DEPTH:	20.7
GRT:	2,164
REGISTRY NUMBER:	US. 155048
ENGINES:	30", 56" Diameter x
	48" Stroke
	Fore & Aft Compound
ENGINE BUILDER:	Shipyard

ONOKO in the Soo Locks

Downbound at Mission Point in 1914

ONOKO leaving Duluth harbor

Photo taken from the deck of the tanker RENOWN, September 14, 1915

J. H. OUTHWAITE

J. H. OUTHWAITE in the Soo Locks

BUILT: 1886
W. H. Radcliffe,
Cleveland, Ohio
HULL
NUMBER:
LENGTH: 224.0
BREADTH: 37.4
DEPTH: 8.6
GRT: 1,304
REGISTRY
NUMBER: US. 76636
ENGINES: 27", 50" Diameter
x 36" Stroke
Fore & Aft
Compound
ENGINE
BUILDER: (#162) Globe
Iron Works
Cleveland, Ohio

The wooden bulk freighter J. H. OUTHWAITE was built in 1886 at Cleveland, Ohio by W.H. Radcliffe for H.J. Webb of the Cleveland Rolling Mills Company for the iron ore trade. In 1894, the vessel was purchased by W.C. Richardson & Company. She was completely refurbished in 1898 to withstand the rigors of lake trade after being ashore in a gale at False Presque Isle Point, Lake Huron with her barge, the H.A. BARR. The OUTHWAITE was released by Captain James Reid and rebuilt at the James Davidson shipyard at West Bay City, Michigan. Later, in 1903, the vessel was transferred back to the Richardson Transportation Company. Photographically elusive, the OUTHWAITE is pictured here in the Soo Locks canal prior to her stranding and burning in a heavy gale on November 28, 1905 at Little Point Sable near Cheboygan, Michigan in the Straits of Mackinac.

257

PHILO PARSONS

Early artist conception of PHILO PARSONS

The wooden passenger steamer PHILO PARSONS, built in 1861 at Algonac, Michigan by Charles Hinman at the Abram Smith yard for Patrick Kean, Selah Dustin and Walter Ashley of Detroit, Michigan for daily service between Detroit and Sandusky, Ohio, was the most famous ship on the Great Lakes during the Civil War. Her engine had been in the vessel LITTLE ERIE and the steamer JOHN OWEN.

September 19, 1864 was the day chosen for a daring plot during the Civil War. This plot, hatched on the Canadian side of the border by Confederate agents, was aimed at releasing a large number of their officers held prisoner on Johnson's Island in Sandusky Bay, about 50 miles south of Detroit. The leader of the conspiracy was Jacob Thompson, a Confederate Commissioner to Canada. His most active agent was a young military captain named Charles H. Cole.

The steamer MICHIGAN, the only naval vessel on the Great Lakes at that time, had been given the assignment of guarding and protecting the prisoner-of-war camp on Johnson's Island. The conspirators hoped either to capture or destroy it, thereby leading to the release of the prisoners on the island. The plan called for Cole to establish friendly relations with the officers on the MICHIGAN and arrange for a cocktail party on board the ship to take place on the night of September 19.

Meanwhile, another young Confederate, John Yates Beall, and a few chosen men from Windsor, Ontario, were to hi-jack a boat and, with a sufficient body of Confederate soldiers, to board and take the steamer MICHIGAN while the sailors on the MICHIGAN were under the influence of alcohol. Unfortunately for Beall, one of his men from Windsor doublecrossed him and turned over all the information to the Union authorities at Detroit.

On Sunday morning, September 18, one of the conspirators approached Walter O. Ashley, the clerk of the PHILO PARSONS, and requested that the steamer stop the next day at Sandwich, Ontario to pick up a party of friends. Ashley agreed and the following day the steamer stopped at Sandwich, a town three miles down river on the Canadian side, and the party took passage to Kelley's Island. At the regular stop at Malden, on the Canadian side at the mouth of the Detroit River, another party of about 20 men came on board. Their baggage consisted of a trunk tied with a rope, which later was found to contain revolvers and large hatchets or axes.

The steamer continued on her regular course and made a stop at North Bass and Middle Bass Islands. The latter was the residence of Captain Atwood of the PHILO PARSONS, and he left the steamer at this point. After a further stop at South Bass Island, the steamer headed for Kelley's Island.

However, instead of leaving the steamer when she arrived there, the party from Sandwich was joined by four men. This development aroused the suspicion of the clerk of the PARSONS. However, he did not have the opportunity to take any action for shortly following the departure from Kelley's Island, the rebels seized the PHILO PARSONS and forced the pilot to change the course of the vessel.

The passengers numbered about 40, and when the vessel was seized by the rebels, all of them were forced into confinement. After securing a guard on the passengers, some of the members of the raiding party learned from the mate and engineer of the vessel that there was not enough fuel to run the vessel many hours. Therefore, the leaders decided to return to Middle Bass Island to obtain a supply of wood.

While the PHILO PARSONS was docked at Middle Bass Island obtaining fuel, the ISLAND QUEEN came alongside the PARSONS and was immediately attacked by members of the raiding party. During the encounter, the engineer of the QUEEN was seriously wounded, and a few others were slightly wounded. The conspirators placed the passengers from both vessels ashore on Middle Bass Island. They then transferred the crew of the ISLAND QUEEN to the PHILO PARSONS, and taking the ISLAND QUEEN in tow, they left for Sandusky. The raiders, having previously cut a hole in the intake pipes of the ISLAND QUEEN, cut loose the steamer and let her drift away, assuming she would sink.

The raiders proceeded to within four miles of their destination. Apparently they had made previous arrangements whereby if Cole's plans were carried out with respect to the officers of the MICHIGAN, a signal would be given and the party on board the PHILO PARSONS would attack the warship and overpower the crew. The signal was never given, however, for the military authorities had previously learned of the conspiracy from the informant in Detroit, and the officers on board the MICHIGAN had been alerted, and Cole and his assistant, Robinson, had been apprehended.

The absence of a signal posed a serious problem to the party. They had captured the PHILO PARSONS and were ready to attack the MICHIGAN. However, many of the raiders were convinced that the absence of the signal indicated that Cole's plans had failed. The leader of the raiders, John Beall, wanted to proceed despite the circumstances, but the majority of the party positively refused. In the face of such opposition, Beall decided the only course was to return to Canada.

The PHILO PARSONS was turned about and proceeded under full steam for the mouth of the Detroit River. The conspirators reached a point six miles beyond Malden at about 5 o'clock the morning of September 20. Here they filled a small boat with plunder and set it ashore on the Canadian side of the river. Proceeding further up the Detroit River, they came to Fighting Island, where they sent all but three of the crew of both steamers ashore in a small boat. They finally docked the PHILO PARSONS at Sandwich and completed the plunder of the vessel. After cutting holes in the injection pipes of the vessel, leaving the PARSONS to sink, they disappeared, the majority walking to Windsor, each with a bundle of plunder taken from the ships.

Fortunately, the pilot of the PHILO PARSONS managed to obtain passage from Fighting Island in a small vessel and was able to recover the PHILO PARSONS before she sank. She was taken in tow to Detroit where she was repaired. Most of the conspirators were able to escape but John Yates Beall later paid the price for his piracy.

The PHILO PARSON's career after this incident was not spectacular. In 1866, Fox Brothers & Co. purchased the vessel. In 1868, it was owned by H. Fuller; the ship was readmeasured (184.71 GRT). In 1869, she was owned by C.D. Chapman. In 1870, the vessel was purchased by John Klug of Chicago, Illinois and taken for new service to Lake Michigan. On October 9, 1871, the PHILO PARSONS was consumed by fire during the famous "Chicago Fire" while she was tied up at her dock in the Chicago River. Her remains were condemned in 1872 and her documents were surrendered on December 31, 1874. The PARSONS' charred bones were found on June 27, 1877 on the North Branch of the Chicago River between Erie and Chicago Avenues, and were removed by dredges.

Fr. Dowling's painting of PHILO PARSONS

BUILT:	1861
	Charles Hinman/Abram Smith,
	Algonac, Mich.
LENGTH:	136.0
BREADTH:	20.0
DEPTH:	8.6
GRT:	221.8
REGISTRY NUMBER:	US. 19678
ENGINES:	40" Diameter x 108" Stroke
	Vertical Beam Low Pressure
ENGINE BUILDER:	Unknown

PERE MARQUETTE 14

A steel railroad carferry designed to haul freight cars between Port Huron, Michigan and Sarnia, Ontario on the St. Clair River, PERE MARQUETTE 14 was launched on December 19, 1903 at Wyandotte, Michigan by the Detroit Shipbuilding Company for the Pere Marquette Railroad. Laid down as F & P.M. 14, the name was changed on the drawing boards because the Flint & Pere Marquette Railroad had been reorganized. This vessel was a prototype of the large river carferries that followed her and a novel idea when built. She had four stacks, while her successors had two. These four smoke stacks actually emanated from two boiler houses, one on each side.

This steamer's humdrum existence was not enhanced by any serious accident or any harrowing experience during her lifetime. Later, she was assigned the duty of ferrying railroad cars across the Detroit River between Windsor, Ontario and Detroit, Michigan. Other than a routine five-year inspection trip to Toledo, Ohio or Ecorse, Michigan, the PERE MARQUETTE 14 did not stray too far out of her area. When longer and larger freight cars were built and a new ferry, the PERE MARQUETTE 10 came out, the old P.M. 14 was surplus. She was retired and taken to Hamilton, Ontario in 1957 where she was cut up for scrap by the Steel Company of Canada Ltd.

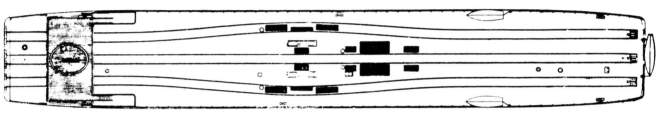

DECK PLANS OF CAR FERRY PERE MARQUETTE NO. 14, FOR SERVICE BETWEEN PORT HURON AND SARNIA.

Deck plans of PERE MARQUETTE 14

PERE MARQUETTE 14 arriving at her dock in Windsor. DETROIT EDISON behind

BUILT:	1904	*DEPTH:*	21.0
	Detroit Shipbuilding Co.,	*GRT:*	2,531
	Wyandotte, Mich.	*REGISTRY NUMBER:*	US. 200611
HULL NUMBER:	156	*TWIN ENGINES:*	28", 52" Diameter x 36" Stroke
LENGTH:	327.6		Fore & Aft Compound
BREADTH:	52.1	*ENGINE BUILDER:*	Shipyard

PERE MARQUETTE 18 (1)

PERE MARQUETTE 18 on Lake Michigan

The launching ceremony of the steel cross-lake carferry PERE MARQUETTE 18, on August 16, 1902 in the yard of the American Shipbuilding Company at Cleveland, Ohio, was at best unusual. Instead of the traditional breaking of a bottle of champagne on her bow, the Japanese custom of releasing a flock of doves was used. The big carferry was built for the Pere Marquette Railroad for cross-lake service between Ludington, Michigan and Kewaunee, Manitowoc and Milwaukee, Wisconsin. She had four railroad tracks on her main deck and 50 elegant staterooms to accommodate passengers for the runs across Lake Michigan.

The PERE MARQUETTE 18 left Ludington at 11:40 p.m. September 8, 1910 bound for Milwaukee with a cargo of 29 loaded cars. Some of the cars were loaded with general merchandise and others with coal. The wind was blowing fresh from the north. A heavy sea was running and continued to build during the night. At 3 o'clock the morning of September 9th, an oiler went aft to oil the bearings for the main shafts which were about 7 feet below the floor of what is known as the "flicker" or sleeping quarters of the oilers, firemen, water tenders and deck hands. The oiler found that the entire compartment was full of water and could not get down to the shafts as the water was almost up to the "flicker" floor. He then returned to the engine room and reported to the engineer on watch. The engineer went to the pilot house and reported to the officer on watch, that "there was something wrong aft. The pumps were on and the water was gaining on them."

The first officer went aft to investigate and returned to the pilot house. The captain was called and took charge of the ship. Along with the first officer and some others of the crew, the captain went to the "flicker" and tried to stop the leak in a deadlight (porthole) which was on the starboard side. Everyone aboard the ship was then alerted and the vessel headed for the west shore. Three more deadlights on the port side gave way, admitting large quantities of water which drove everyone out of the "flicker" and completely filled it and the whole after part of the hull with water.

In order to offset this added weight of water in the hull, the master ordered some of the cars to be run overboard. After putting over 12 or 13 cars, the ship seemed to lighten up aft and the crew felt easier.

At about 4:15 a.m., wireless messages were sent out for help and the life preservers were distributed for the people aboard. Three life boats were safely launched on the port side and men put into them to keep them fended off from the side of the ship. The steamer seemed to be settling aft. At about 6:30 a.m., the steamer PERE MARQUETTE 17 was sighted. Distress signals were blown and flags raised. The PERE MARQUETTE 17 arrived close up to the 18 at about 7:15 a.m. and came alongside on the starboard side, which was the weather side. The master of the 18 then motioned to come up on the lee side, or port side, which was done. Very shortly after, the 18 listed heavily to starboard, the stern started to go down, the bow rose and she sank very rapidly. The people on board the 18 began to jump overboard. The life boats of the PERE MARQUETTE 17 were lowered immediately and work of rescue begun. These boats picked up 32 people. As near as could be ascertained, 27 lives were lost, many because of the sea and floating wreckage.

The cause of the sinking could not be determined because all of the officers of the ship were lost. The case was unique, in the history of Great Lakes navigation at least, in that while other ships have passed out of existence mysteriously they left no soul to give any intimation of what befell. In this case, 32 people were rescued and yet not one knew why the PERE MARQUETTE 18 foundered. Experts who studied the evidence available were of the opinion that the probable point of entry of the water was by way of a fractured stern tube or broken stern tube gland and that later a bulkhead gave way, due to the surging of the water in the after hold caused by the heavy sea running at the time. The PERE MARQUETTE 18 had gone down just 20 miles off Sheboygan, Wisconsin.

BUILT:	1902
	American Shipbuilding Co., Cleveland, Ohio
HULL NUMBER:	412
LENGTH:	338.0
BREADTH:	56.0
DEPTH:	19.5
GRT:	2,909
REGISTRY NUMBER:	US. 150972
TWIN ENGINES:	22½", 36", 59" Diameter x 36" Stroke
	Triple Expansion
ENGINE BUILDER:	Shipyard

PERE MARQUETTE 18 on Lake Michigan

GEORGE W. PERKINS

When the GEORGE W. PERKINS was launched on June 26, 1905 at Superior, Wisconsin by the Superior Shipbuilding Company, she was one of four sisterships that recorded several "firsts" in Great Lakes shipping. Together with the WILLIAM E. COREY (later RIDGETOWN), the HENRY C. FRICK (later MICHPICOTEN) and ELBERT H. GARY (later R.E. WEBSTER), the PERKINS became one of the largest bulk carriers on the lakes, with a carrying capacity of 11,000 gross tons, and one of the first constructed for the Pittsburgh Steamship Co. The four ships also were the first to have arch construction and hoppered side tanks, truly the forerunners of all subsequent bulk carriers designed specifically for the iron ore trade. The PERKINS was initially registered in the 2nd supplement for May-September, 1905 of the Great Lakes Register.

The PERKINS spent a relatively quiet career in the Pittsburgh fleet until her layup at Milwaukee, Wisconsin in June, 1960. She went ashore northeast of Two Harbors, Minnesota in a fog on July 28, 1908, but only required minor repairs. She collided with the WILLIAM P. SNYDER, JR. in Duluth, Minnesota Harbor on June 16, 1918, suffering $5,000 in damage.

The PERKINS sailed relatively unchanged until the Winter of 1935-36 when she received new Babcock & Wilcox boilers. It was at this time that she received a substantially larger funnel and the after mast was moved forward of the stack. During the Winter of 1940-41, the PERKINS received 17 one-piece steel hatches on 24 foot centers and an "iron deckhand," replacing her original 33 hatches. She always was a two cargo-hold vessel during her Pittsburgh career.

After laying idle at Milwaukee until early 1964, the PERKINS was sold by U.S. Steel to Redwood Enterprises of Montreal, one of Captain Reoch's holding companies. She was immediately converted to three compartments, but otherwise remained the same upon entering the seaway trade as WESTDALE (2) (C. 317133). During the Winter of 1972-73, the WESTDALE received the reprieve that extended her career beyond those of her sisters, which were being sold for scrap at about the same time. During layup at Port Colborne, Ontario Herb Fraser and Associates installed oil burners and added two additional screen bulkheads to form five compartments for the parcel grain trade. After these modifications, the WESTDALE traded much more heavily to Georgian Bay ports and Goderich, Ontario and rarely transited the seaway. In 1977, after WESTDALE had become the last Reoch straight-deck bulk carrier, she was purchased by the Soo River Company, but continued in essentially the same trade as c) H.C. HEIMBECKER.

On October 30, 1981, the HEIMBECKER departed Owen Sound, Ontario on one boiler after unloading her final grain cargo. She was bound in ballast for Ashtabula, Ohio and the Triad Salvage scrap berth, where she arrived on November 3, 1981. Traded for the steamer MAXINE, which Triad purchased at auction earlier that year, the scrapping of the HEIMBECKER was the final chapter in the story of four sisterships that represented tremendous progress in Great Lakes vessel design concepts at the time of their construction.

GEORGE W. PERKINS leaving the Poe Lock in 1906, Str. HARLEM astern

GEORGE W. PERKINS downbound at Mission Point, June 17, 1954

GEORGE W. PERKINS,   b) Westdale (2),   c) H.C. Heimbecker

BUILT:	1905
	Superior Shipbuilding Co.,
	Superior, Wisc.
HULL NUMBER:	512
LENGTH:	556.2
BREADTH:	56.4
DEPTH:	26.5
GRT:	6,553
REGISTRY NUMBER:	US. 202166
ENGINES:	Triple Expansion
	24", 39", 65" Diameter
	x 42" Stroke
ENGINE BUILDER:	American Shipbuilding Co.
	Cleveland, Ohio - 1905

On Lake Huron, June, 1960

WESTDALE, July 31, 1975

H. C. HEIMBECKER upbound in the St. Mary's River, July 15, 1981

PESHTIGO

PESHTIGO in Winter Quarters

The wooden bulk freighter PESHTIGO was built in 1869 as a barge for the Peshtigo Company of Chicago. The company was formed around 1860 by W. B. Ogden and Thomas H. Beebe of Chicago. Their first vessels appear to have been the barks HANS CROCKER and TWO FANNIES, which were acquired not long after that date. In 1866 they built the propeller BOSCOBEL for the Lake Michigan west shore trade, but also began acquisition of vessels for the burgeoning lumber business; they bought the saltwater tug ADM. D. D. PORTER and ordered a whole flotilla of barges, all of the latter to be built at the A. A. Turner shipyard at Trenton, Michigan. PESHTIGO was a 200-footer like MAUTENEE and NOQUEBAY, and there were also three 150-footers built around the same time. These six barges were towed by various company tugs during the 1870's and 80's between Chicago and Green Bay ports such as Menominee, Peshtigo, Oconto and Green Bay city.

In 1891, the PESHTIGO was sold by the Peshtigo Company to S. R. Howell of Chicago and, later in the same year, to W. J. Calhoun of the same place. In 1895 she went to Capt. J. C. Pringle and others of Saginaw, Michigan. Pringle contracted with the Wyandotte Boat Company of Wyandotte, Michigan to haul out the old barge and rebuild her as a screw steambarge. The work was done during the winter of 1895-96, at which time the ship was given the machinery of the steambarge GEORGE W. JOHNSON (formerly the D. W. POWERS) which had been built by the Cuyahoga Iron Works in Cleveland in 1870 (817 GRT). The overhaul cost her owners $20,000, and a large but very

conventional-looking lumber steamer emerged. Immediately after her conversion, the PESHTIGO was sold to A. M. and F. P. Chesbrough of Emerson, Michigan, and employed in the lumber trade under the name of the Wolverine Boat Company.

On October 15, 1898, the PESHTIGO was in a collision with the steamer GEORGE W. ROBY near Alpena, Michigan. The PESHTIGO was downbound with lumber when, all of a sudden, she was struck by the ROBY, just forward of the engine room. By the grace of God and good seamanship, the captain managed to steer the vessel toward Alpena, where she settled in 22 feet of water, one-half mile off the river entrance, her decks awash. A tug was summoned, the crew removed and repairs begun. Within a few weeks, she was back in service, having been saved by the quick thinking of her master.

On October 23, 1908, the PESHTIGO was not so fortunate. In very bad weather, she stranded at the east end of the Straits of Mackinac with a full load of 800,000 feet of lumber. The crew was rescued but the fate of the vessel was in doubt. After 10 days of fruitless salvage operations, because of the successive storms that wracked the area, the PESHTIGO was given up as a total loss, although the cargo was salvaged. Soon the devastating weather fronts dashed her remains to pieces and the career of the little steam barge came to an abrupt end. (This vessel is not to be confused with another schooner tow barge of the same name which was built in 1889 and lasted until 1936, ending its days in the Saginaw River.)

BUILT:	1869
	A. A. Turner,
	Trenton, Mich.
LENGTH:	203.4
BREADTH:	34.8
DEPTH:	12.2
GRT:	817
REGISTRY NUMBER:	US. 54218
ENGINES:	17", 36" Diameter x
	36" Stroke
	Steeple Compound
ENGINE BUILDER:	Cuyahoga Iron Works
	Cleveland, Ohio - 1869

PESHTIGO with a load of lumber, downbound at the Soo

PINEBRANCH

The three-masted steel barge MALTA was launched on January 10, 1895 at South Chicago, Illinois by the Chicago Shipbuilding Company for the Minnesota Steamship Company. Her original dimensions were: 302.0 x 40.2 x 19.6; 2,237 gross tons (US. 92637). This vessel had quite a history. Steel barges were built to be consorts for the steamers that were then being turned out by the shipbuilders. The engines of the steamers were very powerful and it was not only practical but also economical to tow a barge. The MALTA saw a variety of owners and ports during her sixty-five year history.

In 1901, along with all the other vessels of the Minnesota Steamship Company fleet, the MALTA was purchased by the Pittsburgh Steamship Company. Being one of the smaller units of this fleet, she did not last long under its ownership. The Western Dry Dock Company purchased the vessel in 1912 and sold her to the Northwest Steamship Company that same year. The vessel was renamed b) THUNDER BAY (C. 131060) and was towed by the steamer PAIPOONGE. In 1917, the Montreal Transportation Company took over her ownership. In 1918, the following owners took possession of the ship: Canadian Towing & Wrecking Company, Collingwood Shipbuilding Company and Cuban interests. The THUNDER BAY was cut in two at Collingwood and towed through the St. Lawrence canals to Lauzon, Quebec in 1919. She was reassembled but shortened 54 feet to canal dimensions after Canada Steamship Lines Ltd. purchased the vessel in 1921 and installed the engine from the steamer NICARAGUA (C. 140936) of 1894.

THUNDER BAY saw service until the Great Depression, when it was laid up from 1930 to 1937 at Kingston, Ontario. Although many other CSL boats were scrapped in 1937, THUNDER BAY was purchased by Marine Industries Ltd., the Branch Line, converted to a tanker at Sorel and renamed c) PINEBRANCH.

The Second World War was already underway when PINEBRANCH was requisitioned by the British Ministry of Shipping in 1941. She was renamed d) EMPIRE STICKLE-BACK in accordance with the British nomenclature system prevalent at that time. She never left the dock at Halifax, N.S. as they did not get her ready before the war ended. In 1946, the vessel was returned to Marine Industries and renamed e) PINEBRANCH, the name she had prior to war service. Her days were rather uneventful now but definitely numbered. At the end of the 1955 season, PINEBRANCH was retired and laid up at Sorel. In 1960, she was purchased to become a permanent part of the breakwater at Mulgrave, Nova Scotia. There she remains to this day.

MALTA with heavy masts and auxiliary sails

a) Malta	
b) Thunder Bay (1)	
c) Pinebranch	
d) Empire Stickleback	
e) PINEBRANCH	

BUILT:	1895
	Chicago Shipbuilding Co.,
	Chicago, Ill.
HULL NUMBER:	13
LENGTH:	247.0
BREADTH:	40.1
DEPTH:	25.0
GRT:	2,237
REGISTRY NUMBER:	C. 131060
ENGINES:	16½", 25", 42" Diameter x 34" Stroke
	Triple Expansion
ENGINE BUILDER:	Frontier Iron Works Detroit, Michigan - 1894

THUNDER BAY as a barge

As a bulk freight steamer

EMPIRE STICKLEBACK at Halifax in 1945

PINEBRANCH in the Welland canal. Steam yacht VENETIA in the background

J. H. PLUMMER

J. H. PLUMMER in 1910

The steel-hulled, canal-sized package freighter J. H. PLUMMER was built in 1903 by Armstrong Witworth & Co. Ltd., at Low Walker-on-Tyne, England for the Canadian Lake and Ocean Navigation Company Ltd., Toronto, a subsidiary of the McKenzie and Mann Group. She was one of three nearly identical sisterships, the other two being A. E. AMES and H. M. PELLATT. All three were named for Toronto financiers.

During 1906, J. H. PLUMMER was operated by the Montreal and Lake Superior Line. This consortium was dissolved prior to the opening of the 1907 season and, in 1907, she ran in the Canadian Lake Line. Still under McKenzie and Mann ownership, she was later operated as part of the Merchants Mutual Line Ltd. This concern was absorbed into Canada Steamship Lines Ltd. Montreal, in 1913 but, although the PLUMMER was operated by C. S. L., she remained under McKenzie and Mann ownership.

J. H. PLUMMER went to salt water in 1917, under the management of the Canadian Maritime Company. Her actual ownership did not change until 1920, when she was acquired by the Soc. Belge d'Armament Marine, of Antwerp, Belgium. Her new owner renamed her b) VAN EYCK.

The steamer returned to the Great Lakes in 1923 under the ownership of the Kirkwood Line Ltd., and she reverted to her original name c) J. H. PLUMMER. Until November,

1923, she was operated in the package freight trade between Lake Ontario ports and the St. Lawrence River. On November 13, 1923, the PLUMMER cleared Hamilton, Ontario, on the start of a new service from the Great Lakes to the west coast of Canada. She called at Toronto and departed that port on November 20. The "Intercoastal Line" was not a success, and on her arrival at Vancouver early in 1924, the PLUMMER was seized by the mortgagee, Sir Thomas Wilson and Company, of Belfast, Northern Ireland.

She was sold in 1924, to the Coastwise Steamship and Barge Company Ltd., Vancouver, and renamed d) AMUR (2). She was placed in service between the Anyox and Britannia mines, of British Columbia, and Tacoma, Washington, carrying concentrates. AMUR was operated under the management of J. Griffiths and Sons.

In 1946, AMUR's registry was transferred to Panama, and she was renamed e) FAR EASTERN CARRIER. Later in 1946, the Tung An Shipping Company Ltd., of Shanghai, China, assumed control of the ship, and she was rechristened f) TUNG AN. Little is known of the operations of any of the lakers that wound up under Chinese ownership, but it was reported that TUNG AN was wrecked on April 10, 1949, six miles southwest of Shaweishan on the Yangtse River.

J. H. PLUMMER	(b) Van Eyck	(c) J. H. PLUMMER	(d) Amur
	(e) Far Eastern Carrier	(f) Tung An	

BUILT:	1903		GRT:	1643
	Armstrong Whitworth and Company Ltd.,	REGISTRY NUMBER:	Br. & C. 114447
	Low Walker-on-Tyne, G. B.	ENGINES:	20½", 33", 54" Diameter x
HULL NUMBER:	740			36" Stroke
LENGTH:	246.4			Triple Expansion
BREADTH:	36.6	ENGINE BUILDER:	Wallsend Slipway Company Ltd.,
DEPTH:	21.7			Newcastle, G. B.

J. H. PLUMMER in the ice

AMUR on the West Coast

Wreck of TUNG AN in the Yangtse River

ROBERT W. POMEROY

The Eastern Steamship Company Ltd., of St. Catharines, Ontario, was formed by the Grammer grain interests, and was managed by Boland and Cornelius, Buffalo. The fleet owned 21 steel-hulled canallers, these having been built in two groups, the first of which comprised ten steamers. Of these ten, two were constructed by each of five British shipyards.

The first to be launched was ROBERT W. POMEROY built by Earles Shipbuilding & Engineering Company, Ltd., which hit the water at Hull, England on March 16, 1923. Quickly completed and registered in Britain (she was not transferred to Canadian registry until 1930), she set out across the Atlantic and arrived safely in Canadian waters.

ROBERT W. POMEROY's first season in lake trade was not a particularly happy one. Upbound on Lake Superior in heavy weather during November, 1923, she broke her back and was very nearly lost. It was only with great difficulty that she managed to reach Fort William, Ontario.

Subsequently repaired, she served the Eastern Steamship Company Ltd. until 1936, although she spent much time in lay-up during the 1930's as a result of the effects of the Great Depression. Most of her periods of inactivity were spent in Muir's Pond, above Lock One at Port Dalhousie in the company of other Eastern canallers.

Along with the other 19 surviving Eastern vessels, ROBERT W. POMEROY was purchased in 1936 by the Upper Lakes and St. Lawrence Transportation Company Ltd., Toronto. She was requisitioned for salt water service during World War Two and was turned over to the British Ministry of War Transport.

Deep-sea service, however, did not agree with the POMEROY. Laden with lumber and bound for the United Kingdom in a North Atlantic convoy, she broke in two in heavy seas. It was found necessary to sink her with gunfire, and she was dispatched to the bottom on April 1, 1942 by an escorting destroyer.

ROBERT W. POMEROY in 1923, her first year on the lakes

Upbound in the St. Mary's River

273

BUILT:	1923
	Earles Shipbuilding &
	Engineering Ltd., Hull, England
HULL NUMBER:	643
LENGTH:	253.0
BREADTH:	43.2
DEPTH:	17.8
GRT:	1,724
REGISTRY NUMBER:	C. 147076
ENGINES:	16", 27", 44" Diameter x
	33" Stroke
	Triple Expansion
ENGINE BUILDER:	Shipyard

ROBERT W. POMEROY in Duluth Harbor, autumn of 1936

Broken in two in a storm in the Atlantic, April 1942

274

ROBERT W. POMEROY at Fort William

At Port Weller, September 1938

PORTADOC (1)

Rare photo of EUGENE C. ROBERTS in the St. Lawrence Canals

The steel canaller EUGENE C. ROBERTS was launched on March 5, 1924 at Birkenhead, England by Cammell Laird & Company for the A. B. Mackay Steamship Company of Hamilton, Ontario. Her first cargo was Welsh coal for Montreal and she left on April 3, 1924 for the lakes. On the journey over, the vessel was damaged by ice and was in drydock at Canadian Vickers at Montreal from April 29 to May 3 for repair of the damage. The Toronto Insurance & Vessel Agency Ltd., had control of the vessel from 1924 to 1925 when it was sold to Captain James Foote's Union Transit Company and renamed b) JAMES B. FOOTE in 1926. She sailed for this fleet until 1939, when Paterson Steamships Ltd., of Fort William, Ontario purchased the vessel on the 26th of April and renamed her c) PORTA-DOC (1).

In 1940, PORTADOC was requisitioned by the British Ministry of Transport for war service on the Atlantic. On April 7, 1941, she was sighted by the German U-124 (Captain Schulz) at 1730 hours in the Atlantic off North Africa and torpedoed. She sank in position 07°. 17'N/16°.53'W. All hands were able to escape before PORTADOC plunged to the bottom. One of the most elusive (photographically) of all the canallers, both as EUGENE C. ROBERTS and PORTADOC, the vessel *was* photographed, and we are pleased to be able to include photographs of the steamer with this history.

a) Eugene C. Roberts
b) James B. Foote
c) **PORTADOC (1)**

BUILT:	1924
	Cammell Laird & Co.,
	Birkenhead, England
HULL NUMBER:	903
LENGTH:	253.0
BREADTH:	43.1
DEPTH:	17.8
GRT:	1,746
REGISTRY NUMBER:	Br. & C. 147246
ENGINES:	16", 27", 44" Diameter x 33" Stroke
	Inverted Triple Expansion, Surface Condensing
ENGINE BUILDER:	Shipyard

JAMES B. FOOTE in 1926

In Winter quarters

PORTADOC in the St. Lawrence River Canals

277

PRESCOTT

The steel bulk freighter WESTERN STAR (U.S. 200376) was launched on October 3, 1903 at Wyandotte, Michigan by the Detroit Shipbuilding Company for M. U. Cummings of Oswego, New York and operated by Sullivan. During the gale of November 28, 1905, the WESTERN STAR was swept ashore at Ontonagon, Michigan on Lake Superior, but suffered little damage. The vessel was released and returned to service in a short time.

In 1912, she was sold to the Cadillac Steamship Company of Detroit, Michigan and wore the large shield and black letter "F" on her smoke stack, the emblem of the Franklin fleet managed by Oakes. In the misty morning of September 24, 1915, the WESTERN STAR, laden with 7,000 tons of coal, was feeling her way up the North Channel of Georgian Bay. Not far from Clapperton Island, the ship ran hard aground on Robertson's Rock. The lifeboats were lowered and the ship settled at an acute angle, her bow seven feet out of the water and her stern down in 114 feet of water. The crew reached shore safely and the owners were quickly informed.

They abandoned her to the underwriters and the work of salvage was begun. One of the greatest feats of marine salvage on the lakes was then accomplished, after much frustration, by the Great Lakes Towing Company of Cleveland, Ohio. The first attempt ended in failure when the timbers of the cofferdam gave out. Winter put an end to the first few weeks of work.

On June 17, 1916, the wrecker FAVORITE and the lighter T. F. NEWMAN, along with numerous tugs, arrived to begin again. Another, stronger cofferdam was built. As this was nearing completion, northwest gales set in and tipped it over. As a result, it had to be reconstructed. The onset of another Winter forced the discontinuation of their salvage efforts.

In the Spring of 1917, work again commenced. This time success was in the salvagers' grasp. The cofferdam finally constructed is believed to have been the largest of its kind ever erected. It involved the use of 430,000 feet of timber, 222,000 square yards of canvas and 73 tons of strut rods. Slowly the water was pumped out and the vessel rose. Finally, on September 18, 1917, the WESTERN STAR was towed into Collingwood, Ontario harbor where it would be repaired. The underwriters, meanwhile, envisioning success in the salvage, had already sold the vessel to the Valley Camp Steamship Company, a division of Playfair's Great Lakes Transportation Company Ltd. After the repairs had been completed, she joined the latter fleet as b) GLENISLA.

In 1924, the vessel was once more taken to Collinwood where it was lengthened 72 feet. Her new dimensions were: 488.0 x 50.2 x 24.0; 5,461 gross tons. In 1926, she was sold to Canada Steamship Lines Ltd. and renamed c) PRESCOTT. The adventurous years were over for this vessel. She served mainly in the grain trade the rest of her life with no serious incidents. During June, 1962, PRESCOTT, while drydocked at Collingwood, was condemned and retired from service. She spent the rest of 1962 laid up at Toronto and, in 1963, was partially scrapped at Hamilton, Ontario by the Steel Company of Canada. A part of the hull, 150 feet x 50 feet, was to be made into a barge. This did not materialize and PRESCOTT was completely scrapped later the same year.

WESTERN STAR upbound at the Soo in 1914

WESTERN STAR on Robertson's Rock in 1917. Tug FAVORITE (2) (stacks visible)

a) **Western Star**   b) **Glenisla**   c) **PRESCOTT**

BUILT:	1903
	Detroit Shipbuilding Co.,
	Wyandotte, Mich.
HULL NUMBER:	155
LENGTH:	416.0
BREADTH:	50.3
DEPTH:	29.0
GRT:	4,764
REGISTRY NUMBER:	C. 138214
ENGINES:	22", 35", 58" Diameter x
	42" Stroke
	Triple Expansion
ENGINE BUILDER:	Shipyard

GLENISLA upbound at Mission Point in 1922

PRESCOTT upbound in the Detroit River

QUEDOC (1)

MARISKA upbound at the Soo in 1901

The steel bulk freighter MARISKA (U.S. 92169) was launched on February 19, 1890 at Cleveland, Ohio by the Globe Iron Works for the Minnesota Steamship Company for use in the iron ore trade. The original dimensions were: 283.4 x 40.3 x 21.1; 2,325 GRT. In 1901, this fleet was one of the many absorbed by the Pittsburgh Steamship Company. In 1916, the vessel was sold Canadian to the Basset Steamship Company and registered at Collingwood, Ontario. In 1918, she was requisitioned by the U.S. War Shipping Board, taken to Buffalo, New York where she was cut in two to transit the canals and prepared for war service. The two halves were rejoined at Montreal at the yard of Canadian Vickers. The vessel saw little war service and, in 1919, was sold to the Transatlantic Steamship Company and again registered at Collingwood.

In 1923, MARISKA was purchased by the Minto Trading Company of Toronto, Ontario which had her lengthened 48 feet at the Canadian Vickers yard in Montreal. (346.4 x 40.2 x 22.0; 3,072 GRT). Again the vessel was cut in two to transit the canals to be brought to the lakes. The two sections were taken to Ashtabula, Ohio where they were rejoined by the Great Lakes Engineering Works. She was renamed b) KAMARIS, a variation of her original name, at that time. In 1926, the vessel was sold to Paterson Steamships Ltd., and renamed c) QUEDOC (1). After a modification to her cabins done in 1931 at Port Arthur, Ontario by the Port Arthur Shipbuilding Company, the QUEDOC served mainly in the grain trade often towing one of Paterson's steel barges.

In 1959, she was sold to the Holden Sand & Gravel Company, renamed d) H.S. & G. No. 1, and used as a barge in the gravel trade. This operation did not last long for the vessel was sold for scrap in 1961 and cut up at the Stelco plant in Hamilton, Ontario later the same year.

a) **Mariska**   b) **Kamaris**   c) **QUEDOC (1)**   d) **H.S. & G. No. 1**

BUILT:	1890 Globe Iron Works, Cleveland, Ohio
HULL NUMBER:	31
LENGTH:	346.4
BREADTH:	40.2
DEPTH:	22.0
GRT:	3,072
REGISTRY NUMBER:	C. 130979
ENGINES:	24½", 38", 61" Diameter x 42" Stroke Triple Expansion
ENGINE BUILDER:	Shipyard

MARISKA upbound, leaving the Soo Locks in 1913

MARISKA just after her sale to Canadian owners

MARISKA pulled apart at Buffalo, September 23, 1918

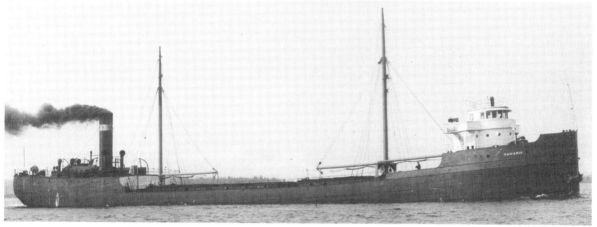

KAMARIS in 1926

QUEDOC downbound out of Lake St. Clair

QUEDOC downbound in the St. Clair River, September 4, 1950

H.S. & G. No. 1, July 8, 1960

RAPIDS QUEEN

COLUMBIAN in the Lachine Rapids of the St. Lawrence River

BROCKVILLE running the Lachine Rapids

    a) Columbian
    b) Brockville
    c) **RAPIDS QUEEN**
    d) **C. D. 110**
    e) **RAPIDS QUEEN**

BUILT:	1892 Deleware River Iron Shipbuilding & Engine Works, Chester, Penn.
HULL NUMBER:	214
LENGTH:	175.0
BREADTH:	39.9
DEPTH:	9.0
GRT:	884
REGISTRY NUMBER:	US. 126860
TWIN ENGINES:	12½", 19", 30" Diameter x 15" Stroke Triple Expansion
ENGINE BUILDER:	Shipyard

COLUMBIAN was the name given to the steel passenger steamer built in 1892 at Chester, Pennsylvania by the Delaware River Iron Shipbuilding & Engine Works for the Joy Line (Morgan Iron Works) of New York City. It was originally planned to operate her to the Columbian Exposition, which was held in 1893 at Chicago. It was in honor of the fair that she was named. However, she was not completed in time for the Exposition, and entered service in the New York City area.

In 1893, George Shea of St. John's, Newfoundland purchased the vessel and registered her British (B. 101254). Two years later, the vessel was taken over by the Montreal Safe Deposit Company as mortgagee of the Richelieu and Ontario Navigation Company Ltd. It was operated by them and ran between Toronto and Montreal, running the Rapids of the St. Lawrence River which was an exciting feature of the trip downbound.

In 1901, COLUMBIAN was chartered for service to the Pan American Exposition at Buffalo, New York. Later that same year, she was remodeled slightly at Sorel and her tonnage changed to 703 GRT. In 1905, the ship was renamed b) BROCKVILLE and in 1906 came into Canadian registry.

Title to BROCKVILLE was officially taken over by the Richelieu and Ontario Navigation Co., in 1907. There was no change in her route. In 1909, the vessel received a major rebuild at Sorel. She was lengthened to 194.4 x 33.5 x 8.8; 1,607 GRT, and her twin engines were modified to 15½", 24" diameter of cylinders x 22" stroke. She then also had a second smoke stack as well as a new name, c) RAPIDS QUEEN.

Canada Steamship Lines absorbed the R & O fleet in 1913, along with several other fleets, to form the C.S.L. conglomerate. The Great Depression idled many ships. RAPIDS QUEEN was idled for awhile, but in 1930 was purchased by John E. Russell of Toronto who owned her only a short period of time. She was sold to Sin-Mac Lines Ltd., later that year. (Russell was vice-president of Sin-Mac Lines Ltd.)

From 1930 to 1932, RAPIDS QUEEN was chartered to Dr. Locke's Clinic for use as a floating hotel for patients at Morrisburg, Ontario. In 1933, she was chartered to run between Fort William, Ontario and Isle Royale on Lake Superior. In 1935, she was chartered to the Ontario & Quebec Lines Ltd., to run between Toronto and Montreal. However, her days as a passenger vessel were ended. In 1937, Sin-Mac Lines laid her away in the "boneyard" at Portsmouth (Kingston), Ontario.

In 1938, all the superstructure and engines were removed at Kingston, Ontario after the ship was purchased by the Canadian Dredge & Dock Company. The RAPIDS QUEEN was converted into a fuel oil bunkering barge (412 GRT), and renamed d) C.D. 110. In this capacity, the vessel was engaged until 1960 when she was laid up at Kingston. She remained there in a partially sunken condition until 1978, when the once proud rapids runner was sold to the Queen City Yacht Club in Toronto. The vessel was towed to Ward's Island in Toronto harbor, filled with stone and allowed to settle to the bottom to act as a breakwall for the yacht club. There she lies all painted and festooned, her name, RAPIDS QUEEN, painted on her bows and decorated by park benches, a perfect memory of her glory days.

RAPIDS QUEEN at Isle Royale

Shooting the Rapids

RAPIDS QUEEN leaving Toronto

C. D. 110 as an oil barge

RAPIDS QUEEN at Wards Island, Toronto Harbor

PETER REISS

The steel bulk freighter PETER REISS was built in 1910 for the Wisconsin Transportation Company by the Superior Shipbuilding Company at West Superior, Wisconsin. She was launched on May 9th, and went into service on May 27th in the iron ore and coal trades. The North American Steamship Company took over its ownership later the same year. The PETER REISS ran for this company for 11 years. In 1921, this vessel and others in the fleet was transferred to the Reiss Steamship Company of Sheboygan, Wisconsin.

The only major conversion done to this vessel was the modernization and conversion to a self-unloader in 1949 at Manitowoc, Wisconsin by the Manitowoc Shipbuilding Company. This conversion was deemed necessary to her owners to keep up with the economy and save time at unloading ports. It also gained them greater dispatching flexibility.

In 1969, the Reiss Steamship Company decided to divest itself of its fleet. It sold the name and assets of its several companies to American Steamship Company of Buffalo, New York. The popular name of this firm, BoCo, is taken from the original partnership days when Messrs. Boland and Cornelius managed the American Steamship Company fleet under a separate management agreement. "BoCo" repainted all the former Reiss boats in its own colors but the vessels retained their Reiss names. PETER REISS was retired by "BoCo" early in 1972 and sold to Clepro Marine Corp., which had her converted to a barge at Toledo, Ohio by the Hans Hansen Welding Company. She saw little service as the owning firm went out of business. The PETER REISS was scrapped at Port Colborne, Ontario by Marine Salvage Ltd., in 1973.

An early view of PETER REISS in the St. Clair River

BUILT:	1910
	Superior Shipbuilding Co.,
	W. Superior, Wisc.
HULL NUMBER:	522
LENGTH:	512.0
BREADTH:	54.0
DEPTH:	30.0
GRT:	5,923
REGISTRY NUMBER:	US. 207471
ENGINES:	23½", 38", 63" Diameter x
	42" Stroke
	Triple Expansion
ENGINE BUILDER:	American Shipbuilding Company
	Cleveland, Ohio

PETER REISS downbound in the Detroit River

As a self-unloader, May 31, 1963

In Boland & Cornelius colors

PETER REISS in 1973

Being scrapped, July 13, 1963 at Ramey's Bend, Welland Ship Canal, tug YVONNE DUPRE alongside

RELIANCE

The composite (steel and wood) tug RELIANCE was built in 1892 at Collingwood, Ontario by the Collingwood Dry Dock Company for its own use around the yard. Ten years later, the tug went to the Midland Towing & Wrecking Company and was employed in their main concern . . . to help raise shipwrecks and stranded vessels and tow them to repair yards.

In September of 1903, the RELIANCE burned while at Spanish River, Ontario near Sprague, Ontario. The hull was towed to Midland, Ontario for a thorough rebuild. Joseph Ganley of Sault Ste. Marie, Ontario purchased the tug in 1915 to be used in the towing of log rafts to the Abitibi paper mill at the Soo from ports on Lake Superior. A new career, her third, had begun.

On December 15, 1922, the RELIANCE was homeward bound to the Soo from the Superior Paper Company logging camps on the eastern shores of Lake Superior. She carried a crew of 14, 20 lumberjacks and two officials, all heading home for the Holidays, and ran into a vicious storm. The RELIANCE was dashed onto the rocks surrounding Lizard Island, 70 miles northwest of the Soo. The tug and men were in a precarious position. One man volunteered to try to swim ashore with a line. He succeeded and all the people on board were painstakingly led to safety on the island. The temperature plummeted to way below zero.

The Captain and six men succeeded in launching a lifeboat and reached the mainland. Slowly they made their way through the blizzard to a telegraph line after a grueling hike to tell the world about the shipwreck. Two tugs rushed to the scene from the Soo. The two officials and two of the passengers set out in another lifeboat before the arrival of the tugs but never made it to safety. The boat was discovered days later, smashed on the shore. These four men were the only ones who lost their lives. The rest reached a safe haven at the Soo.

The RELIANCE was recovered the following spring, not damaged beyond repair. She was fixed up and resumed her duties soon after. The Lake Superior Paper Company purchased the vessel in 1925. The Abitibi Power & Paper Company took over her ownership in 1932. The tug's duties remained the same throughout these transfers. In 1945, Roderick McLean of Sault Ste. Marie bought the tug. The RELIANCE went into the sand and gravel business, towing a scow out into Lake Superior to recover the gravel in the vicinity of Gros Cap.

In 1947, Donald Clark of Port Arthur, Ontario assumed her ownership but the old tug's days were limited. RELIANCE was dismantled and her register closed on May 23, 1949.

RELIANCE at the Soo

BUILT: 1892
                 Collingwood Dry Dock Co.,
                 Collingwood, Ont.
LENGTH: 124.0
BREADTH: 23.0
DEPTH: 11.6
GRT: 311
REGISTRY NUMBER: C. 97115
ENGINES: 21", 38" Diameter x 24" Stroke
                 Fore & Aft Compound
ENGINE BUILDER: Sutton Brothers

RELIANCE in the lock with a raft of pulpwood

RENVOYLE (2)

GLENLEDI upbound at Mission Point in 1926

The second RENVOYLE was built as the GLENLEDI in 1925 at Newcastle-on-Tyne by Swan, Hunter & Wigham Ricardson Ltd., for Playfair's Great Lakes Navigation Company of Midland, Ontario. This steel canaller carried her own 126 foot midsection in her holds across the Atlantic as ballast. She went immediately to Collingwood, Ontario where she was cut in two and the midbody installed late that same year.

In 1926, Canada Steamship Lines took over the ownership and later the same year renamed her b) RENVOYLE. Most of her time in CSL was spent in the package freight business between Toronto, Windsor, Sarnia, Sault Ste. Marie and Fort William/Port Arthur, Ontario. Occasionally, she was diverted to other ports with a variety of cargoes.

After the opening of the St. Lawrence Seaway in 1959, RENVOYLE made trips into the St. Lawrence as far as Montreal. On June 1, 1967, the RENVOYLE was at the Point Edward, Ontario (Sarnia) CSL dock. As the vessel started to make her left turn to go down the St. Clair River to Windsor, the swift current under the Blue Water Bridge caught her bow, and before compensation could be made, she rammed into the steamer SYLVANIA which was unloading coal at the Peerless Cement dock on the Port Huron, Michigan side, directly across the river. The RENVOYLE had a huge dent in her bow and managed to come to anchor a short distance below the cement company dock. The SYLVANIA began to sink but was held to the dock by her steel mooring cables. She settled there and no one was injured in the collision. The SYLVANIA was later repaired, pumped out and returned to service but the RENVOYLE was through.

The vessel went to Kingston, Ontario, where she lay in ordinary until a decision could be made about her repair. On November 15, 1967, CSL surrendered title to RENVOYLE to the U.S. Marshall who sold her at auction at Cleveland, Ohio in a legal maneuver to limit their liability arising from the sinking of SYLVANIA. The vessel was sold to Acme Scrap & Metal Company of Ashtabula, Ohio where she was scrapped the following year.

	BUILT: 1925
	Swan, Hunter & Wigham Richardson,
	Newcastle-on-Tyne, England
HULL NUMBER:	1271
LENGTH:	379.1 (as lengthened)
BREADTH:	44.2
DEPTH:	23.9
GRT:	3,571 (as lengthened)
REGISTRY NUMBER:	C. 148133
ENGINES:	22½", 37", 62" Diameter x
	42" Stroke
	Triple Expansion
ENGINE BUILDER:	N. E. Marine Engineering Company
	Wallsend-on-Tyne, England

a) Glenledi
b) RENVOYLE (2)

RENVOYLE in the Welland Ship Canal

After the collision with SYLVANIA at Port Huron, June 2, 1967

ROSEDALE

Built in 1888 at Sutherland, England by the Sunderland Shipbuilding Company, the steamer ROSEDALE was a steel bulk carrier of the flush-deck, ocean-going type, with her bridge and machinery amidships. Constructed for Thomas Marks and Company Ltd., of Port Arthur, Ontario, she sailed directly to the Great Lakes upon completion. Her first lake cargo, consisting of 1,300 tons of coal consigned to Fort William, was loaded at Ashtabula, Ohio on July 18, 1888. ROSEDALE originally carried two masts which were equipped with auxiliary sails.

ROSEDALE passed to the ownership of Messrs. Hagarty and Crangle of Toronto who operated the St. Lawrence and Chicago Steam Navigation Company, Ltd. These new owners had her lengthened by 72 feet at Owen Sound in 1891. Her new hull section was inserted amidships between the bridge and the engine, and a third mast was added (1,507 gross tons).

The year 1897 was an extremely unlucky one for ROSEDALE. She was involved in five separate accidents. Strangely enough, each of these occurred on the fourth day of a month. In April, she ran ashore near Rock Island Light in the St. Lawrence River and the damage she sustained forced her to go on the drydock at Detroit for repairs on April 17.

The most serious of the 1897 accidents occurred in December when she stranded on Charity Shoal in the St. Lawrence. She was released on December 13 by the Donnelly Towing and Wrecking Company, and was then towed to Kingston. The St. Lawrence and Chicago Steam Navigation Company Ltd. abandoned ROSEDALE to the underwriters, who sold her to the Edwardsburg Starch Company. This firm then resold her to her previous owner, St. Lawrence and Chicago for $55,000.

In 1907, ROSEDALE was acquired by Rosedale Ltd., of Hamilton, a subsidiary of Inland Navigation Company Ltd. which was operated by R. O. and A. B. Mackay. James Playfair gained control of this fleet in 1910, and it became known as Inland Lines Ltd., Midland, Ontario.

During the consolidation of 1913, ROSEDALE passed to the ownership of Canada Steamship Lines Ltd., Montreal. She remained in lake trade until 1916, when she was requisitioned for wartime service on salt water. She was still actually owned by CSL when, on April 8, 1919, she foundered in the North Atlantic after a collision with the steamer LUELLA.

Although ROSEDALE always had a reputation for being a ship that was very difficult to handle, she is remembered today for something more positive. She was the first vessel ever to carry a cargo straight through from Montreal to Chicago without transshipment.

ROSEDALE downbound in the St. Clair River

ROSEDALE at Owen Sound

BUILT:	1888	*GRT:*	1,040
	Sunderland Shipbuilding Co.,	*REGISTRY NUMBER:*	Br. & Can. 95265
	Sunderland, England	*ENGINES:*	17", 28", 46" Diameter x
HULL NUMBER:	147		30" Stroke
LENGTH:	173.0		Triple Expansion
BREADTH:	35.0	*ENGINE BUILDER:*	North Eastern Marine Engineering Co.,
DEPTH:	14.7		Ltd.
			Sunderland, England

ROSEDALE in Inland Lines' colors

ROTHESAY

The wooden-hulled, beam-engined, sidewheel passenger steamer ROTHESAY was built in 1867 at Carleton, New Brunswick, by J. & S. E. Oliver for Enoch Lunt. She was launched on February 2, 1867, and registered at Fredericton, N. B. Her sidewheels were of the non-feathering type.

Lunt operated her on the St. John River between Fredericton and St. John. Enoch Lunt died in 1873, but his sons, Joseph A. and Reuben G. Lunt, carried on as Enoch Lunt and Sons. ROTHESAY was taken off the St. John River after the summer of 1876, for she was no longer needed in the trade for which she was built. She made her last trip there on September 10, 1876.

ROTHESAY was re-registered at Prescott, Ontario, on July 20, 1877, for service on the Upper St. Lawrence River. She was still owned by the Lunts, and the Richelieu and Ontario Navigation Company Ltd. took exception to the appearance of ROTHESAY as competition on its river routes. An agreement was eventually reached, whereby the Lunts agreed not to compete directly with the R & O steamers. As a result, ROTHESAY was sent in 1878 to Toronto, where she was operated on the Niagara River service in opposition to the Niagara Navigation Company's steamer CHICORA. An intense rate war soon developed and it lasted until the close of the 1880 season.

ROTHESAY was refused a licence for Lake Ontario service in 1881 and she returned to the St. Lawrence for a run from Kingston to Prescott. By this time, the Lunts had established a new operating company, in which former Governor Smith of Vermont held an interest.

By 1882, the registered owner of ROTHESAY was Ambrose E. Lalande, Montreal, and in 1883, her owner was listed as J. R. Oughtred. On June 27, 1883, while bound downriver from Clayton to Dickinson's Landing, ROTHESAY took a sudden sheer and stranded near Thou-sand Island Park. She was quickly repaired. By 1886, she had passed to the ownership of J. G. Ross, Quebec City. Some references showed Ross as her managing owner as early as 1884, with Ross supposedly acting for the St. Lawrence Steamboat Company.

On December 6, 1886, ROTHESAY steamed downriver from Gananoque to Ogdensburg so that she could go on the marine railway during the winter for repairs and a partial rebuilding. She showed up back on Lake Ontario, again, briefly, in either 1888 or 1889 and she is believed to have run between Toronto and Oakville, with a stop at Lorne Park.

ROTHESAY was back in the Thousand Islands service by late summer of 1889. On the evening of September 12, 1889, whilst downbound from Kingston and about one-half mile above Prescott, her destination, she collided with the wooden tug MYRA of the Ogdensburg Coal and Towing Company. Both steamers were severely damaged. MYRA sank with the loss of two lives, but was later salvaged and repaired. ROTHESAY was beached on the Canadian shore, where she settled, and was later abandoned to the underwriters as a total loss.

The 1889 Canadian register listed ROTHESAY's owner as J. J. Kenney, Toronto. Kenney was the manager of the Western Assurance Company, and he represented the interests of ROTHESAY's insurers. The wreck remained half-submerged at the spot where she had been beached after the collision. In 1901, the wreck, which had been declared a nuisance to local navigation, was dynamited. The hull did not disintegrate completely however, and it still lies today in some 35 feet of water. It has been explored by divers who have recovered a number of artifacts from the steamer.

ROTHESAY on the St. Lawrence River

BUILT:	1867
	J. & S. E. Oliver,
	Carleton, New Brunswick
HULL NUMBER:	
LENGTH:	179.3
BREADTH:	29.0
DEPTH:	8.0
GRT:	839
REGISTRY NUMBER:	C. 54485
ENGINES:	Beam
ENGINE BUILDER:	Fleming & Humbert,
	St. John, New Brunswick

ROYALITE

ROYALITE entering Cleveland harbor

Built in 1916 at Collingwood, Ontario by the Collingwood Shipbuilding Company and launched on December 15, 1915 for Imperial Oil Limited, Toronto, the tanker ROYALITE was one of three almost identical sisterships. The other two were SARNOLITE (IMPERIAL HAMILTON) and IOCOLITE (IMPERIAL KINGSTON), and all three enjoyed long careers in the Imperial Oil fleet. In fact, ROYALITE holds the record for the longest period of service ever by any powered vessel owned by Imperial Oil.

ROYALITE originally was intended for Great Lakes trade but, because of the demand for tonnage created by World War I, she saw much service on salt water during the hostilities. Even after the armistice, she made a number of trips between Halifax and France.

Between the two wars, ROYALITE operated on the lakes but, when World War II began, she was once again sent to the east coast. After the war ended, she was brought back to the lakes and, in 1947, she was renamed IMPERIAL WELLAND. During the 1950's, she was used as a bunkering tanker in the St. Lawrence River around Montreal.

IMPERIAL WELLAND was eventually replaced by the bunkering barges IMPERIAL VERDUN and IMPERIAL LACHINE (2) which were built for the Montreal service. IMPERIAL WELLAND was returned to lake trade in 1963, and she spent her last two years of operation on the lakes. In 1964, it was decided that she was due for retirement and, at the close of the season, she was withdrawn and laid up at Sarnia.

IMPERIAL WELLAND was sold to Steel Factors Ltd., Montreal, early in 1965, and she left the lakes under her own power with a cargo of oil loaded at Sarnia and consigned to Kingston, Ontario. Steel Factors then sold her, via a New York broker, to a German firm and she was subsequently resold to Spanish shipbreakers.

The old tanker was finally taken across the Atlantic in a tandem tow with IMPERIAL SIMCOE, but she seemed determined to avoid the breakers' torches. Twice during the voyage she broke tow, but each time she was retrieved by the tug. IMPERIAL WELLAND arrived at Santander, Spain on October 13, 1965 and was subsequently cut up for scrap.

IMPERIAL WELLAND upbound in the St. Clair River, August 6, 1958

a) ROYALITE   **b) Imperial Welland**

BUILT:	1916	*DEPTH:*	16.6
	Collingwood Shipbuilding Co.,	*GRT:*	2,052
	Collingwood, Ont.	*REGISTRY NUMBER:*	C. 134513
HULL NUMBER:	45	*ENGINES:*	16", 26", 44" Diameter x
LENGTH:	250.0		36" Stroke
BREADTH:	43.1		Triple Expansion
		ENGINE BUILDER:	Shipyard

Below Lock 3 in the Welland Ship Canal

299

ROYAN

WACCAMAW upbound at the Soo in 1911

The steel canaller WACCAMAW was launched on September 16, 1900 at Toledo, Ohio by the Craig Shipbuilding Company for J. L. Crosthwaite of Buffalo, New York and went to the East Coast trades almost immediately. In 1907, she was sold to William B. Price of Boston, Massachusetts. On July 27, 1911, the vessel was in the Buffalo Dry Dock yard for replacement of 30 plates as a result of a grounding in the St. Lawrence River.

For 1916-1917, the WACCAMAW was chartered to Canada Steamship Lines Ltd., for deep water service. On January 25, 1917, she was sold to the French government and renamed b) ROYAN. At the end of World War I, she lay in ordinary and was then sold to the George Hall Coal Company of Canada in 1921 (C. 150356). Her dimensions now were: 250.2 x 40.2 x 14.8; 1,471 gross tons.

In 1926, the vessel was sold to Canada Steamship Lines Ltd. of Montreal. From 1929 to 1937, she was not used and lay at Kingston, Ontario along with many other vessels idled by the Great Depression. Marine Industries Ltd. of Sorel purchased the vessel in late 1937 and moved her to Sorel. At the end of 1945, after some service during World War II, the ROYAN was scrapped at Sorel.

ROYAN in Hall colors upbound at Mission Point

BUILT:	1900
	Craig Shipbuilding Co.,
	Toledo, Ohio
HULL NUMBER:	79
LENGTH:	249.7
BREADTH:	40.5
DEPTH:	15.4
GRT:	1,359
REGISTRY NUMBER:	US. 81715
ENGINES:	20", 32½", 55" Diameter x
	40" Stroke
	Triple Expansion
ENGINE BUILDER:	Shipyard

a) Waccamaw
b) ROYAN

In C.S.L. colors

301

SACRAMENTO

The wooden bulk freighter SACRAMENTO was launched on July 24, 1895 at West Bay City, Michigan by James Davidson for his own Davidson Steamship Company. He used her in various bulk trades up and down the lakes and never sold or renamed her.

Few serious incidents happened to this vessel in her career but one particular work of mercy stood out. The steamer COTTONWOOD had stranded on Coppermine Point on Lake Superior on November 15, 1926. The crew abandoned the vessel and she was frozen in for the Winter of 1926-27, one of the most severe in years, and titled by newspapers around the country as "The Big Freeze." Literally hundreds of ships were trapped in the Upper and Lower St. Mary's River for weeks. The COTTONWOOD was held fast all Winter.

In the early Spring of 1927, preparations were made to attempt salvage of the vessel. The SACRAMENTO and other vessels were called to assist. After much work, the COTTONWOOD was released on May 30, 1927 and taken to a drydock for repairs. The SACRAMENTO was instrumental in that release operation.

The Great Depression of the 1930's hit the lakes shipping business very hard. Of some 390 vessels available, only 67 were used in one particular season. The SACRAMENTO was one of those not used. She was idled at Bay City early in 1930 and never moved again. Gradually the elements reduced the vessel's planks to rot, vandals took whatever was loose and ordinary people in need of firewood came to the riverbank to feed on this plentiful supply of ancient oak. In 1936, she still looked like a boat. By 1939, there was not much left when the SACRAMENTO was abandoned and removed from documentation. Parts of her are still there today.

Launch of SACRAMENTO at Bay City, July 24, 1895

SACRAMENTO in 1910

BUILT:	1895	*GRT:*	2,380
	James Davidson,	*REGISTRY NUMBER:*	US. 116682
	W. Bay City, Mich.	*ENGINES:*	20", 33", 54" Diameter x
HULL NUMBER:	69		42" Stroke
LENGTH:	308.2		Triple Expansion
BREADTH:	42.6	*ENGINE BUILDER:*	Frontier Iron Works
DEPTH:	21.2		Detroit, Michigan

At Bay City, September 13, 1936

SAGINAW VALLEY

An early photo of GRAND TRAVERSE, similar to the SAGINAW VALLEY

The wooden package freighter SAGINAW VALLEY was launched on April 12, 1881 at West Bay City, Michigan by F. W. Wheeler for the Saginaw Transportation Company, J. Roberts of Bay City, manager. According to the U.S. Steamboat Inspection Service Report of June 1883, her original engine was a compound of 24" and 54" diameter cylinders x 36" stroke but it gives no builder or place. Her second engine was installed in 1886. In 1888, the vessel was lengthened to 226.0 x 31.5 x 19.3; 1,112 gross tons.

From 1886 to 1895, she was owned by W. W. Tyler of Buffalo, New York and chartered by the Lackawanna Transportation Company to carry package freight between Buffalo, New York and Green Bay, Wisconsin. In 1896, she was purchased by M. J. Galvin of Buffalo and in 1897, by Thomas M. Ryan of the same city. He renamed her b) MERIDEN.

Captain Ryan decided to make the vessel a single decker and put her in the lumber trade. In 1899, he had the vessel converted. The 'tween deck was removed and a new career begun. On September 27, 1903, she was partially burned at the dock in Toledo, Ohio. The ship was then sold to H. M. Loud & Co. of AuSable, Michigan who rebuilt and renamed her c) KONGO in 1904. The new dimensions were: 215.0 x 31.0 x 10.2; 672 gross tons. Her engine was also rebuilt to: 18" and 36" diameter cylinders x 30" stroke. This was done by the Marine Iron Works at Bay City in 1905.

From 1913 to 1916, the KONGO was owned by H. H. Salmon Company of New York City, but the vessel never left the lakes. She became the first auto carrier on the lakes, travelling between Detroit, Buffalo and other ports.

On October 3, 1916, Salmon sold her to the Reid Wrecking Company of Sarnia, Ontario who, in turn, sold her to Robert S. Misener et al, of Sault Ste. Marie, Ontario early in 1917. The vessel was renamed d) OVERLAND (C.134520). In 1920, Robert Laing of the Niagara Sand Company was the owner and, in 1921, the boat was purchased by Harold Robertson of Toronto, Ontario, owner of the Harbour Brick Company. The sand and gravel trade was her main pursuit. During the summer of 1925, she broke her back on Lake Ontario and was towed to Toronto. The engine was removed and the hull was towed to the south shore of Lake Ontario near Port Dalhousie and abandoned.

a) SAGINAW VALLEY
   b) Meriden
   c) Kongo
   d) Overland

BUILT:	1881
	F. W. Wheeler & Co.,
	W. Bay City, Mich.
HULL NUMBER:	11
LENGTH:	161.0
BREADTH:	31.0
DEPTH:	10.0
GRT:	720
REGISTRY NUMBER:	US. 115769
SECOND ENGINES:	20", 36" Diameter x 30" Stroke
	Steeple Compound
ENGINE BUILDER:	J. B. Wilson
	Detroit, Michigan

SAGINAW VALLEY upbound at Mission Point

MERIDEN

KONGO upbound in the St. Clair River

OVERLAND in Toronto Harbor

Entering the Eastern Gap, Toronto Harbor

ST. IGNACE

The wooden railroad carferry ST. IGNACE was built in 1888 at Detroit, Michigan by the Detroit Dry Dock Company for the Mackinac Transportation Company to ferry railroad cars across the Straits of Mackinac from Mackinaw City in the lower peninsula of Michigan to St. Ignace in the upper. She was designed by Frank E. Kirby and had two tracks to accommodate ten cars. This vessel was the first American ship to have propellers both fore and aft and her bow was strengthened for ice breaking. The open sides of the vessel were enclosed in the late 1890's.

On June 10, 1902, while loading ore cars, she sank at the slip when too much load was put aboard her port track. There were no fatalities involved but the consternation was considerable. Seeing the big ship on her side made those involved rather red-faced. The vessel was raised and put back into service soon thereafter.

In 1913, her usefulness came to an end and she was replaced by a new ferry. ST. IGNACE was then sold to the West Superior Dock Company and, in 1914, to James Whalen of Port Arthur, Ontario (C. 134017) to be used as a wrecking steamer. On August 30, 1916, she burned while tied up at the Western Dry Dock & Shipbuilding Company at Port Arthur. The hull was converted into a barge.

In 1917, the barge was sold to T. L. Durocher of DeTour, Michigan who used her as a lighter and to haul heavy stone. The vessel lasted in this trade until 1929 when she was purposely sunk in the St. Mary's River because of age and condition.

ST. IGNACE bucking ice in the Straits

BUILT:	1888	REGISTRY NUMBER:	US. 116191
	Detroit Dry Dock Co.,	ENGINES:	One Forward 26", 48" Diameter
	Detroit, Mich.		x 40" Stroke
HULL NUMBER:	85		Two Aft 28", 53" Diameter x
LENGTH:	215.6		48" Stroke
BREADTH:	52.3		Fore & Aft Compounds
DEPTH:	15.8	ENGINE BUILDER:	Dry Dock Engine Works,
GRT:	1,199		Detroit, Michigan

Breaking ice in 1906

307

SAINTE MARIE (2)

SAINTE MARIE when she was chartered by the State

A steel railroad carferry that replaced the ST. IGNACE, the SAINTE MARIE, was launched on January 22, 1913, at Toledo, Ohio by the Toledo Shipbuilding Company for service across the Straits of Mackinac. She received her engines from the wooden carferry SAINTE MARIE (1). This new vessel had four tracks and a capacity for 14 railroad cars.

The SAINTE MARIE spent most of her life as the spare boat for the venerable CHIEF WAWATAM and was chartered extensively each spring and late fall by the Lake Carriers' Association for use as an ice-breaker. In this capacity the vessel was well known to lake sailors. In the 1920's, she was also used to break the ice to release a blockade of freighters during severe early winters when vessels were held up because a few became stuck and blocked the channels.

An especially harrowing experience for the vessels and their crews occurred in the 1926 season, called by the newspapers "The Big Freeze." Storms in late November and early December left many vessels behind schedule. The temperature at Duluth, Minnesota plunged to 50 degrees below zero and the ice set in early. The St. Mary's River became plugged with ice and one vessel was caught in the West Neebish Channel, completely blocking it. SAINTE MARIE was called to try to release the vessels which were now accumulating in the river. Close to 100 were anchored or tied up until the grounded vessel could be released. They were literally frozen in. The huge carferry succeeded in releasing the vessels that were stuck in the upbound channel and then turned her attention to the ones stuck downbound. The way was cleared when the grounded vessel was released. Sailors who spent the two weeks locked in the ice will remember SAINTE MARIE well as she plowed her way through the ice to rescue the trapped vessels.

When the U.S. Coast Guard icebreaker MACKINAW was built in 1942, SAINTE MARIE was not used as frequently. The MACKINAW took over the majority of ice breaking duties. In 1961, SAINTE MARIE was sold to the Sadoff Company for scrapping. The vessel was towed to Ashtabula, Ohio and cut up.

BUILT:	1913
	Toledo Shipbuilding Co.,
	Toledo, Ohio
HULL NUMBER:	127
LENGTH:	250.0
BREADTH:	62.2
DEPTH:	21.7
GRT:	2,383
REGISTRY NUMBER:	US. 210944
ENGINES:	One Forward 28", 52" Diameter
	x 40" Stroke
	Two Aft 32", 58" Diameter x
	48" Stroke
	Vertical Inverted
	Fore & Aft Compound
ENGINE BUILDER:	Dry Dock Engine Works,
	Detroit, Michigan, 1893

SAINTE MARIE leaving the Soo Locks to break ice

Leaving her dock to cross the Straits of Mackinac

WILLIAM F. SAUBER

On April 15, 1891, the wooden bulk freighter WILLIAM F. SAUBER was launched at West Bay City, Michigan by F. W. Wheeler for Mitchell & Company of Cleveland, Ohio. In 1900, the vessel was purchased by the Inland Transportation Company of which W. H. Becker and Martin Mullen were the principal stockholders.

The steamer had left Ashland, Wisconsin on Saturday afternoon, October 24, 1903, with a cargo of iron ore destined for a Lake Erie port. While off Keweenaw Point, the steamer ran into a severe gale. In the vicinity of Manitou Island, she sprang a leak and the water gained steadily on the pumps. At nightfall Sunday, when it was observed that the SAUBER was in great peril, two steamers were sighted and signals of distress were displayed. One of the steamers, the YALE, came alongside and positioned herself to windward to afford more protection.

Slowly the two vessels crept to the safety of Whitefish Bay, but by 11 P.M. of the 25th, it became obvious that the wooden freighter would not make it. The captain of the YALE brought his vessel as close to the SAUBER as he could and the crew began the four hour long process of abandoning ship. Captain W. E. Morris, master of the SAUBER, ordered the crew to take to the yawls and go to the YALE. Captain Morris remained aboard the vessel after all the others had left. Frank Robinson, an oiler, was in the yawl. The circumstances of Robinson's death are not known, but it is supposed that he lost his hold on the rope when it was thrown to him from the YALE. When the cold waters of Lake Superior hit the red-hot boilers of the SAUBER, she blew up and sank immediately. Captain Morris was observed floating among the wreckage and crying for help. A line was thrown to him but, benumbed with cold, he was unable to grasp it. He perished in sight of help. The SAUBER sank on October 26th, 30 miles off Whitefish Point, just a few miles from safety. The YALE took the 15 survivors to the Soo where they were cared for and sent home.

WILLIAM F. SAUBER upbound at the Soo in 1901

BUILT:	1891
	F. W. Wheeler & Co.,
	West Bay City, Mich.
HULL NUMBER:	78
LENGTH:	291.0
BREADTH:	41.0
DEPTH:	19.8
GRT:	2,053
REGISTRY NUMBER:	US. 81317
ENGINES:	20", 32", 54" Diameter x
	42" Stroke
	Triple Expansion
ENGINE BUILDER:	Frontier Iron Works
	Detroit, Michigan

SHENANGO No. 2

a) SHENANGO NO. 2   **b) Muskegon**   **c) Pere Marquette 16**   **d) Harriet B.**

BUILT:	1895
	Craig Shipbuilding Co.,
	Toledo, Ohio
HULL NUMBER:	69
LENGTH:	282.6
BREADTH:	53.0
DEPTH:	19.4
GRT:	1,938
REGISTRY NUMBER:	US. 116695
ENGINES:	One Forward 20", 40" Diameter x
	36" Stroke
	Two Aft 23", 46" Diameter x
	36" Stroke
	Fore & Aft Compound
ENGINE BUILDER:	S. F. Hodge
	Detroit, Michigan

SHENANGO NO. 2 breaking ice

The wooden railroad carferry SHENANGO No. 2 was built at Toledo, Ohio by the Craig Shipbuilding Company and launched on October 25, 1895 for the United States & Ontario Steam Navigation Company. She had four tracks and a capacity of 26 railroad cars which she would shuttle between Conneaut, Ohio and Port Dover, Ontario on Lake Erie. One unusual feature of this vessel was the fact that she had three propellers, two aft and one forward, the latter used frequently to break up ice. In 1897, the vessel was leased to the Detroit, Grand Rapids & Western Railway and was sold to this firm in 1898. This company renamed her b) MUSKEGON and she began work on Lake Michigan, operating from Muskegon, Michigan to Milwaukee, Wisconsin.

This vessel seemingly had a propensity for accidents. On October 20, 1898, she slammed into a grain elevator which was being built in Milwaukee. Her steering gear failed in a storm on December 18, 1899, but the vessel was rescued. Because of inadequate power, her rudder broke in another storm on February 23, 1900 and she was severely damaged. The steamer hit the pierhead at Ludington, Michigan on December 21, 1901, broke in two and sank. One life was lost in this accident. She was severely damaged in a storm in 1907 and this time was not repaired.

Previous to this, she was sold to the Pere Marquette Railroad in 1901 and renamed c) PERE MARQUETTE 16. From 1907 until 1917, when it was sold to Peter Edwards of Sault Ste. Marie, Michigan, it lay in ordinary at Ludington. In 1918, the Hammermill Paper Company purchased the vessel and had it converted to a steam barge. She was renamed d) HARRIET B. Her new job was hauling pulpwood from ports on Lake Superior to the Hammermill paper mill at Erie, Pennsylvania. On the return trips she hauled coal north bound. Her dimensions at this time were: 282.6 x 53.6 x 17.0; 1,938 gross tons. The engine was removed in 1921; 2,340 gross tons.

Just off Two Harbors, Minnesota in a dense fog, the HARRIET B., in tow of the steamer C. W. JACOB, was struck by the steamer QUINCY A. SHAW on May 3, 1922. The collision ripped the old vessel apart and she sank 20 minutes later but not before the crew was able to escape to safety. The JACOB, the barge CRETE and the barge HARRIET B. were at anchor at the time of the accident to await the lifting of a fog before going into Two Harbors for a load of lumber. The career of the accident-prone vessel ended in one last disaster.

MUSKEGON entering harbor in icy conditions

PERE MARQUETTE 16 broken in two at Ludington in 1901

HARRIET B. upbound at Mission Point in 1919

312

HOME SMITH

When the steel bulk freighter WILLIAM S. MACK was launched on September 21, 1901 by the American Shipbuilding Company at Lorain, she was one of the larger vessels on the Great Lakes but she was soon far outclassed by much longer steamers constructed by lake shipyards. She was built for the Lake Erie Transportation Company of Mentor, Ohio and was named for one of its founders, who had died on September 15, 1896. Mack had joined forces with the Becker interests of Cleveland in 1890 and, after the death of Mack's son in 1902, the Beckers took over control of the entire combined fleet. WILLIAM S. MACK was later transferred to another Becker affiliate, the Valley Steamship Company.

In 1915, she was purchased by the Valley Camp Coal Company. She was operated by its Canadian affiliate, the Great Lakes Transportation Company Ltd., of Midland (James Playfair, manager). Although painted in Playfair colors, the MACK remained under U.S. registry during this period.

Late in 1917, WILLIAM S. MACK was acquired by the Algoma Central and Hudson Bay Railway Company, Sault Ste. Marie, Ontario in a trade which saw Algoma send its canaller THOMAS J. DRUMMOND to the Playfair fleet.

The MACK was renamed b) HOME SMITH (C. 138212) when she was fitted out in Algoma colors in 1918. She was to remain under the same ownership for the rest of her life, although the official name of the operating subsidiary would undergo various changes.

The steamer was rebuilt in 1920 and was renamed c) ALGORAIL (1) in 1936. She was given a new tank top in 1947 and a new pilothouse several years later. Until the end, however, she retained her tall and thin stack, whose top was cut parallel to the water rather than at right angles to the rake.

ALGORAIL was retired at the close of the 1962 season. She was sold in early 1963 to the Industrial Metal Company Ltd., Toronto, and she fitted out for one last trip. She sailed from Owen Sound to Saginaw, where she loaded a cargo of scrap and then onward to Toronto where she arrived during the night of May 4-5, 1963. She was scrapped at the company's yard on the Ship Channel, just outside the Cherry Street bridge, during the summer of 1963 although the work was delayed when the hull, cut down almost to the tank top, sank. It was later raised and the scrapping operation completed.

WILLIAM S. MACK downbound at Mission Point in 1915

HOME SMITH and NORWAY in the ice in the St. Mary's River

a) William S. Mack, b) HOME SMITH, c) Algorail

BUILT:	1901
	American Shipbuilding Co.,
	Lorain, Ohio
HULL NUMBER:	311
LENGTH:	346.0
BREADTH:	48.0
DEPTH:	28.0
GRT:	3,720
REGISTRY NUMBER:	US. 81791
ENGINES:	20", 33½", 55 ⅜ " Diameter x
	40" Stroke
	Triple Expansion
ENGINE BUILDER:	Shipyard

HOME SMITH, SENATOR and ROBERT J. PAISLEY at Owen Sound, Winter quarters

ALGORAIL downbound at Mission Point

Downbound out of Lake Huron, September 29, 1960

T. W. SNOOK

The T. W. SNOOK was typical of scores of small lumber steamers built around Lake St. Clair, with a single deck, one large schooner-rigged mast forward, and her cabins aft. She was built in 1873 at Mt. Clemens, Michigan by Frank C. Leighton in William Dulac's shipyard for T. W. Snook of Mount Clemens, and powered with the engine of Snook's older steambarge, the ARIZONA (1867). Interestingly, the ARIZONA became a towbarge, consort of the SNOOK and both operated from St. Clair River and lower Lake Huron ports to Sandusky, Toledo and Cleveland. The SNOOK carried 200,000 feet of lumber.

In 1879 the little steamer was sold to C. H. Cook and others of Whitehall, Michigan, and newspapers indicate that she traded out of the smaller Lake Michigan ports for the next several seasons. In the Fall of 1883, she holed herself on the pier at South Haven, Michigan and settled in 18 feet of water, but suffered little damage and she was repaired during the winter; she had been bound from Chicago to White Lake on the last trip of the season.

In 1888, the SNOOK was sold to W. E. Rice and others of St. Clair, Michigan, and they ran her for the next six years; Van Buskirk, Griffith, and Crockett also owned shares. Early in 1894, they sold the steamer to Detroit Captain Harris W. Baker, who rebuilt her as a wrecker.

Baker operated several run-down old vessels in the wrecking business, and racked up an impressive list of successful salvage jobs during the 1890's and the first ten or fifteen years of the present century.

In 1916, Baker disposed of the SNOOK and she was purchased by D. W. Lockhart of Sandusky, Ohio who outfitted the craft with sand-dredging gear and put her to work on Lake Erie. It appears that the ship was shuffled to Jacob Roth of Erie, Pennsylvania in 1918 and to John Boland of Buffalo in 1919 but she was laid up and abandoned in 1921 someplace on the St. Clair River. She spent her last days dredging on Lake St. Clair.

T. W. SNOOK (rt.), OCEANICA, COMPANION and WILLIAM CHISHOLM at the head of Belle Isle, Lake St. Clair on August 14, 1896

T. W. SNOOK in the Buffalo Dry Dock, August 29, 1918

BUILT:	1873
	Leighton/DuLac,
	Mt. Clemens, Mich.
LENGTH:	113.6
BREADTH:	24.7
DEPTH:	9.2
GRT:	168
REGISTRY NUMBER:	US. 24949
SECOND ENGINES:	16" Diameter x 18" Stroke
	High Pressure
	Non-Condensing
ENGINE BUILDER:	Unknown (1879)

SOO CITY (1)

SOO CITY (1) in Northern Michigan Line colors

The wooden passenger and freight steamer SOO CITY was launched on May 19, 1888 at West Bay City, Michigan by F. W. Wheeler & Co. for the Owen family of Escanaba, Michigan (Delta Transportation Company) and was designed for the Soo River run. She remained on this route for her first three seasons, but in 1891 was chartered to the Northern Michigan Line, to supplement the services of CITY OF CHARLEVOIX and LAWRENCE between Chicago and Mackinac Island, stopping at Traverse City, Petoskey and Harbor Springs, Michigan. In 1892, she was chartered to the St. Joseph and Lake Michigan Transportation Company (Vandalia Line) running opposite OSSIFRAGE, between St. Joseph, Michigan and Chicago. In 1893 and 1894, she ran between Michigan City, Indiana and Chicago for the Chicago and Michigan City Line, which was apparently a Delta Transportation operation originated to serve the World's Fair in Chicago.

In 1894, SOO CITY entered by far her longest period of service on a single route. Under a pool arrangement, the boat was transferred to the newly-formed Grand Rapids and Chicago Steamboat Company, owners of the CITY OF HOLLAND, with W. R. Owen as president. Under this management the two boats were operated between Holland and Chicago for a number of years.

In the spring of 1901, with a new steel boat on order at the Craig yard at Toledo, Ohio, the company sold the CITY OF HOLLAND to the Thompson Line of Rogers City, Michigan. Shortly afterward, the company itself was sold to Graham & Morton, of Benton Harbor, including the new steamer, which came out in June as PURITAN (2). This put G&M on the Holland route, with SOO CITY and the new PURITAN holding down the service.

In 1903, Graham & Morton traded SOO CITY and C. W. MOORE to the A. Booth Packing Company for its Craig-built steel steamer ARGO (1901), but SOO CITY was not immediately sent to Lake Superior. In the spring of 1903, Booth chartered her to the Michigan Steamship Company to operate between South Haven and Chicago opposite their new steel steamer EASTLAND. She remained on this route for three seasons, until October, 1905, when the Michigan Steamship Company merged with Dunkley-Williams, making the SOO CITY surplus on the South Haven route. Accordingly, she was chartered for the balance of the season to the Hackley Transportation Company of Muskegon and ran between Muskegon and Chicago until winter layup.

For the season of 1906, the SOO CITY left Lake Michigan for the first time in 15 years and went north to run between Duluth, Minnesota and Port Arthur, Ontario for her owners, the A. Booth Packing Company. She was back on Lake Michigan the following year, having been sold to the Indiana Transportation Company, to replace INDIANAPOLIS, running opposite THEODORE ROOSEVELT between Chicago and Michigan City. She was a "make-do" boat on this route. With their new UNITED STATES coming out in 1909, the Company sold SOO CITY in the fall of 1908, to Felix Jackson of Velasco, Texas. On November 1st, she left Michigan City for the last time, headed for New York for repairs and then to the Gulf Coast. As she neared Newfoundland, a gale swept in which lasted two days, and on December 2, 1908 the SOO CITY was lost with all hands (19). Her wreckage came ashore at Cape Race, December 4, 1908.

SOO CITY in Michigan Steamship Co. colors

BUILT:	1888	*GRT:*	670
	F. W. Wheeler & Co.,	*REGISTRY NUMBER:*	US. 116217
	W. Bay City, Mich.	*ENGINES:*	22", 42" Diameter x
HULL NUMBER:	40		36" Stroke
LENGTH:	171.1		Fore & Aft Compound
BREADTH:	33.5	*ENGINE BUILDER:*	S. F. Hodge & Company
DEPTH:	12.0		Detroit, Michigan

At Grand Haven

SOO CITY (2)

The steel passenger steamer MABEL BRADSHAW was built in the spring of 1889 by Edward W. Heath at Benton Harbor, Michigan for Thomas V. Waters of Muskegon, Michigan (her first Captain) and Hugh Bradshaw of Chicago, Illinois. She was built to sail between Holland, Michigan and Chicago, and held to this run the first three seasons. Probably owing to the frequent closures of Holland harbor because of sand in the channel, the boat was transferred in 1892 to the Benton Harbor/St. Joseph-to-Chicago run, in connection with the Farnum & Company Transporation line.

After two seasons the owners were in financial trouble, as a result of claims of the Montague Iron Works, her engine builder and first mortgagee. At a U.S. Marshal's sale, Captain Waters' interest was sold to Charles T. Hills, of Muskegon. Hills' interest was promptly assumed by Hugh Bradshaw who, as sole owner, transferred the boat back to the Holland-Chicago run in 1894.

The Holland and Chicago Transportation Company, having been organized by Holland businessmen, evidently did not appreciate the competition, and in 1895, the BRADSHAW was denied dockage at Ottawa Beach and Macatawa. Hugh Bradshaw then put the vessel on a pioneer run between Chicago, White Lake and Pentwater, Michigan. She kept this route for five seasons, through 1899, and was then sold in April of 1900 to the newly organized Chicago and Muskegon Transportation Company (Barry Brothers). The BRADSHAW proved to be too small for this service, however, and was sold that fall to W. H. Singer's White Line Transportation Company, Duluth, Minnesota.

She sailed for Singer through the 1905 season and was then sold, along with the BON AMI and the EASTON, to A. Booth & Company for the same route, Duluth to Port Arthur, Ontario. After two more seasons on the north shore, she was sold in June 1907, to Herbert Cleland of Collingwood, Ontario. In July, she was renamed b) SOO CITY (C. 117085), and placed on a run between Parry Sound and the Soo.

She changed hands a number of times during the next decade, but because the name "Georgian Bay Navigation Company Ltd." keeps occurring in her ownership records, it is believed her operation remained much the same. She was finally cut down to a barge in 1917 and abandoned in 1918.

MABEL BRADSHAW in Chicago & Holland colors

a) Mabel Bradshaw
b) SOO CITY (2)

BUILT:	1889
	Edward W. Heath,
	Benton Harbor, Mich.
LENGTH:	135.0
BREADTH:	26.0
DEPTH:	9.0
GRT:	331
REGISTRY NUMBER:	US. 92096
ENGINES:	16", 28" Diameter x 26" Stroke
	Fore & Aft Compound
ENGINE BUILDER:	Wilson & Hendrie
	Montague, Michigan

MABEL BRADSHAW in Booth Line colors leaving Duluth harbor

SOO CITY at her dock at the Soo

SOUTH AMERICAN

SOUTH AMERICAN just before the launch at Ecorse

At her Winter lay-up dock at Holland

BUILT:	1914	*GRT:*	2,662
	Great Lakes Engineering Works,	*REGISTRY NUMBER:*	US. 212244
	Ecorse, Mich.	*ENGINES:*	21½", 30¾", 44½", 64"
HULL NUMBER:	133		Diameter x 36" Stroke
LENGTH:	290.6		Quadruple Expansion
BREADTH:	47.1	*ENGINE BUILDER:*	Shipyard
DEPTH:	18.3		

The steel cruise passenger cruise steamer SOUTH AMERICAN was built in 1914 at Ecorse, Michigan by the Great Lakes Engineering Works for the Chicago, Duluth & Georgian Bay Transit Company to operate between Chicago, Illinois and Duluth, Minnesota in conjunction with her near-sister NORTH AMERICAN. One of the differences in the two ships' operation was that the SOUTH AMERICAN would go to Duluth and the NORTH AMERICAN to Buffalo, New York. When the St. Lawrence Seaway opened in 1959, the SOUTH AMERICAN also made trips to Montreal.

On September 9, 1924, when the ships were already in winter lay-up quarters at Holland, Michigan, a fire started on board the SOUTH AMERICAN and completely destroyed her upper works. The vessel was taken back to Ecorse and completely rebuilt. In 1925, she came out almost brand new and now sporting a second smokestack, the forward one a dummy which housed electrical equipment.

For more than a half a century, the SOUTH AMERICAN regally sailed the Great Lakes, carrying more than half-a-million passengers between Detroit, Chicago, Montreal and Duluth. Her name came to represent a touch of elegance that no longer exists. Other cruise vessels have tried to take her place since her last trip to Montreal for Expo '67, but none has succeeded for very long. Late in 1967, she was sold to the Seafarers International Union. Plans called for SOUTH AMERICAN to replace the lost NORTH AMERICAN as a floating barracks for students at the Lundeberg School for Seamanship at Piney Point, Maryland. The plans fell through partly because of the new federal laws that banned the use of passenger vessels with wooden superstructures because of the danger of fire. That, incidently, was the same reason the ship was withdrawn from service in the first place.

The SOUTH AMERICAN made it to Norfolk, Virginia, where her engine was removed. (The NORTH AMERICAN had previously sunk off Nantucket, Massachusetts, on her delivery voyage under tow.) Work stopped and SOUTH AMERICAN was relegated to a dock at Camden, New Jersey, where she began to deteriorate. Many plans were made to have her towed back to the lakes, to such places as Mackinac Island and Holland. All these schemes so far have not been successful. She remains in extremely bad shape. Vandals have reduced her royal highness to a "Cinderella after midnight."

SOUTH AMERICAN upbound in the St. Clair River

After the fire, September, 1924. NORTH AMERICAN at right.

SOUTH AMERICAN upbound on Lake St. Clair, July 9, 1950

At Mackinac Island, July 7, 1951

SOUTH AMERICAN downbound on Lake Huron, August 18, 1960

At Camden, New Jersey, December 30, 1976

SPOKANE

The first steel ship ever built on the Great Lakes was the bulk freighter SPOKANE, which was launched on June 6, 1886 at Cleveland, Ohio by the Globe Shipbuilding Company for Thomas Wilson of Cleveland. She immediately entered the iron ore trade, also carrying cargoes of coal and grain. In 1892, the vessel was lengthened by the Cleveland Shipbuilding Company at Cleveland. Her new dimensions were: 311.8 x 38.2 x 20.8; 2,356 gross tons. Later, when huge 600 footers were coming out of the shipyards on the lakes, the SPOKANE was relegated to the background.

In 1910, she was sold to James Reid of Port Huron for his Spokane Steamship Company. In 1920, the vessel was taken to Ecorse, Michigan, where she was converted into a combination package freighter and auto carrier. The SPOKANE spent most of the 1920's carrying cars from the auto plants to various ports on the lakes and returning with grain or coal, depending on where the cars had been delivered. Nicholson-Universal Steamship Company assumed control of the vessel in 1929 but the Reid Transit Company of Port Huron resumed ownership in 1930.

When the Great Depression struck, the SPOKANE, along with hundreds of American and Canadian vessels, was laid up. The SPOKANE gathered rust at her dock at Port Huron until 1935. She was then taken to Cleveland and reduced to scrap. Her document was surrendered on December 6, 1935. After almost 50 years, the first steel vessel built on the lakes was dismantled.

SPOKANE upbound in the St. Clair River

BUILT:	1886
	Globe Shipbuilding Co.,
	Cleveland, Ohio
HULL NUMBER:	11
LENGTH:	249.5
BREADTH:	39.0
DEPTH:	20.0
GRT:	1,741
REGISTRY NUMBER:	US. 116104
ENGINES:	26", 50" Diameter x
	42" Stroke
	Fore & Aft Compound
ENGINE BUILDER:	Globe Iron Works
	Cleveland, Ohio

SPOKANE downbound at Mission Point

In Lake St. Clair

HENRY STEINBRRENNER (1)

Traffic at the Soo in 1901. R. L. IRELAND, HENRY STEINBRENNER, JOHN W. GATES foreground, barge ANTRIM, tug C. L. BOYNTON and PHILIP MINCH in background

Built for the Kinsman Transit Company, the steel bulk freighter HENRY STEINBRENNER (1) was launched on September 28, 1901 at Port Huron, Michigan by the Jenks Shipbuilding Company. On December 6, 1909 the STEIN-BRENNER, downbound loaded, collided in a blinding snowstorm with the HARRY A. BERWIND, upbound in ballast in the lower St. Mary's River near Round Island. The STEINBRENNER went to the bottom in 30 feet of water with a hole, 40 feet wide from top to bottom on her starboard side. The crew was rescued but the owners abandoned the ship to the underwriters, who awarded the contract to salvage the vessel to the Reid Wrecking Company. She was raised and put back into service the following spring. The BERWIND had damage to her bow and stern and proceeded to Duluth, Minnesota, where she arrived on December 22nd to be repaired.

In a severe fog on October 11, 1923, the STEINBREN-NER collided with the JOHN McCARTNEY KENNEDY on Whitefish Bay, Lake Superior. This time damage was not serious and both vessels continued to their destination.

It was a balmy day in Duluth on Saturday, May 9, 1953, as the STEINBRENNER was loading ore at the Great Northern Railway's Allouez docks, just across the bay in Superior, Wisconsin. Shortly before she left on Sunday at 7 A.M., gale warnings were raised because a severe cold front was approaching. May storms aren't too much of a problem for steel ships, but this one was one of the worst in recent memory.

The gale grew worse as the front moved eastward. Waves were reported to be 19 feet high and the temperature was plummeting. The hatch covers were secure on the vessel but they were not covered by tarpaulins. The waves pounded the vessel mercilessly. During the night, water seeped into the cargo hold. The ship settled lower in the water and, in early morning, when 14 miles off Rock of Ages Light, a monstrous wave suddenly struck her stern and carried away the three aft hatch covers. Desperately, the captain called on the radio telephone for help. The STEINBRENNER started filling and settled down at the stern. The captain ordered "abandon ship" at 6:25 A.M. on the 11th, but before this order could be completed, the HENRY STEIN-BRENNER went down stern first, her boilers exploding and her pilot house blown apart by the air pressure. The entire crew was either thrown into the icy waters or trapped in the sinking vessel. Only one life raft and two lifeboats floated from the wreck.

Fortunately, at least three vessels heard the distress call and raced, in spite of 70 mph winds, to the last reported position of the ill-fated vessel. The JOSEPH H. THOMPSON, WILFRED SYKES and D. M. CLEMSON rushed to the rescue. Shortly after 10 A.M., the three vessels found the survivors. The THOMPSON picked up the raft with the captain and four men. The CLEMSON rescued seven men from one lifeboat and the SYKES picked up two in the other boat. Seventeen were dead as Lake Superior's waters had claimed another vessel.

HENRY STEINBRENNER sunk in the St. Mary's River in 1909

BUILT:	1901 Jenks Shipbuilding Co., Port Huron, Mich.
HULL NUMBER:	14
LENGTH:	420.0
BREADTH:	50.0
DEPTH:	24.0
GRT:	4,719
REGISTRY NUMBER:	US. 96584
ENGINES:	23", 38", 63" Diameter x 40" Stroke Triple Expansion
ENGINE BUILDER:	Shipyard

Downbound in the St. Clair River in 1916

HENRY STEINBRENNER downbound past Port Huron, August 10, 1947

Downbound at Mission Point, August 25, 1952

I. WATSON STEPHENSON

One of the handsomest of the lumber-carrying fleet and among the last lumber-hookers built on the lakes was the I. WATSON STEPHENSON. She was launched on May 11, 1895 by the F. W. Wheeler Company at West Bay City, Michigan for Isaac Stephenson of Peshtigo, Wisconsin. He operated her under the name of the Stephenson Transportation Company. She was reportedly a duplicate of the MINNIE E. KELTON. The STEPHENSON worked the Lake Michigan and Lake Superior lumber trades, ordinarily towing the Stephenson barge ADVANCE. She carried 725,000 feet of lumber, and was named for the son of a well-known Marinette businessman and financier, who also served three terms in Congress. She was owned by his firm from the time of her construction until 1923. During that time she had few accidents, although she suffered a grounding at Sturgeon Bay on August 23, 1898, when she was struck by her barge and had a hole stoved in her stern. In 1911, the ship was rebuilt and reboilered with a new scotch boiler from the Manitowoc Boiler Works. She also received major repairs in 1920.

In 1923, the STEPHENSON was sold to the J. O. Nessen Lumber Company of Chicago, and in 1926 to E. M. Carleton of Cleveland who did business as the "Northern Ohio Lumber & Timber Company". She was sold to the Saginaw Bay Transportation Company the following year. The ship was sold again in 1933 for scrap, and her machinery was removed at Cleveland. The oak hull was scuttled at the Stadium Yacht Basin on the Cleveland waterfront on July 11, 1935 to serve as a breakwater and what remained of it was burned to the waterline in the Spring of 1946.

I. WATSON STEPHENSON upbound in the St. Clair River

BUILT:	1895
	F. W. Wheeler & Co.,
	W. Bay City, Mich.
HULL NUMBER:	107
LENGTH:	172.0
BREADTH:	35.0
DEPTH:	11.9
GRT:	639
REGISTRY NUMBER:	US. 100597
ENGINES:	18", 36" Diameter x
	32" Stroke
	Fore & Aft Compound
ENGINE BUILDER:	Shipyard

I. WATSON STEPHENSON with a load of lumber

At Cleveland in the 1930's

DONALD STEWART

The bulk carrier DONALD STEWART was one of the most handsome canal-sized lakers ever built. She was launched on April 14, 1923, by the Smith's Dock Company Ltd. at South Bank-on-Tees, England. Similar in appearance to KEYSTATE and KEYBAR, which she followed from the shipyard, she was rather more heavily constructed.

DONALD STEWART was built for the Bruce Trading Company Ltd., Toronto, which was managed by J.F.M. Stewart, and she was named for Stewart's younger son. She was taken over in 1927 by the International Waterways Navigation Company Ltd., Montreal, which was operated by R. A. Campbell, Montreal, and John E. Russell, Toronto. She joined the fleet of Canada Steamship Lines Ltd., Montreal, in 1929, as a result of a court decision that DONALD STEWART had been responsible for damages suffered by the wooden C.S.L. steamer CATARACT in a collision on the St. Lawrence River.

Shortly after the outset of World War II, DONALD STEWART was requisitioned for salt water service, and she passed to the control of the British Ministry of War Transport. It was her misfortune that she fell victim to the little-known Battle of the St. Lawrence, which took place during the late summer of 1942, and which was not generally reported at the time because of the reluctance of officials to admit that German U-boats had penetrated the St. Lawrence River.

On September 3, 1942, U-517, under the command of Lt. Cmdr. Paul Hartwig, attacked a convoy outbound from the Gulf of St. Lawrence, in position 50.32 N. by 58.45 W., in the westerly approaches to the Strait of Belle Isle, between the northwest coast of Newfoundland and the Quebec shore. Before being chased by naval escorts, the submarine fired two torpedoes, one of which struck DONALD STEWART. She was carrying a cargo of aviation fuel in barrels, and the resulting explosion and searing fire sank the STEWART in less than twelve minutes.

Despite her embarrassing proximity to the Canadian mainland, the voyage of U-517 netted her nine scores, including one warship, one troop transport, and seven freighters, this latter group including the lakers DONALD STEWART and OAKTON.

DONALD STEWART just after her builder's trials in 1923

DONALD STEWART downbound in Lake St. Clair

BUILT:	1923
	Smith's Dock Co. Ltd.,
	South Bank-on-Tees, England
HULL NUMBER:	779
LENGTH:	250.0
BREADTH:	42.9
DEPTH:	18.7
GRT:	1,781
REGISTRY NUMBER:	C. 147765
ENGINES:	16", 26", 44" Diameter x
	33" Stroke
	Triple Expansion
ENGINE BUILDER:	Shipyard

SULPHITE

BALLEW upbound in the St. Clair River

The steel tug BALLEW (US. 217678) was built in 1919 at Elizabeth, New Jersey by the Bethlehem Shipbuilding Corporation for the wartime United States Shipping Board. This was one of the many tugs built during World War I and shortly after to a standard design. In 1924, she was purchased by the Detroit Sulphite Transportation Company and brought to the lakes to tow pulpwood barges from Lake Superior ports to its mill in Detroit, Michigan. In 1926, she was renamed b) SULPHITE.

In 1939, the entire fleet was transferred to Canadian operators, the Driftwood Lands & Timber Company Ltd. The SULPHITE would tow the barges DELKOTE, SWEDE-ROPE, and MITSCHFIBRE from Port Arthur/Fort William, Ontario to the mill at Detroit on the Rouge River. One barge would be at the Canadian Lakehead being loaded with pulpwood, another would be unloaded at the mill. The third would be in tow underway between the ports in tow of the tug SULPHITE. She was always busy.

The operation of the tug and barges was sold in 1956 to the Hindman Transportation Company Ltd., of Owen Sound, Ontario. Water transportation for pulpwood was severely restricted in the middle 1960's and the services of the tug and barges were no longer needed. This came about as a result of the high cost to maintain and operate the floating equipment at a time when rail competition was increasing. Eventually, the railroads won all the pulpwood-hauling business from the Great Lakes. In 1966, the SULPHITE was dismantled at Goderich, Ontario, her parts placed in the hold of the barge MITSCHFIBRE which was then towed to Ashtabula, Ohio in November. There both barge and tug were cut up for scrap. The pilot house nameboard now hangs in the Dossin Marine Museum on Belle Isle, Detroit. It shows both of the tug's names, BALLEW on one side and SULPHITE on the other.

	BUILT: 1919
	Bethlehem Shipbuilding Co.,
	Elizabeth, N. J.
a) Ballew	**HULL NUMBER:** 2123
b) SULPHITE	**LENGTH:** 142.0
	BREADTH: 27.5
	DEPTH: 16.0
	GRT: 433
	REGISTRY NUMBER: C. 170560
	ENGINES: 17", 25", 43" Diameter x
	30" Stroke
	Triple Expansion
	ENGINE BUILDER: Shipyard

SULPHITE at Owen Sound, August, 1955

Downbound at Mission Point

SUMATRA

EMPIRE CITY was the third of five steel steamers built for the Zenith Transit Company of Duluth, which was managed by Augustus B. Wolvin. She was launched on June 17, 1897, by the Cleveland Shipbuilding Company at Cleveland, Ohio. Along with the other four Zenith bulk carriers, ZENITH CITY, QUEEN CITY, CRESCENT CITY and SUPERIOR CITY, she was absorbed into the Pittsburgh Steamship Company, the lake shipping division of the United States Steel Corporation, in 1901.

EMPIRE CITY was reboilered in 1925 and, in 1927, was sold to G. A. Tomlinson's Empire Steamship Company, Cleveland. In 1929, she was sent to the American Shipbuilding Company's yard at Lorain, where she was converted to a scraper-type self-unloader. That same year, Tomlinson renamed her b) SUMATRA and transferred her to his Sumatra Steamship Company, Cleveland. She was given a new square pilothouse and texas during the 1940's, and was transferred in 1955 to the Tomlinson Fleet Corporation.

In 1961, SUMATRA was sold to Law Quarries Transportation Ltd., Port Colborne, a subsidiary of R. E. Law Crushed Stone Ltd. Refitted at Port Colborne, she was painted in dark red colors similar to those of Tomlinson, except that her two silver stack bands were replaced by the vertically-mounted letters 'LAW' in white. She was re-named c) DOLOMITE (C. 316031) in 1962. DOLOMITE was operated 1961-64 for Law by the Reoch interests, in 1965 and 1966 by Law for its own account, and in 1967 under a purchase agreement by Bayswater Shipping Ltd., Brockville. That sale was never completed, the result of financial problems which beset Bayswater after the death of its founder.

By 1967, her last year of service, DOLOMITE was having mechanical problems. It was becoming ever more difficult to find coalpassers to service her hand-fired boilers, and her crew accommodations could most charitably be described as spartan. DOLOMITE was sold in 1968 to Marine Salvage Ltd., Port Colborne, and was then resold to Spanish breakers. She passed down the Welland Canal under her own power on September 11, 1968, and was towed across the Atlantic by the Dutch tug HUDSON. She avoided the loss of her tandem tow-mate, EDWARD Y. TOWNSEND, and arrived safely at Santander, Spain, on October 20, 1968.

DOLOMITE will best be remembered for the very melodious triple-chime steam whistle that she carried for her entire life. It was one of the last of its type to be in regular use on a lake freighter.

EMPIRE CITY upbound at Mission Point in 1922

Empire City
b) SUMATRA
c) Dolomite

BUILT:	1897
	Cleveland Shipbuilding Co.,
	Cleveland, Ohio
HULL NUMBER:	28
LENGTH:	405.4
BREADTH:	48.0
DEPTH:	24.4
GRT:	4,118
REGISTRY NUMBER:	US. 136623
ENGINES:	17 1/2", 26 1/8", 39 1/8",
	60 1/8" Diameter x 40" Stroke
	Quadruple Expansion
ENGINE BUILDER:	Shipyard

SUMATRA passing Marine City, May 31, 1937

Downbound in Lake St. Clair

DOLOMITE upbound, passing Sarnia, June 24, 1965

SWEEPSTAKES

The tug SWEEPSTAKES was one of the proudest and prettiest tugs ever to grace fresh water. She was designed to be powerful and fast, as her name implied, and was built in 1867 by Quayle & Martin for H. N. Strong of Detroit. Strong also owned the SATELLITE, STRANGER, I. U. MASTERS, and later a number of other tugs.

SWEEPSTAKES was built with one deck, a sleek, yacht-like silhouette, and distinctly ornate appearance, although she always was meant to be a real workhorse. Indeed, she earned a fine reputation for her towing abilities and was always a forerunner in the competition for fastest, longest, or heaviest tows. Her greatest rivals were the CHAMPION, FRANK MOFFATT, THOMAS QUAYLE and the WINSLOW.

The tug was rebuilt in 1873 and "housed-in," as were most of her contemporaries, so that they could better stand up to conditions on the open lakes when towing log rafts.

It was at this time that the SWEEPSTAKES' gross tonnage was increased to 228, and she was readmeasured to 130.7' x 21.8' x 12.5'.

The tug changed hands several times during the 1880's, going from the Strong Estate to Thomas Pitts of Detroit in 1884; to John Pridgeon Jr. of Detroit in 1887, and to Benjamin Boutell of Bay City in 1892. Boutell took the tug to the East Coast in 1898 to work the coal trade with several of his own barges, and in 1904, he sold her to the Davis Coal & Coke Company of Baltimore. SWEEPSTAKES' name was changed to b) SEA KING in 1913, when she was acquired by the Western Maryland Railroad Company (George Weaver, managing owner). In 1923 her owners were listed as the Eastern Transportation Company of Wilmington, and she was reported abandoned and sunk in that year.

Norton painting and advertizement of SWEEPSTAKES

SWEEPSTAKES at the Soo

SWEEPSTAKES in Boutell colors

a) SWEEPSTAKES	**b) Sea King**	*DEPTH:*	11.0
		GRT:	205
BUILT:	1867	*REGISTRY NUMBER:*	US. 22383
	Quayle & Martin,	*ENGINES:*	20", 40" Diameter x
	Cleveland, Ohio		32" Stroke
HULL NUMBER:			Steeple Compound
LENGTH:	130.0	*ENGINE BUILDER:*	S. F. Hodge
BREADTH:	21.0		Detroit, Michigan

SEA KING on the East coast

TADOUSSAC

A steel overnight passenger steamer, an almost exact duplicate of the ill-fated QUEBEC, and a slightly larger model of her near-sister ST. LAWRENCE, the TADOUSSAC was built for Canada Steamship Lines Ltd., in 1928 at Lauzon, Quebec by the Davie Shipbuilding & Repair Company, Ltd. She operated out of Montreal to Quebec City, Tadoussac and Bagotville, the headwaters of navigation on the Saguenay River.

This popular cruise route took its passengers through the St. Lawrence River, past quaint French villages with their towering cathedral-like spires, arriving at Quebec City and the Chateau Frontenac, high up on the cliffs above. The late afternoon departure from Montreal enabled commuters or businessmen a comfortable overnight voyage and early arrival at Quebec. After her passengers had spent a day in the old and new town of Quebec, the steamer would sail down the St. Lawrence to stop at another CSL hotel, the Manoir Richelieu at Pointe-au-Pic (Murray Bay) and thence to Tadoussac, at the confluence of the St. Lawrence and Saguenay Rivers. The tour continued up the Saguenay past towering Capes Trinity and Eternity to Bagotville, Quebec. The return voyage was just as exciting. Stops could be made at any of these three hotels and a resumption of the voyage could be arranged at a time later. After the opening of the St. Lawrence Seaway in 1959, TADOUSSAC made a few trips through the new canals and once even came as far west as Detroit, Michigan on a cruise.

Unfortunately, good things seem always to come to an end. The three surviving C.S.L. Saguenay cruise ships, RICHELIEU, ST. LAWRENCE and TADOUSSAC, were withdrawn from service in 1965 because of stringent new laws governing passenger vessels with wooden superstructures or interiors and their propensity for being fire hazards. In 1966, the three vessels were sold to Joseph de Smedt of Antwerp, Belgium. The TADOUSSAC, renamed b) PASSENGER NO. 2 for the journey, and the RICHELIEU, renamed b) PASSENGER NO. 3, were towed in tandem by the tug ROBBENPLATE, leaving Sorel on May 15, 1966 and arriving at Antwerp on June 9. The RICHELIEU was eventually cut up for scrap as was the ST. LAWRENCE. Before the TADOUSSAC could be cut up, she was purchased by Danish interests and refurbished to serve as a floating hotel in Copenhagen harbor. She was renamed c) ST. LAWRENCE (2) and towed to the Danish port, where she did yeoman service for tourists and became the temporary home for thousands of refugees from Eastern Block countries who stayed on her until clearance would arrive from their adopted "free nation". (The original ST. LAWRENCE also was to go into this service and was even renamed KOBENHAVN for this purpose but these plans did not materialize and she was scrapped.)

In 1975, ST. LAWRENCE (2) was again sold, this time to Arabian interests. On July 18, 1975, she was under tow at Suez, eastbound behind the West German tug FAIRPLAY X, enroute to Sharjah, United Arab Emirates, on the Persian Gulf near Oman, for use as either a hotel or workers' barracks. In 1981, she was observed there with her hull completely embedded in sand. As far as we know, she is still there. Quite a change of scenery . . . from the cool St. Lawrence to the salty air of Copenhagen to the brown sands of Arabia.

TADOUSSAC entering Montreal harbor

TADOUSSAC entering the harbor at Tadoussac, July 9, 1964

In the Welland Ship Canal returning from a trip to Detroit

	BUILT:	1928
		Davie Shipbuilding & Repair Co., Ltd.,
		Lauzon, P. Q.
TACOUSSAC	HULL NUMBER:	496
b) Passenger No. 2	LENGTH:	350.0
c) St. Lawrence	BREADTH:	70.1
	DEPTH:	18.8
	GRT:	7,013
	REGISTRY NUMBER:	C. 153447
	2 ENGINES:	4 cyl. Triple Expansion
		24", 38", 44", 44" Diameter
		x 36" Stroke
	ENGINE BUILDER:	Richardsons, Westgarth & Co., Ltd.
		West Hartlepool, England

PASSENGER NO. 2 at Sorel

ST. LAWRENCE (2) at Copenhagen, September, 1969

TAMPICO

The steel canaller TAMPICO was launched on May 4, 1900 at Toledo, Ohio by the Craig Shipbuilding Company for the Hawgood Lines. She was intended for the canal-to-ocean service, along with the EUREKA of 1899 and the METEOR of 1901. Her bridge was amidships and the vessel was fit for salt water service. Late in 1900, TAMPICO was sold to the Globe Navigation Company of Seattle, Washington, and left for the Pacific. In 1912, she was sold to the Pacific Coast Steamship Company and, in 1916, to Crowell & Thurlow Steamship Company. The ship was used mainly in the coal trade out of Boston, Massachusetts for this firm.

The F. D. Gleason Coal Company purchased the TAMPICO in 1922 and brought her back to the lakes. In 1924, her dimensions and gross tonnage were changed slightly. She was rebuilt at Ecorse, Michigan to 22.0 foot depth and 1,894 gross tons for her new service as a sand dredge. Her cabins were moved forward and she assumed the usual lake freighter silhouette. Nicholson Transit Company of Detroit, Michigan purchased the vessel in 1937 and converted it to a crane vessel at Ecorse to run in the scrap iron trade in 1938.

World War II broke out in 1939. The United States was plunged into the war in 1941, and many vessels on the lakes were requisitioned for war service the following Spring. The TAMPICO, because of her former ocean service, and because she could pass through the canals, was reconverted again, this time by the American Shipbuilding Company yard at Buffalo, New York (1,995 gross tons). The vessel was sent to the Atlantic in 1942 and chartered by the British War Ministry of Transport in 1944. A whole fleet of ships followed TAMPICO to salt water for war service and more canallers were sent overseas in 1944. They were reconditioned at Port Dalhousie, Ontario by Muir Brothers Drydock Company. Among these were FELLOWCRAFT, FLEETWOOD, IRONWOOD, LAKE CHELAN, COVALT, BENNINGTON, BROCTON and BACK BAY.

After the war, TAMPICO was returned to Nicholson, who brought her back to the Great Lakes in 1947. She worked for this firm until 1961, when Hyman-Michaels Company, a scrap dealer in Duluth, Minnesota purchased the vessel. Instead of being reduced to scrap, the TAMPICO was cut down to a barge and her engine removed at Ashtabula, Ohio in 1962. There followed a series of owners but TAMPICO lay idle at the foot of Riopelle Street in Detroit for three years. She was officially out of documentation but the hull lived on. U.S.-Canada Transit Company were her owners in 1962; Seaway Cartage Company of Detroit in 1963; and Bultema Dredge & Dock Company in 1965. After 1967, she belonged to the Luedke Engineering Company of Frankfort, Michigan. The hull was towed to Two Creeks, Wisconsin and used as a breakwater with the ADRIAN ISELIN when a power plant was built there. In 1968, they were raised and towed to Frankfort where they lay in the inner harbor partially listing and seemingly resting. Subsequently, both vessels were made into docks. They now lie at the eastern end of Frankfort harbor.

TAMPICO at the Soo, early in her career

TAMPICO in Crowell & Thurlow S.S. Co. colors

BUILT:	1900
	Craig Shipbuilding Co.,
	Toledo, Ohio
HULL NUMBER:	77
LENGTH:	247.0
BREADTH:	42.0
DEPTH:	24.0
GRT:	2,133
REGISTRY NUMBER:	US. 145840
ENGINES:	19", 30", 52" Diameter x
	40" Stroke
	Triple Expansion
ENGINE BUILDER:	Dry Dock Iron Works
	Detroit, Michigan, 1895

As a crane vessel

TAMPICO in War colors

TAMPICO upbound in the Detroit River

As a dock at Frankfort, July 24, 1982

EDWIN S. TICE

EDWIN S. TICE almost brand new

Many of the Great Lakes' best proportioned lumber steamers came from the Burger yards at Manitowoc, Wisconsin. The EDWIN S. TICE is a good example. She was built there for Edward Smith and others of Buffalo, New York and was intended for the Lake Michigan and Lake Superior lumber trades. With her tall spars and substantial shear, she cut a fine figure and was always well kept-up. Her machinery is thought to have come from the old propeller SUSQUEHANNA (1858); the latter ship, one of the old Erie Railway Line package freighters, was given one of the lakes' first steeple compound engines in 1867, and the ship was dismantled at Milwaukee in 1880. Some records indicate that the TICE was re-engined with another steeple engine from the Bay City Iron Works in 1889, with cylinders 19-7/8" and 38" in diameter and a stroke of 36". It is not clear whether or not this was the ship's original powerplant or a replacement.

The TICE had a whole list of owners. She was sold to H. W. McCormack of Bay City, Michigan in 1892. In 1895, she went to Samuel Neff of Milwaukee. In 1901, she went to William Mueller & Company of Chicago (Mueller Cedar Company), at which time she was rechristened

b) MUELLER, and readmeasured to 172.0 x 30.1 x 12.5; 699 gross tons. She usually towed the barge BUTCHER BOY at this time, and sometimes the PARANA, RICHARD MOTT or BELLE BROWN. In 1912, the ship was bought by the Wisconsin Land and Lumber Company of Chicago, and was managed by the W. F. Holmes Company, who operated three other lumber hookers and four consort barges; MUELLER was paired with the barge HALSTED. In 1915, she was again readmeasured to 160.0 x 32.0 x 12.0; 567 gross tons. In 1918, the ship was sold to the Central Transportation Company of Gary, Indiana, after which time she towed the ROBERT L. FRYER. In 1929, both vessels went to the Central Paper Company of Muskegon. The MUELLER and the FRYER were finally purchased by Winand Schlosser of Milwaukee in 1930, and during her last years the MUELLER towed both the FRYER and the famous OUR SON in the pulpwood trade, largely from Georgian Bay to Chicago. The steamer was laid up at Sturgeon Bay in 1932 and dismantled in the boneyard a year later. The hull was burned and scuttled about four miles North of the city of Sturgeon Bay in 1935.

BUILT:	1887
HULL NUMBER:	
LENGTH:	159.9
BREADTH:	32.1
DEPTH:	12.5
GRT:	728
REGISTRY NUMBER:	US. 135954
SECOND ENGINE:	20", 38" Diameter x 36" Stroke Steeple Compound
ENGINE BUILDER:	Bay City Iron Works Bay City, Michigan

a) EDWIN S. TICE
b) Mueller

EDWIN S. TICE at her dock

MUELLER upbound at the Soo

Downbound with a load of pulpwood in the St. Mary's River

348

PAUL L. TIETJEN

On January 12, 1907, at Cleveland, Ohio, Miss Marcella Andrews christened the steel steamer named for her father, Mr. Matthew Andrews. Built by the American S. B. Co. for the Kinsman Transit Company, this was the beginning of the ship's 71-year career. She was well appointed and the favorite of many, having five modest-sized staterooms with total accommodations for ten.

In 1913, the ANDREWS became one of the many casualties of the "Great Storm." Proceeding down Lake Huron in heavy seas and loaded with iron ore, the steamer's Captain decided to anchor rather than attempt to make the St. Clair River. The ANDREWS stranded on Corsica Shoals because the keeper of the LIGHTSHIP 61, Corsica Shoals light, neglected to return the lightship back to its proper station after it had been driven two miles off. There were no casualties, however, and the ship was salvaged and repaired.

In 1933, the ANDREWS was renamed b) HARRY L. FINDLAY. In 1954, she was given "new blood" in the form of a new three-cylinder Skinner Uniflow engine 28" diameter of cylinder x 36" stroke and new boilers by the American Shipbuilding Co. at Lorain, Ohio. The year 1965 saw this ship renamed for the last time as c) PAUL L. TIETJEN.

On August 10, 1967, the TIETJEN almost ended her career in collision with the CSL package freighter FORT WILLIAM, 25 miles north of Port Huron, Michigan. Repaired again, she continued hauling grain, ore, coal, stone, and company guests until July, 1977. At that time, under the command of Captain R. I. McGrath, the TIETJEN sailed into the "Frog Pond" in Toledo, where he rang "finished with engines" for the last time. Little more than a year later, in October, 1978, the tug OHIO took the TIETJEN in tow to the Triad Salvage Co. in Ashtabula, Ohio where she was dismantled.

On a final note, the TIETJEN was the last boat which Kinsman had built as well as owned throughout her entire career.

MATTHEW ANDREWS upbound in the St. Clair River

a) Matthew Andrews (1)
b) Harry L. Findlay
c) PAUL L. TIETJEN

BUILT:	1907
	American Shipbuilding Co.,
	Cleveland, Ohio
HULL NUMBER:	437
LENGTH:	532.0
BREADTH:	56.0
DEPTH:	31.0
GRT:	7,014
REGISTRY NUMBER:	US. 203907
ENGINES:	23½", 38", 63" Diameter x
	42" Stroke
	Triple Expansion
ENGINE BUILDER:	Shipyard

HARRY L. FINDLAY downbound in Lake St. Clair, June 23, 1951

Downbound in the Detroit River, July 17, 1954

HARRY L. FINDLAY downbound in Lake Huron, August 31, 1960

PAUL L. TIETJEN, August 18, 1970

SIR S. L. TILLEY

SIR S. L. TILLEY in the locks at the Soo

The composite-hulled (iron frames, wooden planking) package freighter SIR S. L. TILLEY was built in 1884 by the celebrated St. Catharines shipyard of Louis Shickluna. Her first owners were Sylvester Neelon and James Norris of St. Catharines. They placed her in service with the Merchants Lake and River Steamship Lines, which was a joint venture of G. E. Jaques and Company, Montreal, Sylvester Neelon, James Norris, Capt. Peter Larkin, of St. Catharines, and Aeneas D. Mackay and Capt. J. B. Fairgrieve, of Hamilton.

On August 26, 1899, SIR S. L. TILLEY burned on Lake Erie near Fairport, Ohio and her superstructure was completely destroyed. She was carrying a heavy load of cement on deck at the time of the fire, and, when heated, the heavy iron deck beams, together with the stanchions, ties and stringers, were crushed downward, and were so buckled and twisted that the ship's sides were pulled out of shape. The hull was abandoned to the underwriters, and later was sold to J. and J. T. Mathews, of Toronto, who turned the TILLEY over to Polson Iron Works for rebuilding at Toronto under the supervision of W. E. Redway.

By 1902, SIR S. L. TILLEY was owned by James Carruthers of Toronto. On October 25, 1903, while loaded with coal, she caught fire at Sault Ste. Marie, Ontario, and her upperworks were again destroyed. Later towed to Kingston, the hull was purchased by the Montreal Transportation Company and rebuilt. When she again re-entered service, she did so under the name b) ADVANCE. She was still a package freighter but, in 1913, she was cut down to a bulk carrier by the Muir Bros. Dry Dock Company Ltd., at Port Dalhousie.

Roy M. Wolvin and his Montreal Transportation Company formed an operating agreement with Canada Steamship Lines Ltd., Montreal, in 1916, but the ownership of ADVANCE was not actually transferred to C.S.L. until 1921. She lay idle in Muir's Pond, above Lock One at Port Dalhousie, during the 1924, 1925 and 1926 navigation seasons.

ADVANCE returned to active service in 1927, but she stranded on Manitoulin Island on December 5, 1927, with the loss of two lives. She was salvaged by Wallace and Bingley, of Cornwall, and was towed to their drydock at Cornwall, where she was repaired. Nevertheless, ADVANCE did not return to service and, about 1934 or 1935, she was stripped of any salvageable equipment. The tired old hull was discarded in the St. Lawrence River downstream from Cornwall.

ADVANCE in the Soo Locks in 1910

At a grain elevator in Montreal

a) **SIR S. L. TILLEY**
   b) **Advance**

BUILT:	1884
	Louis Shickluna's Shipyard,
	St. Catharines, Ontario
LENGTH:	168.0
BREADTH:	35.3
DEPTH:	15.0
GRT:	1,178
REGISTRY NUMBER:	C. 88632
ENGINES:	25½", 52" Diameter x
	42" Stroke
	Fore & Aft Compound
ENGINE BUILDER:	G. N. Oille at Louis Shickluna's yard
	St. Catherines, Ontario

G. A. TOMLINSON (2)

D. O. MILLS at the iron ore dock

Entering service in 1907 after her launch on March 12 at Ecorse, Michigan by the Great Lakes Engineering Works, the steel steamer D. O. MILLS was the last of four ships commissioned for the Mesaba Steamship Company which had been formed in 1905 by Harry Coulby. The Mesaba fleet and seven others were merged to form the Interlake Steamship Company in 1913. That same year, the MILLS nearly met her end in the "Great Storm," when she was driven aground on a reef off Harbor Beach, Michigan, where she settled to the bottom. The irony of the situation was that a distress signal was never sent by the MILLS, that the lifesaving crew who fought the fierce seas to reach the stranded vessel returned to Harbor Beach without seeing even one crewmember after circling the vessel several times, and that, when the seas subsided, the ship was pumped out, worked free and sailed to the shipyard for repairs of $45,000 covered by her owners' sinking fund.

The MILLS remained an Interlake boat until 1960, when she was sold to the Tomlinson Fleet Corporation, converted to a self-unloader at the Fraser-Nelson shipyard, Superior, Wisconsin and renamed G. A. TOMLINSON (2) after the deceased owner who was one of the most famous vessel men in Great Lakes' history.

In 1971, the TOMLINSON was sold to the Columbia Transportation Division, Oglebay Norton Company, along with the steamers SYLVANIA and JAMES DAVIDSON, ending the "life" of the once gigantic Tomlinson fleet. (These boats had been under charter to Columbia since 1969.) The TOMLINSON served her last owners well until 1979 when, on December 13th, she entered Ashtabula Harbor, blowing three long and two short. There she shut down steam for the last time. The Triad Salvage Company finished her scrapping in 1980.

	BUILT: 1907
	Great Lakes Engineering Works,
	Ecorse, Mich.
HULL NUMBER:	29
a) D. O. Mills **LENGTH:**	532.0
b) G. A. TOMLINSON (2) **BREADTH:**	58.2
DEPTH:	32.0
GRT:	6,598
REGISTRY NUMBER:	US. 203979
ENGINES:	23", 38", 65" Diameter x
	42" Stroke
	Triple Expansion
ENGINE BUILDER:	Shipyard

G. A. TOMLINSON downbound in Lake Huron, July 17, 1961

In Columbia colors, June 5, 1974

TOPEKA

TOPEKA was a wooden bulk freighter, similar in construction and dimension to PUEBLO, DENVER and OMAHA. All were built by the Milwaukee Ship Yard Company. TOPEKA was built in 1889 for J. B. Merrill and others of Milwaukee, primarily for the Milwaukee grain business. The ship was described as having the first hydraulic steering gear employed on the Lakes, although such equipment was in use on the Inland Rivers some years earlier. She had a capacity of 2,100 tons of bulk freight, with one compartment and six hatches spaced at 24-foot intervals.

In 1894, Richard P. Fitzgerald became managing owner of the ship, and in 1899 W. E. Fitzgerald succeeded him. In 1901 they sold the ship to Frank W. Smith, one of the principals in the Lake Shore Stone Company of Milwaukee.

The same firm owned the bulk freighters E. M. PECK, PUEBLO, DENVER, OMAHA, and the MARY H. BOYCE. In 1906 the HENNEPIN was added to the fleet. The latter craft was the first self-unloader on the Great Lakes. The TOPEKA also was rebuilt into a self-unloader in 1912, the work being done by the Leathem Smith Dry Dock Company at Sturgeon Bay, Wisconsin where HENNEPIN and several later ships were converted.

In an unfortunate confusion over passing signals, the TOPEKA was sunk on the Detroit River abreast of Sandwich, Ontario on August 15, 1916 when she was struck by the steel steamer CHRISTOPHER. Her coal cargo was salvaged, but the ship was dismantled by Trotter & Company of Amherstburg, and cleared away with dynamite later that same year.

TOPEKA upbound at the Soo in 1905

As a self-unloader in the coal and stone trades

BUILT:	1889	*GRT:*	1,376
	Milwaukee Shipyard Company,	*REGISTRY NUMBER:*	US. 145510
	Milwaukee, Wisc.	*ENGINES:*	24", 44" Diameter x 42" Stroke
LENGTH:	228.3		Fore & Aft Compound
BREADTH:	36.0	*ENGINE BUILDER:*	Samuel F. Hodge & Company
DEPTH:	19.2		Detroit, Michigan

TOPINABEE

TOPINABEE on Mullet Lake

a) **TOPINABEE** b) Pe-To-Se-Ga

In 1899, a small wooden steamboat was built at Charlevoix, Michigan for Herbert Hamill of Petoskey, Michigan to run the Inland Waterway between Cheboygan, Michigan, through the inland lakes of Mullett and Burt and Crooked Lake past Indian River to Conway on Lake Michigan. It was and is a delightful journey through what is now known as Hemingway territory in the northern half of the lower peninsula of Michigan. There were many such small steamers but the TOPINABEE was "The Queen of the Inland Waterways." Not much is known today of this turn-of-the-century "Queen" except that she had twin screws to help her maneuver the sharp turns in Crooked River. She had an unique smokestack that was on hinges so it could be lowered to pass under bridges. The photographs herewith tell the story of this unique little vessel.

In 1911, TOPINABEE was used as a ferry on Traverse Bay and renamed b) PE-TO-SE-GA. William H. Umlor of Traverse City, Michigan owned her in 1913 and E. N. Emory of Mapleton, Michigan in 1914. She was slightly rebuilt in 1910, 64.8 x 14.5 x 4.7; 36 gross tons, to accommodate the wider expanse she was to travel on Traverse Bay. In 1916, she was further altered to 56.3 x 14.5 x 4.5; 25 gross tons. In 1920, the little vessel was purchased by J. F. Divell of Erie, Pennsylvania and taken to that port to be used as a tug. In 1925, she was abandoned there because of age. The end of the "Queen of the Inland Waterways" was uneventful compared to the wonderful excursions she had given in the upper reaches of Michigan's water wonderland.

BUILT:	1899	*DEPTH:*	2.5
	at Charlevoix, Mich.	*GRT:*	16
	builder unknown	*REGISTRY NUMBER:*	US. 145809
LENGTH:	64.9	*ENGINES:*	Unknown
BREADTH:	14.5	*ENGINE BUILDER:*	Unknown

At a dock on the Inland Waterway

EDWARD Y. TOWNSEND

EDWARD Y. TOWNSEND upbound at the Soo

The Cambria Steamship Company was formed in 1906 by the Cambria Steel Company to own two new steamers, EDWARD Y. TOWNSEND and DANIEL J. MORRELL, which had been ordered from the Superior Shipbuilding Company and the West Bay City Shipbuilding Company, respectively. TOWNSEND was launched, amid much celebration, on August 18, 1906. For a brief period of time, she was the largest vessel in operation on the Great Lakes.

TOWNSEND and MORRELL were to remain under the same ownership for their entire careers, although the management of the Cambria Steamship Company was transferred in 1924 from the M. A. Hanna Company to the Bethlehem Transportation Corporation. It was at that time that both boats traded their Hanna colors for Bethlehem livery.

EDWARD Y. TOWNSEND was reboilered in 1946 and in 1954, was repowered with a three-cylinder Skinner uniflow engine, with cylinders of 30" and a stroke of 36". She received a new tank top in 1956. Her sistership, the MORRELL, was updated in the same manner, and the two remained almost identical in appearance.

During the night of November 17, 1966, both MORRELL and TOWNSEND were upbound on Lake Huron and encountering extremely heavy weather. MORRELL foundered with the loss of all but one of her crew, while TOWNSEND managed to reach the safety of the St. Mary's River. It was discovered while fueling at Lime Island, however, that the TOWNSEND had developed a crack in her deck and she was taken to the old Algoma Central coal dock at Sault Ste. Marie, Ontario. She was laid up permanently there following Coast Guard inspection and condemnation.

In 1968, she was sold to Sea Land Service Inc., which purchased her only for use as a trade-in to the U. S. Maritime Administration for other tonnage. She was resold to Marine Salvage Ltd., Port Colborne, who then dealt her to Spanish breakers. She was towed from Sault Ste. Marie to Quebec City, and then set out across the Atlantic in tandem tow with DOLOMITE, behind the Dutch tug HUDSON.

On October 7, 1968, while some 400 miles southeast of St. John's Newfoundland, EDWARD Y. TOWNSEND broke in two in a gale and foundered. Her loss, albeit on salt water, vindicated the Coast Guard's earlier decision to bar her from service as a result of the structural damage which she had suffered in the storm that sank her sistership.

Upbound at Mission Point

EDWARD Y. TOWNSEND downbound past the Old Club, Harsens Island July 5, 1950

BUILT:	1906	GRT:	7,438
	Superior Shipbuilding Co.,	REGISTRY NUMBER:	US. 203449
	Superior, Wisc.	ENGINES:	24", 39", 65" Diameter x
HULL NUMBER:	515		42" Stroke
LENGTH:	586.5		Triple Expansion
BREADTH:	58.2	ENGINE BUILDER:	Detroit Shipbuilding Company
DEPTH:	27.4		Detroit, Michigan

Downbound in Lake Huron, August 4, 1960

JOHN B. TREVOR

The steel whaleback bulk freighter JOHN B. TREVOR was built at West Superior, Wisconsin and launched on May 1, 1895 at the yard of the American Steel Barge Company for Alexander McDougall's own fleet. He was the inventor of the whaleback design and operated both the shipyard and the American Steel Barge fleet. In March, 1900, he sold the TREVOR to the Bessemer Steamship Company which, on June 3, 1901, merged with the Pittsburgh Steamship Company and others to form the 101 ship fleet owned by the United States Steel Corporation.

The TREVOR had a few peculiar incidents in her life. On August 10, 1899, she was rammed and sunk by her own barge #131, another whaleback, at the Southeast Bend of the St. Clair River, opposite Star Island. The crew scampered onto the barge and the big whaleback settled to the bottom of the river. Salvage was begun almost immediately and the vessel was again in service in less than six weeks.

On October 13, 1909, the TREVOR stranded on Rocky Reef, Isle Royale in Lake Superior in a gale. She went on between Grace Harbor and Rainbow Cove, while upbound with a cargo of coal. Her crew was rescued when salvagers could reach her after the waves subsided. For over a month, the work of getting the vessel off the rocks continued. Finally her owners gave up and turned her over to the underwriters. She lay there all that Winter. She was eventually raised and towed to the Canadian port of Port Arthur, Ontario. There she lay until purchased by Franklin Samuel Wiley on September 16, 1912. The vessel was repaired, completely rebuilt and renamed b) ATIKOKAN (C.131053).

Her dimensions were now: 362.0 x 38.8 x 24.0; 2,004 gross tons.

On January 14, 1913, the Canadian Northwest Steamship Company Ltd., purchased the vessel. Her troubles, however, were not over. Again, on the St. Clair River on August 17, 1913, the ATIKOKAN had a rather embarrassing experience. Because of circumstances beyond anyone's control, her steering gear let go just as she was passing Marine City, Michigan and she collided with Pesha's Photography Studio located on the bank of the river. The ATIKOKAN was high and dry on the beach but the famous lake ship photographer was not there. He had passed his business to others a few years before but Sol Foster, another Marine City photographer, was on the scene. Even to this day, the incident has become a legend for citizens of the surrounding territory.

Beginning on April 13, 1917, the ATIKOKAN switched owners quickly. The Montreal Transportation Company was the first, followed by Canada Steamship Lines Ltd. on December 4, 1920, and Dominion Iron & Steel Company Ltd., Nova Scotia on September 8, 1925. The ship had been cut in two at American Shipbuilding in Cleveland and transitted the Welland and old St. Lawrence canals in 1918 and never returned to the Great Lakes again.

She seems to have run on the St. Lawrence River for a few years but was damaged by fire at Halifax, Nova Scotia in 1922; damage that was apparently not repaired. Whether she was used again is not known to us. We do know that she was eventually scrapped at Halifax in 1935 but her document was not surrendered until October 20, 1938.

JOHN B. TREVOR leaving the Poe Lock in 1901

JOHN B. TREVOR upbound at the Soo in 1909

a) JOHN B. TREVOR   b) Atikokan

BUILT:	1895
	American Steel Barge Co.,
	Superior, Wisc.
HULL NUMBER:	135
LENGTH:	308.0
BREADTH:	38.0
DEPTH:	24.0
GRT:	1,713
REGISTRY NUMBER:	US. 77173
ENGINES:	18¾", 32", 54" Diameter x
	42" Stroke
	Triple Expansion
ENGINE BUILDER:	S. F. Hodge & Company
	Detroit, Michigan

ATIKOKAN upbound in the St. Mary's River in 1916

ATIKOKAN on the beach at Marine City, August 17, 1913

Downbound at Mission Point in 1917

TRISTAN

LAIRG of the Moorecraft Transportation Corporation in 1928

In 1911, just prior to World War I, many ships were being built for ocean service in Great Lakes' shipyards. As the years dwindled down to the opening of hostilities in 1914, and during the years of the "war to end all wars", the yards on the lakes were even busier. The Harper Transportation Company of New York City ordered a steel canal-sized bulk freighter to run on its East Coast routes. The PENOBSCOT was launched on June 10, 1911 at Ecorse, Michigan by the Great Lakes Engineering Works. The PENOBSCOT left the lakes and began her ocean tour; no one could guess that she would be back for service on the lakes.

In 1915, the Shawmut Steamship Company of Philadelphia, Pennsylvania purchased the vessel. The following year the Oriental Navigation Company of Uruguay took over and almost immediately transferred the ship's ownership to Soc. Nationale D'Affretments, a French firm which renamed her b) P.L.M. No. 2 in 1917 and sent her off to war service. (The French gross registered tonnage for this vessel was 2,649.) After surviving the war, P.L.M. No. 2 was sold in 1926 to a British firm, the Intercoastal Steamship Company. They renamed her c) LAIRG (Br. 143986). The same year, A. B. MacKay of Hamilton, Ontario, the "famous" ship broker, bought her and brought the vessel back to the lakes where he sold her to the St. Lawrence

Navigation Company of Nova Scotia. This firm did not keep the vessel long and she went to the Moorecraft Transportation Company in 1928. This firm sold her to the Hammermill Paper Company of Erie, Pennsylvania the same year. Hammermill renamed her d) PENOBSCOT, her original name, and used the steamer to transport coal to Lake Superior ports and pulpwood back to its mill at Erie. Later the same year, she was renamed, e) TRISTAN.

In 1932, TRISTAN was purchased by the Buckeye Steamship Company, Hutchinson & Co., managers and converted to a crane ship. For nine years she was in this service but, in 1941, the TRISTAN went to the coast once again, under the ownership of the Madrigal Shipping Company. She served during World War II for this company. In 1949, still owned by Madrigal, she was transferred to their Manila offices and renamed f) LEPUS of the Philippines. On a voyage from Lagazpi to Hirohata on October 24, 1956, when 200 miles ENE of Luzon, the LEPUS foundered in the terrific storm called "Typhoon Jean". Only 11 crewmen were later rescued out of a complement of 36. The LEPUS had served eleven owners under the flags of six different nations, had been in two World Wars and had adventures from the lakes to the Atlantic, back to the lakes and then to the Pacific. TRISTAN was quite a traveller.

Penobscot
b) P.L.M. No. 2
c) Lairg
d) Penobscot
e) TRISTAN
f) Lepus

BUILT:	1911
	Great Lakes Engineering Works,
	Ecorse, Mich.
HULL NUMBER:	84
LENGTH:	247.0
BREADTH:	43.7
DEPTH:	28.4
GRT:	2,294
REGISTRY NUMBER:	US. 209001
ENGINES:	21", 34½", 57" Diameter x
	42" Stroke
	Triple Expansion
ENGINE BUILDER:	Shipyard

PENOBSCOT upbound at Mission Point in 1928

TRISTAN just after being sold to Hutchinson in 1932

Downbound at the Soo

Upbound at Mission Point

TRISTAN after her cranes were removed, upbound past Detroit September 6, 1940

TURRET CAPE

William Doxford and Sons Ltd., of Sunderland, England, built 176 turret steamers between 1892 and 1911. The twelfth of this series was completed in 1895 as TURRET CAPE. Very few turrets traded regularly in Canadian coastal waters, and only five ever came to the Great Lakes. Built for the Turret Steam Shipping Company Ltd., but transferred in the late 1890's to the St. Bede Trading Company Ltd., she was managed by Petersen, Tate and Company. Used in 1900 and 1901 to carry coal from Sydney, N.S., to Montreal, she was purchased in 1901 by the Canadian Ocean and Inland Navigation Company Ltd., and she first appeared on the lakes in 1902.

TURRET CAPE was acquired in 1904 by the Canadian Lake and Ocean Navigation Company Ltd., Toronto, and management of its boats was assumed in 1911 by the Canadian Interlake Line Ltd. On November 18, 1911, she grounded on Cove Island, Lake Huron. Salvaged the following year by the Reid Wrecking Company, she was repaired at Collingwood and re-entered service in June, 1912. Management of TURRET CAPE was taken over in 1913 by Canada Steamship Lines Ltd., and she was brought into Canadian registry in 1915.

Sent to the east coast for wartime service in the coal trade, she was acquired on December 1, 1915, by the Cape Steamship Company Ltd., Halifax, although C.S.L. continued to operate her until management was taken over in 1917 by the Dominion Iron and Steel Company Ltd. Corporate changes led to a transfer of ownership and management to the British Empire Steel Corporation Ltd. in 1926.

TURRET CAPE was returned to the lakes in 1927 by the Inland Waterways Navigation Company Ltd., Montreal, and by 1929 she had passed to the Inland Waters Navigation Company Ltd. (Mapes and Ferdon Ltd., managers). That company failed in 1930 and TURRET CAPE was laid up at Port Colborne. Her machinery was condemned and was removed in 1932, and the hull was towed to Port Dalhousie in 1934. Taken over in 1935 by the Fort William-Montreal Navigation Company Ltd., Montreal, she was refitted by the Muir Bros. Dry Dock Company as a barge. She entered service in 1936, hauling bagged flour from Fort William to Toronto for Robin Hood Flour Mills Ltd.

Out of service by 1940, she was sold in 1941 to Saguenay Terminals Ltd., Montreal. She was rebuilt at Lauzon by Davie Shipbuilding and Repairing Ltd., emerging as a diesel-powered bulk carrier with all cabins aft. She ran bauxite from British Guiana to Trinidad and to Port Alfred, Quebec, during the war but, in 1944, she was converted briefly to a sandsucker by Sprostons Ltd., Georgetown, for dredging obstructions from the Demerara River. Renamed b) SUN CHIEF in 1947, she was retired in 1948 and laid up at Mobile, Alabama.

She was purchased in 1949 by Capt. R. Scott Misener for his Sarnia Steamships Ltd., which brought her back to the lakes and refitted her at Port Colborne, renaming her c) WALTER INKSTER in 1950. She was transferred in 1951 to Colonial Steamships Ltd. She saw but limited service. Most of this was in shuttling grain screenings from the Canadian Lakehead to Duluth/Superior in 1950-51. Those two seasons saw particularly large quantities of screenings moved to Duluth/Superior. (The reason was a good price for screenings in Duluth.). She lay idle at Fort William from 1952 through 1955, and was sold in 1956 to A. Newman and Company, St. Catharines, for scrapping. She sailed under her own power to Toronto with grain, and then laid up on July 1, 1956, in Muir's Pond, Port Dalhousie. She was scrapped there during the summer of 1959.

TURRET CAPE upbound at the Soo in 1909

TURRET CAPE as a barge in 1936

a) TURRET CAPE   **b) Sunchief**   **c) Walter Inkster**

BUILT:	1895	*GRT:*	1,827
	William Doxford & Sons Ltd.,	*REGISTRY NUMBER:*	Br. & C. 104283
	Sunderland, England	*ENGINES:*	22", 36", 59" Diameter x
HULL NUMBER:	234		39" Stroke
LENGTH:	253.0		Triple Expansion
BREADTH:	44.0	*ENGINE BUILDER:*	Shipyard, 1894
DEPTH:	19.4		

WALTER INKSTER downbound at the Soo

WALTER INKSTER in Duluth Harbor

Awaiting the scrapper's torch at Port Dalhousie

368

UGANDA

Wooden ships were seldom constructed as twin sisters, and never as sextuplets, until six identical vessels were built at West Bay City, Michigan by F. W. Wheeler & Company for various fleets in the early 1890's. The six sisters were WILLIAM F. SAUBER, C. F. BIELMAN, L. R. DOTY, TAMPA, IOSCO and UGANDA. On April 12, 1892, the wooden bulk freighter UGANDA was launched for James McBrier of Erie, Pennsylvania. In 1902, Edward Mehl of Erie purchased the vessel. She was remodeled in 1904 (2,298 GRT). UGANDA was employed in various trades but most of her cargoes were grain.

On April 19, 1913, with a load of corn, she was cut by ice in the Straits of Mackinac 1 and 3/4 miles north and east of White Shoals on Lake Michigan. At first, the crew did not realize the extent of the damage. The ice had cut a severe gash below the waterline and the icy waters filtered in on her corn cargo. Soon, everyone knew what predicament they were in and the captain raised the distress signal. Fortunately, the steamer JOHN A. DONALDSON was nearby and stood by the stricken vessel. The rescued crewmen watched from the DONALDSON as the UGANDA took her final plunge about 2½ hours after she had been holed, four miles east of White Shoals.

BUILT:	1892
	F. W. Wheeler & Co.,
	W. Bay City, Mich.
HULL NUMBER:	88
LENGTH:	291.0
BREADTH:	41.0
DEPTH:	19.8
GRT:	2,053
REGISTRY NUMBER:	US. 25289
ENGINES:	20", 32", 54" Diameter
	x 42" Stroke
	Triple Expansion
ENGINE BUILDER:	Frontier Iron Works
	Detroit, Michigan

UGANDA early in her career

Upbound in the St. Clair River

UNITED STATES

It has been said of the UNITED STATES that she should never have been built in the first place, and certainly her strange career was one long series of failures. But this was no fault of the ship, since she was one of the finest of the steel passenger steamers on the lakes.

She was built at Manitowoc, Wisconsin in 1909, under supervision of George Craig, at the Manitowoc Dry Dock Company as the running mate for THEODORE ROOSE-VELT of the Indiana Transportation Company of Michigan City, Indiana. She ran originally between Chicago, Illinois and Michigan City for that company and later between Chicago and Saugatuck, Michigan. In 1916, she was first chartered, then sold to the Crosby Transportation Company to replace the NYACK in service between Milwaukee, Wisconsin and Grand Haven and Muskegon, Michigan.

At the end of that season, the vessel was sold to "Colonel" Ned Green and sailed down to Brooklyn, New York to be converted to a yacht. She was lengthened by 54 feet to a new length of 259 feet (1,711 gross tons) and otherwise refurbished at great expense. Under Green's ownership, she made two trips to Galveston, Texas, and a number of short cruises, but spent most of her time idle at a leased dock at Padanarum Harbor, South Dartmouth, Massachusetts, near New Bedford. Following one of her shorter trips, and while anchored inside Padanarum break-water, on August 20, 1919, she swung with the tide and struck a rock ledge, holing herself and lying over at an angle of 45° in shallow water. Patched and raised, the vessel was towed to Moore Drydock, Brooklyn, for repairs and was then laid up at Tebos Basin, where she remained for four years, an abandoned plaything.

Bought in 1923 by Penninsula and Northern Navigation Company, she was reconverted to a passenger steamer and deepened 6' at Tebo Yacht Basin, Brooklyn, New York. She was brought back to the lakes to run between Houghton, Michigan, Isle Royale and Port Arthur, Ontario. This service was a financial disaster and, in 1924, UNITED STATES went back to her 1916 route between Milwaukee, Grand Haven and Muskegon. Considerable litigation followed owing to claims that she was in violation of the cabotage law, being more than 25% owned by Canadian interests and sailing between U.S. ports. On July 26, 1926, the ship was seized by the Coast Guard cutter TUSCARORA while attempting to pass through the Straits of Mackinac, and was brought back to Milwaukee. Finally released by the courts, she sailed for Sarnia, Ontario in September.

The following Spring, as she was being fitted out for a new run between Toronto, Ontario and Rochester, New York, she burned and once again heeled on her starboard side. Salvage was begun by the Reid Wrecking Company of Sarnia and lasted until August 10th. Cleanup operations took up the Fall and Winter. She lay at Reid's dock in Sarnia until she finally sailed in September, 1929, for the Davie yard at Lauzon, Quebec, where she was rebuilt as a package freighter for Canada Steamship Lines. She was re-registered in January, 1930 as b) BATISCAN (C. 154476) (1,656 gross tons) and went in the package freight trade between Montreal and Quebec. After two years, the vessel was laid up at the end of the 1931 season at Sorel. There she lay until she was finally scrapped, her registry being closed in 1945.

UNITED STATES entering Saugatuck Harbor

UNITED STATES leaving Milwaukee

In Port Arthur Harbor

	a) UNITED STATES	b) Batiscan
BUILT:	1909	
	George Craig/Manitowoc Dry Dock Co.,	
HULL NUMBER:	Manitowoc, Wisc.	
LENGTH:	28	
BREADTH:	193.0	
DEPTH:	41.0	
GRT:	16.0	
REGISTRY NUMBER:	1,374	
ENGINES:	US. 206330	
	22", 36½", 60" Diameter x 40" Stroke	
ENGINE BUILDER:	Triple Expansion	
	Gunnell Machine Company	
	Manitowoc, Wisconsin	

BATISCAN as a package freighter

At Sorel in 1938

UNITED STATES GYPSUM

Launched on June 25, 1910, the steel bulk freighter THEODORE H. WICKWIRE, JR. was built by the Great Lakes Engineering Works at their St. Clair, Michigan yard for the American Steamship Company, Boland & Cornelius, managers. For this fleet, she served her entire life, carrying ore, grain, stone, sand, coal and gypsum to many Great Lakes ports. In 1932, the vessel was converted to a self-unloader at Lorain, Ohio by the American Shipbuilding Company and renamed b) THUNDER BAY QUARRIES (1). (6,612 GRT).

On October 18, 1936, she came to the rescue of seven sailors clinging to two overturned lifeboats just outside of Cleveland, Ohio harbor. These men had been in the water from 12 to 14 hours after their vessel, the SAND MER-CHANT, had sunk in a storm. The THUNDER BAY QUARRIES had spotted the lifeboats and effected the rescue. Nineteen others were lost.

In 1939, the ship was renamed c) UNITED STATES GYPSUM in honor of the firm for whom she hauled so many cargoes. Toward the end of 1972, the handwriting was on the wall for this once proud vessel. She was relegated to the coal run from Toledo, Ohio to Detroit, Michigan and was not certified by the Coast Guard for trips past Port Huron, Michigan. She grounded at Toledo on November 4, 1972. Her propeller was removed, her wheel locked and she was to finish the season as a barge. Her towing tug, MAINE, collided with the barge on November 10, 1972 near Amherstberg, Ontario and UNITED STATES GYPSUM had to be beached and pumped out. After temporary repairs, she completed the voyage and unloaded her last cargo the next day.

The now "ripe" vessel was sold for scrapping in 1973 and left Quebec with the steamer HENRY G. DALTON in tow of the tug FAIRPLAY X on May 12, 1973. She never made it to the scrap pile for, on May 26, during heavy weather, the tow line broke and she sank in deep water off Sydney, Nova Scotia.

THEODORE H. WICKWIRE, JR., June 25, 1910

Downbound in the St. Mary's River in 1916

THUNDER BAY QUARRIES just after being converted at Lorain, Ohio

THUNDER BAY QUARRIES unloading coal at Toronto

	BUILT:	1910
		Great Lakes Engineering Works,
		St. Clair, Mich.
	HULL NUMBER:	78
a) **Theodore H. Wickwire, Jr.**	*LENGTH:*	504.0
b) **Thunder Bay Quarries (1)**	*BREADTH:*	56.2
c) **UNITED STATES GYPSUM**	*DEPTH:*	26.2
	GRT:	6,077
	REGISTRY NUMBER:	US. 207766
	ENGINES:	22½", 37", 63½" Diameter
		x 42" Stroke
		Triple Expansion
	ENGINE BUILDER:	Shipyard

UNITED STATES GYPSUM downbound in the Detroit River, September 19, 1965

Downbound in Lake St. Clair

Awaiting the tugs to tow her to the scrapyard

VALLEY CAMP

LOUIS W. HILL downbound at the Soo in 1922

The steel bulk freighter LOUIS W. HILL was launched on July 14, 1917 at Lorain, Ohio by the American Shipbuilding Company for the Producers Steamship Company, M. A. Hanna Co., managers. She carried this name and fleet colors until June, 1955, when the Wilson Transit Company swapped its BEN MOREELL (2) for the smaller LOUIS W. HILL and ALBERT E. HEEKIN (a. WILLIAM A. AMBERG) of the Hanna fleet for the Cuyahoga River iron ore trade to Republic Steel. Wilson promptly renamed them b) VALLEY CAMP and c) SILVER BAY, respectively. Two years later, in 1957, Wilson sold six boats to Republic Steel Corporation after taking over Great Lakes Steamship Co.

Both vessels were relatively small — and the VALLEY CAMP was still a coal burner — when Republic sold her to Le Sault de Sainte Marie Historical Sites, Inc., early in 1968 for $10,000. She had been laid up at Duluth, Minnesota the previous season.

"She will be a floating museum." These words, and a drive beyond telling, brought the vessel to fruition as a museum at Sault Ste. Marie, Michigan. In tow of the Roen tug JOHN PURVES, the VALLEY CAMP arrived at the Soo on July 3, 1968 amid a fanfare that had not been seen there in many a day. After hard labor, a few coats of paint, many sleepless nights and pestering recurring problems for those involved, the VALLEY CAMP opened as a museum at the site of the former Kemp's Coal Dock.

She now lies in a slip in a more permanent berth at the foot of Johnstone Street behind the Pullar Ice-Skating Arena and next to the Famous Soo Locks Boat Tour dock, a fitting and (hopefully) lasting memorial and museum. There are guided tours, come rain or shine, that take visitors from the pilot house to the engine room, and a huge portion of her former cargo hold is now festooned with shipping company flags, life rings, photographs and models of ships and artifacts. Even the lifeboats (what's left of them) of the EDMUND FITZGERALD are preserved for visitors' inspection. The VALLEY CAMP still lives.

Downbound entering the Rock Cut in the lower St. Mary's River

VALLEY CAMP in Wilson colors upbound in the Detroit River in 1956

In the Cuyahoga River, Cleveland with tug NEBRASKA

VALLEY CAMP upbound at the Soo, August 5, 1962

Arriving at the Soo from Duluth to become a museum. Tug JOHN PURVES ahead

a) Louis W. Hill	b) VALLEY CAMP
BUILT:	1917
	American Shipbuilding Co.,
	Lorain, Ohio
HULL NUMBER:	721
LENGTH:	525.0
BREADTH:	58.0
DEPTH:	31.0
GRT:	7,038
REGISTRY NUMBER:	US. 215518
ENGINES:	23½", 38", 63" Diameter x
	42" Stroke
	Triple Expansion
ENGINE BUILDER:	Shipyard

Today as a Museum Ship

VERNON

It has been said that the wooden passenger and freight propellor VERNON was built with too much sheer and too little beam. It was also said by her one survivor that she was very heavily loaded on her final voyage. In any event, she had lasted just fourteen months when tragedy ended her brief career.

The VERNON was built in Chicago, Illinois by J. P. Smith during the Summer of 1886 for the A. Booth Company, intended for a route running the length of Lake Michigan between Chicago and Manistique, Michigan. These plans changed when the propellor A. BOOTH was lost on her Lake Superior run, and VERNON was sent north in September to run between Duluth, Minnesota and Port Arthur, Ontario.

For the season of 1887, she was engaged to tow ore schooners between Lake Superior and Cleveland, Ohio, but she was attached by Captain John Pridgeon for damages for having put one of her consorts on the rocks in the Straits of Mackinac. The VERNON was very soon resold to

Booth and was then chartered to Northern Michigan Lines, to replace their CHAMPLAIN, which had been very badly damaged by fire off Fisherman's Island, near Charlevoix, Michigan. The CHAMPLAIN's route, resumed by VERNON, was between Chicago, Illinois, Milwaukee, Wisconsin and Cheboygan, Michigan with stops at intermediate ports.

On October 28, 1887, on a return trip from Cheboygan the VERNON came through the Manitou Passage in the afternoon, making a stop at Good Harbor Bay. She then passed Sleeping Bear and headed across the lake, presumably for Manitowoc, Wisconsin, the weather then being fair. At about 9:00 p.m., a gale sprang up from the northeast, and, after a long night of grim struggle with the seas, the VERNON foundered during the early morning hours of October 29th, just a few miles off Two Rivers, Wisconsin. Axel Stone, fireman, was the sole survivor. Thirty-six perished.

VERNON backing away from her dock

BUILT:	1886	*DEPTH:*	18.8
	J. P. Smith,	*GRT:*	694
	Chicago, Ill.	*REGISTRY NUMBER:*	US. 161557
LENGTH:	158.7	*ENGINES:*	Unknown
BREADTH:	25.5	*ENGINE BUILDER:*	Unknown

VIGILANT

The wooden tug VIGILANT was launched on April 23, 1896 at Port Huron, Michigan by the Jenks Shipbuilding Company with A. M. Carpenter as the master builder, for the Huron Transportation Company. Her engine was formerly in the large river tug ALANSON SUMNER. In 1898, H. N. Loud & Sons of Au Sable, Michigan purchased her to tow log rafts to their mill at Oscoda, Michigan. In 1899, the Thompson Towing & Wrecking Company of Port Huron bought the vessel. This firm was one of the many that merged into the conglomerate known as the Great Lakes Towing Company in 1900. In 1901, VIGILANT again changed hands, this time going to the Nestor Estate.

The Calvin Transportation Company of Ogdensburg,

New York acquired the tug in 1909, and then the Daly-Hannan Dredging Company did likewise in 1911. The Norton-Griffiths Dredging Company Ltd., purchased the steam tug in 1913, renamed her b) MUSCALLONGE (C. 133752; 360 gross tons) and had her registered at St. John, New Brunswick. Roger Miller & Company of Prince Edward Island were her owners in 1916 and Sincennes MacNaughton (Sin-Mac) in 1917. After nine different owners, the MUSCALLONGE no longer traded hands. She served this firm until her career ended at Brockville, Ontario on August 15, 1936, when she was consumed by fire and reduced to ashes. Her remains were disposed of in quick order.

VIGILANT in the St. Clair River

	BUILT:	1896
		Jenks Shipbuilding Co.,
		Port Huron, Mich.
	LENGTH:	128.0
	BREADTH:	24.5
a) **VIGILANT**	DEPTH:	12.0
b) **Muscallonge**	GRT:	372
	REGISTRY NUMBER:	US. 161767
	ENGINES:	20", 38" Diameter x 32" Stroke
		Steeple Compound
	ENGINE BUILDER:	King Iron Works
		Buffalo, New York, 1872

VIGILANT as a rafting tug

MUSCALLONGE at Prince Edward Island

WELLANDOC (2)

SHERBROOKE at Milwaukee

Launched on November 25, 1922, the steel-hulled, canal-sized bulk carrier EDWARD L. STRONG was built for the George Hall Coal and Shipping Company Ltd., Montreal at Three Rivers, Quebec by Fraser Brace, Ltd. She was acquired in 1926 by Canada Steamship Lines Ltd., Montreal, and renamed b) SHERBROOKE in 1927.

The steamer served the C. S. L. fleet until the outbreak of the Second War. She was chartered from 1940 until 1945 by the British Ministry of War Transport for service on salt water, and remained in deep-sea service long after the cessation of hostilities. C. S. L. sold her in 1946 to the Cia. Ponca de Vapores, Panama, and she was renamed c) AROSA. Still on salt water in 1951, she was sold in that year to the Cia. Finanzioria Agricola Commerciale & Industriale, of Naples, Italy, and they renamed her d) IDA O.

Looking for additional canal-sized tonnage as a result of

wartime losses, N. M. Paterson and Sons Ltd., Fort William, found IDA O. in 1952 and purchased her. She was brought back to the lakes and renamed e) WELLANDOC (2). By this time, she looked rather different than she had when she first sailed the lakes for, during her years on salt water, her pilothouse and texas cabin, which had originally been located on the forecastle, were moved back to a position abaft the first hatch.

The Paterson fleet operated WELLANDOC for several years but, with the opening of the St. Lawrence Seaway in 1959, she, as well as many other canallers, became excess tonnage. WELLANDOC was sold in 1961 to A. Newman and Company, a St. Catharines scrap dealer. She lay in Muir's Pond, above Lock One at Port Dalhousie, until she was finally cut up for scrap in the Port Dalhousie drydock during 1963.

With PENETANG in Winter Quarters at Toronto

WELLANDOC downbound in the Detroit River, July 11, 1953

a) Edward L. Strong	**b) Sherbrooke**	**c) Arosa**	*DEPTH:*	18.0
			GRT:	2,077
BUILT:	1922		*REGISTRY NUMBER:*	C. 150823
	Fraser Brace & Co. Ltd.,		*ENGINES:*	17", 32", 56" Diameter x
	Three Rivers, P. Q.			36" Stroke
HULL NUMBER:	19			Triple Expansion
LENGTH:	250.7		*ENGINE BUILDER:*	Worthington Pump & Machinery
BREADTH:	43.2			Corporation
				Ampere, New Jersey

In the old St. Lawrence River Canals

FREDERICK B. WELLS

This many-named steel bulk freighter was launched on October 5, 1901 as FREDERICK B. WELLS at South Chicago, Illinois by the Chicago Shipbuilding Company for the Peavey Steamship Company, Wolvin & Co., managers, primarily for the grain trade.

In 1916, the Reiss Steamship Company of Sheboygan, Wisconsin purchased the vessel for the coal and iron ore trades and renamed it b) OTTO M. REISS (1). In 1918, the tonnage of the vessel was changed to 4,463 gross tons and in 1923 to 4,378 gross tons, primarily to reflect the addition of an after deck house above her original sunken quarters. The Chicago Navigation Company acquired the vessel, which was idled by the Great Depression, in 1931 and, later the same year, the Gartland Steamship Company (Sullivan & Co., Managers) purchased the vessel and renamed her c) SULLIVAN BROTHERS (1) in 1934. This transaction apparently was part of a trade for the steamer LYNFORD E.

GEER, later the OTTO M. REISS (2). The steamer was a familiar sight to all boat watchers who liked to see the huge columns of smoke pour from her smokestack and listen to her triple chime whistle. In 1958, Gartland renamed her the d) HENRY R. PLATT, JR. (1) shortly before her retirement.

The Pillsbury Company of Buffalo, New York, the well-known flour miller, purchased the PLATT, JR. in 1959 to use as a grain storage barge at Buffalo, and renamed the vessel e) PILLSBURY'S BARGE in 1960. She acted in this capacity, never leaving Buffalo Harbor, until 1966. The vessel was then purchased by Marine Salvage Ltd., of Port Colborne, Ontario, renamed f) PILLSBURY and taken to Lake Michigan for use as a breakwater at the newly constructed port of Burns Harbor, Indiana. She was filled with stone and sunk there as part of a dock, where she remains to this day.

FREDERICK B. WELLS upbound in the St. Clair River

At the Soo in 1913

FREDERICK B. WELLS in Reiss colors alongside the FRANK H. PEAVEY

FREDERICK B. WELLS,   b) Otto M. Reiss (1),   c) Sullivan Brothers (1),
d) Henry R. Platt, Jr. (1),   e) Pillsbury's Barge,   f) Pillsbury

BUILT:	1901	*GRT:*	4,897
	Chicago Shipbuilding Co.,	*REGISTRY NUMBER:*	US. 121208
	Chicago, Ill.	*ENGINES:*	15", 23¾", 36½", 56" Diameter
HULL NUMBER:	50		x 40" Stroke
LENGTH:	430.0		Quadruple Expansion
BREADTH:	50.2	*ENGINE BUILDER:*	Shipyard
DEPTH:	24.5		

OTTO M. REISS upbound in the Detroit River

SULLIVAN BROTHERS upbound, leaving the locks at the Soo

HENRY R. PLATT, JR. downbound in the St. Clair River

PILLSBURY'S BARGE at Buffalo

PILLSBURY, October 6, 1966

WESTERN RESERVE

The steel bulk freighter WESTERN RESERVE was launched on October 20, 1890 at Cleveland, Ohio by the Cleveland Shipbuilding Company for Captain Peter Minch. The most outstanding feature of this vessel's life was its unfortunate demise.

Late in August, 1892, Captain Peter Minch, his wife and daughter and one of his sons, a boy of ten, and Mrs. Minch's sister and her daughter, climbed aboard the WESTERN RESERVE in Cleveland for a combination pleasure and business trip to Two Harbors, Minnesota. The vessel was in ballast and was to pick up a cargo of iron ore. The trip as far as Whitefish Bay in Lake Superior was delightful but uneventful.

While WESTERN RESERVE was on the bay, a moderate wind began kicking up and the captain decided to drop the anchor and study the weather. The wind and waves showed no signs of increasing, so it was decided to weigh anchor and proceed on out into the open lake. Late in the evening of August 30, the vessel rode into a full gale. Shortly after, a loud crack was heard and a fissure appeared on the deck ahead of the boiler house. This began to widen with the continual pounding the ship took in the now heavy seas. Suddenly, with almost a deafening roar, the vessel broke in two. Within ten minutes, the seemingly staunch vessel slipped beneath the waves.

A metal lifeboat and a wooden yawl managed to survive the plunge of the sinking ship and all the crew of 21 and six passengers scrambled into them. The wooden yawl held 18, the metal boat nine. Five of the crew went down with the ship. It was then discovered that the metal boat was in a sinking condition. As the people in the wooden yawl tried to transfer the others into their already overcrowded boat, only two, the youngster and another man made it.

The wooden yawl managed to survive for a period of time until it was turned over and engulfed by waves as it reached the shore outside of Grand Marais, Michigan. Only two survived the capsizing, the young boy and one seaman. The boy's strength ebbed quickly and he too sank beneath the waves. The seaman, Harry Stewart, managed to reach shore where he lay exhausted. Finally, he was able to walk the ten miles to the Deer Park Life Saving Station where he told his story. The bodies of 16 people washed ashore, including four of the Minch family.

After the sinking of the WESTERN RESERVE and its near sister, the W. H. GILCHER, two months later, it was determined that the structural steel used in these vessels was brittle and from then on, more close attention was paid to the tempering of steel used in shipbuilding so that vessels could withstand the sometimes violent twisting and pounding without cracking.

WESTERN RESERVE at the dock

BUILT:	1890
	Cleveland Shipbuilding Co.,
	Cleveland, Ohio
HULL NUMBER:	13
LENGTH:	300.7
BREADTH:	41.2
DEPTH:	21.0
GRT:	2,392
REGISTRY NUMBER:	US. 81294
ENGINES:	24", 38", 61" Diameter x
	42" Stroke
	Triple Expansion
ENGINE BUILDER:	Shipyard

WESTERN RESERVE upbound light

WESTERN STATES

WESTERN STATES — artist's conception

Early in 1901, the Detroit & Buffalo Navigation Company decided to build two identical overnight, steel-hulled passenger boats to run from Detroit, Michigan to Buffalo, New York. Frank E. Kirby of the Detroit Shipbuilding Company designed the two vessels which were to be named WESTERN WORLD and EMPIRE STATE. The ships were ordered and their keels laid but the names given them were WESTERN STATES and EASTERN STATES. The WESTERN STATES was launched at Wyandotte, Michigan on January 18, 1902.

In 1904, the Detroit & Cleveland Navigation Company took over the vessels and, for the time being, left them on the Detroit-to-Buffalo run. When larger ships were put into service, the WESTERN STATES went on the Detroit/Mackinac Island/Chicago Division, running cruises in competition with the Georgian Bay Line. The company also operated charter cruises to the Soo and various ports carrying, on many occasions, the Detroit Chamber of Commerce.

After World War II, the WESTERN STATES ran for a while to Put-In-Bay and the Lake Erie Islands from Detroit, sometimes also filling in for another vessel to Buffalo or Cleveland. In 1955, after the dissolution of the D&C fleet, she was towed to Tawas City, Michigan on Lake Huron to become a floating hotel. Overnighter Inc. of Tawas City was her owner and the vessel was unofficially renamed b) OVERNITER. When the "flotel" idea proved to be unprofitable, Siegel Iron & Metal Company of Detroit purchased the ship in 1958.

Before the OVERNITER could be taken away for scrap, the aging vessel burned at the dock at Tawas City on March 31, 1959 and was declared a total loss. The Bay City Scrap Company took over ownership of the hulk, had it towed to Bay City, Michigan and dismantled it at the old Davidson shipyard slip during July and August of that year.

Upbound in the Detroit River past Belle Isle

389

WESTERN STATES upbound in the Detroit River (notice the white forecastle)

Another view of WESTERN STATES

As the S. S. OVERNITER at Tawas City

BUILT:	1902
	Detroit Shipbuilding Co.,
	Wyandotte, Mich.
HULL NUMBER:	145
LENGTH:	350.0
BREADTH:	44.0
DEPTH:	19.9
GRT:	3,077
REGISTRY NUMBER:	US. 81811
ENGINES:	52", 72", 72" Diameter x
	84" Stroke
	Inclined 3 cylinder
ENGINE BUILDER:	Shipyard

WESTERN STATES being scrapped at Bay City in 1959

WHITE STAR

WHITE STAR in C.S.L. colors

The iron-hulled, beam-engined, sidewheel passenger steamer WHITE STAR was built in 1897 at Montreal. She was powered by one of the twin engines from the Allan Line tug ROCKET, which had been rebuilt in 1892 as BRITANNIC. WHITE STAR was first documented in 1898, with her builder, W. C. White, of Montreal, shown as her owner. In 1899, she was acquired by Capt. W. W. Paterson, of Oakville, Ontario, for the Oakville Navigation Company, and she was placed in service between Toronto, Oakville and Hamilton.

During the season of 1901, WHITE STAR was chartered to the International Navigation Company, Buffalo, for service on the Niagara River to the Pan American Exposition at Buffalo. The charter, however, lasted for only part of the season and, late in the year, WHITE STAR was reportedly sold to the Dunkirk (New York) Cruising Club, which proposed to rename her CITY OF DUNKIRK. The sale was never completed, and she returned to her old route on Lake Ontario in 1902.

On July 11, 1903, WHITE STAR was seriously damaged in a fire of suspicious origin, which broke out whilst she was moored at her dock at the foot of Bay Street, Toronto. The hull was abandoned, and was later purchased by Charles Mignault, of Montreal, and the Montreal firm known as the St. Lawrence and Ontario Navigation Company. Towed to Cornwall, Ontario, she was rebuilt there in 1905 by Oliver Gillespie and shortened 9'1" in the process. (308 gross tons)

In 1908, WHITE STAR was owned by the St. Lawrence Canadian Navigation Company Ltd., Montreal, of which Alexandre Desmarteaux was manager. She was placed on the route between Montreal and Quebec, and ran there, along with IMPERIAL, (a) SOVEREIGN, in opposition to the long-established service of the Richelieu and Ontario Navigation Company Ltd., Montreal. This opposition service was not successful and, by 1910, still under the management of Desmarteaux, WHITE STAR was running from Montreal to King Edward Park for the King Edward Park Company.

In 1915, WHITE STAR was traded to Canada Steamship Lines Ltd., Montreal, in exchange for its ferry BOUCHER-VILLE. C. S. L. placed WHITE STAR on a service from Toronto to Oakville, Hamilton and Jordan Harbour, and later operated her on Hamilton Bay, running from downtown Hamilton to Wabasso Park.

WHITE STAR burned while in winter quarters at Hamilton on March 1, 1926. The burned-out hull was purchased in 1927 by Capt. John F. Sowards of Kingston, and he converted her into a coal barge (224 gross tons). She operated for Sowards until 1940, when she was abandoned and her registry closed. For many years, the hull lay in the inlet behind the De Wattville Island Range Lights.

The remains of WHITE STAR were purchased in 1949 by the Simpson Sand Company Ltd., of Brockville, and the hull was towed to the Simpson yard, where it was rebuilt as a sandsucker and equipped with a diesel engine. Remeasured as 160.6 x 25.4 x 8.1, (286 gross tons), she returned to service in 1950 as b) S. M. DOUGLAS. She operated in the Upper St. Lawrence River area, and was acquired in 1968 by Black Douglas Contractors Ltd., of Ivy Lea, Ontario.

S. M. DOUGLAS, by then having passed three-quarters of a century in lake and river service, lay idle at Brockville in 1973, and was finally dropped from the Canadian register in 1974. The hull has since been moved to various locations in the upper river and, most recently, was reported as being used as a breakwater in the Kingston area.

WHITE STAR, b) S. M. Douglas

BUILT:	1897
	W. C. White,
	Montreal, P. Q.
LENGTH:	167.2
BREADTH:	25.3
DEPTH:	8.2
GRT:	451
REGISTRY NUMBER:	C. 103961
ENGINES:	35" Diameter x 96" Stroke
	Beam
ENGINE BUILDER:	W. Smith
	Montreal, P. Q.

WHITE STAR at Quebec

S. M. DOUGLAS at Brockville, July 27, 1963

CHARLES M. WHITE

MOUNT MANSFIELD at a dock on the coast

During World War II, many standard-design ships were built, including the C4-S-A4 class cargo ships. In 1951, three of these cargo ships were modified for service on the Great Lakes by the Nicholson-Universal Steamship Company (70% owned by Republic Steel Corporation) to plans prepared by the J. J. Henry Company. These three sister ships were named TOM M. GIRDLER, CHARLES M. WHITE, and TROY H. BROWNING (later THOMAS F. PATTON), and came to the lakes in that order. Among shipwatchers, the trio quickly became known as the "red tomatoes" because of their huge reddish-orange funnels. In Cleveland shipping circles, they became known as the hermaphrodites (a 2-masted vessel square-rigged forward and schooner-rigged aft) as a result of their design.

The CHARLES M. WHITE was built as a) MOUNT MANSFIELD at Vancouver, Washington by Kaiser Company, Inc. for the U. S. Maritime Commission (American President Lines, operator). After the war, many of the C-4 cargo ships became surplus, and these ships were laid up in the James River, Virginia reserve fleet. The Maryland Drydock Company converted five of these ships in total for Great Lakes use, including the JOSEPH H. THOMPSON (a. MARINE ROBIN) and MCKEE SONS (a. MARINE ANGEL) from C4-S-B2 fast troop transports.

The existing turbine propulsion machinery was overhauled. The original vessel was cut in half, and the stern section cut down to a new depth of 35 feet. All new equipment was installed to conform to requirements for Great Lakes services, but the vessels retained their saltwater DC electrical systems. The original bow section was scrapped and a new bow of fuller form was constructed and connected to the modified after section. This new section was built by Ingalls Shipbuilding Co. at Pascagoula, Mississippi and towed to Baltimore where it was joined and outfitted. Superstructure above the forecastle deck and poop deck was fabricated and stowed on the spar deck for bridge clearance during delivery.

The WHITE was christened at Baltimore on September 20, 1951, and then towed to New Orleans, Louisiana, pushed up the Mississippi River by the towboat H. A. BAYLESS and towed through the Chicago Sanitary Canal to the South Chicago yard of the American Shipbuilding Company. This yard also built the forward passenger house and the funnel. The wheelhouse was constructed in Baltimore and erected at South Chicago where the CHARLES M. WHITE entered service early in the 1952 season. The conversion of the other two boats was accomplished in a similar manner, with the GIRDLER making a few trips in late 1951 and the BROWNING commencing service later in 1952. The new registered dimensions were: 585.0' x 71.6' x 35.0'; 9,115 gross tons.

Republic Steel Corporation remained the owner of the three sisters throughout their entire lives on the Great Lakes. The Nicholson-Universal Steamship Company (T. H. Browning, manager) was the operator until 1955 when Wilson Marine Transit Company won the Republic iron ore hauling contract and took over as operator. When this happened there were only minor visible changes in the vessels; their huge red funnels still made them stand out in striking contrast to other ships. In 1957, six smaller vessels were added to the Republic fleet when Wilson purchased Great Lakes Steamship Co.

One interesting highlight of the career of the WHITE was when the vessel was in several "unofficial" races with the steamer CLIFFS VICTORY in 1953. In July, the two ships raced upbound on Lake Huron and Lake Superior, and in early August came down Lake Huron loaded with iron ore. Although the Cleveland newspapers declared the WHITE the winner, both skippers, Captain C. R. "Let-her-go" Gallagher of the VICTORY and Captain John Tonge of the WHITE, declared that their vessels were not operating at maximum speed. Captain Gallagher had a reputation for living up to his nickname, however, and Captain Tonge was immensely proud of the WHITE after years sailing the old

Nicholson-Universal and Browning boats, so it seems likely that the pair did enter into an "all-out" test to determine the fastest cargo vessel on the Great Lakes.

In 1972, Wilson Marine Transit Company lost the Republic contract and went out of business. The WHITE and her sisters were then chartered to Cleveland-Cliffs Steamship Company from 1973 to 1980 while they held the Republic business. They were all painted in the traditional Cliffs color scheme — black funnels with a huge red "C" and olive green superstructure.

Because of their small carrying capacity (14,000 gross tons at mid-summer draft) and high fuel costs, Cleveland-Cliffs dropped their charter early in the 1980 season when business slumped. All three ships had been fitted out at the beginning of the season, but the PATTON's orders were cancelled and she never left Toledo. The GIRDLER sailed briefly until May, and then tied up at the old B&O coal dock up the Black River in Lorain. On June 19, 1980 the WHITE cleared the Upper Republic docks at the head of the Cuyahoga River in Cleveland, and went to Lorain for layup alongside the GIRDLER. Ironically, her last trip

was up the river that probably caused her early demise. When converted, the three vessels were designed for the Cuyahoga's depth and curving course, but had become obsolete by the time they could traverse the river. If they had been converted with deeper hulls, they probably could have been lengthened (much like the JOSEPH A. THOMPSON was originally converted — 714 feet in overall length with a depth of 38'6") and avoided the hermaphrodite label.

Republic Steel was in the process of adopting all self-unloader deliveries through a new terminal in Lorain, Ohio and quickly disposed of the vessels for scrapping overseas. The WHITE departed Lorain on August 24, 1980 in tow of the tug SALVAGE MONARCH. Catching up to the PATTON at Quebec City, the pair departed in tandem tow of the West German tug FAIRPLAY IX and arrived at Karachi, Pakistan on December 23rd. They were sold to Metal Scrap Trade Corp., Ltd. of India for dismantling by Haryama Steel Company. Scrapping on the WHITE began in January 1982 at Bombay, India. Along with her outstanding speed, this great laker probably holds the unofficial record for most miles towed anywhere for a Great Lakes freighter.

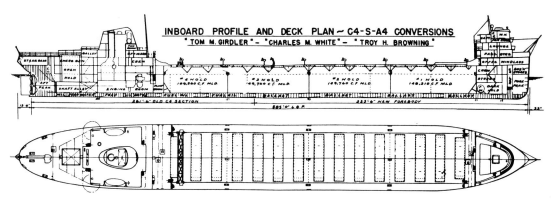

Inboard profile and deck plan — C4-S-A4 conversions

a) Mount Mansfield
b) CHARLES M. WHITE

BUILT:	1946
	Kaiser Company, Inc.,
	Vancouver, Washington
HULL NUMBER:	516
LENGTH:	497.2
BREADTH:	71.7
DEPTH:	29.9
GRT:	10,654
REGISTRY NUMBER:	US. 249263
ENGINES:	2 cylinder turbine
ENGINE BUILDER:	Joshua Hendy Iron Works
	Vancouver, Washington

CHARLES M. WHITE at Ashtabula in her first year of operation

CHARLES M. WHITE downbound in the St. Mary's River, August 13, 1973

Being towed out of Lorain by the tug SALVAGE MONARCH, August 24, 1980

Being scrapped at Bombay in 1982

WIARTON (1)

One of several American steel canallers built after the turn of the century, the JOHN SHARPLES (US. 77587) had a long and varied career. She was launched on June 13, 1903 at West Superior, Wisconsin by the Superior Shipbuilding Company for A. B. Wolvin's Great Lakes & St. Lawrence Transportation Company for service between Duluth, Minnesota, Chicago, Illinois and St. Lawrence River ports. JOHN SHARPLES was one of ten identical canallers built for Wolvin, the largest group of sistership canallers ever built at Great Lakes shipyards.

On December 9, 1910, she stranded on Galops Island on Lake Ontario, 9 miles from Main Duck Island. The vessel was in such bad condition that she was abandoned to the underwriters. Reid & Baker became her joint owners and attempted salvage. They were successful after many setbacks and the SHARPLES was released, taken to Buffalo, New York and repaired by the Buffalo Dry Dock Company. In a way, the stranding was fortunate, because all her sisterships were taken to the East Coast and served during World War I under the French flag. JOHN SHARPLES was the only one not sent overseas. Reid and Baker were successful in selling the steamer in 1916 to the Charcoal Iron Company of America who converted her to a crane-equipped freighter. This firm renamed her b) CICOA, an acronym for the company name. Her history then became more involved.

The U.S. Government took over the vessel in 1917, and removed the deck cranes, intending to take her to the coast to serve in a wartime capacity. They did this, but the war ended before the vessel could be made ready for war service. CICOA went to the Paisley Steamship Company of Cleveland, Ohio in 1919. The Waukau Transit Company, also of Cleveland, took over ownership later the same year. In June, 1920, she was sold Canadian, (C. 150231) to the

Glen Transportation Company, Ltd. (Mathews Steamship Company, managers). In 1923, the vessel was renamed c) GLENVEGAN in conformity with James Playfair's method of naming vessels; Playfair had combined with Mathews in a joint venture, operating several ships together.

The GLENVEGAN carried this name until 1925, when Playfair and Mathews broke up the joint venture. Mathews Steamship Company took over and renamed the vessel d) WIARTON (1) that same season. When Mathews went into receivership in 1931, Frederick C. Clarkson was named receiver. During the interim, WIARTON was used as a storage barge for grain by Toronto Elevators Ltd. in 1932 and 1933. R. Scott Misener purchased the WIARTON in 1933 and resold her to Nicholson Transit Company of Detroit, Michigan the following year.

Again in American registry, (1,588 GRT), Nicholson renamed the vessel e) FLEETWOOD (2) to be used in the scrap metal trade. She carried a variety of other cargoes as well and survived the Great Depression. In 1939, the FLEETWOOD was altered slightly. Her dimensions were: 246.7 x 41.2 x 15.7; 1,593 gross tons.

FLEETWOOD's World War II career was interesting, but fortunately without serious injury. In 1941, she went to the coast. In 1943, she was back on the lakes under direction of the U.S. War Shipping Administration which turned the vessel over to the U.S. Maritime Commission that year. This agency brought her back to the coast in 1944 and then transferred it under charter to the British Ministry of War Transport under management of Montreal Shipping Ltd. In 1945, FLEETWOOD went to the U.S. Navy Department. They kept her until 1947, when she again reverted to the U.S. War Shipping Administration. After all this shuffling, the now exhausted FLEETWOOD was scrapped on the East Coast in 1947.

JOHN SHARPLES upbound in the St. Clair River

CICOA upbound at the Soo in 1917

GLENVEGAN upbound in the St. Mary's River in 1924

WIARTON in Toronto, Winter of 1931-1932

a) John Sharples   b) Cicoa   c) Glenvegan

d) WIARTON (1)   e) Fleetwood (2)

BUILT:	1903
	Superior Shipbuilding Co.,
	Superior, Wisc.
HULL NUMBER:	507
LENGTH:	255.0
BREADTH:	41.0
DEPTH:	18.0
GRT:	1,614
REGISTRY NUMBER:	C. 150231
ENGINES:	14", 25", 42" Diameter x
	30" Stroke
	Triple Expansion
ENGINE BUILDER:	Shipyard

FLEETWOOD at Ecorse

FRANCIS WIDLAR

FRANCIS WIDLAR downbound at Mission Point in 1919

Hull 421 of the American Shipbuilding Company's Cleveland yard was a steel bulk carrier launched on April 7, 1904 for the Columbia Steamship Company, Cleveland, which was managed by W. H. Becker. She was christened FRANCIS WIDLAR. Transferred by 1920 to the Valley Steamship Company, her service in the Becker fleet came to an end on November 12, 1920 when she stranded in eastern Lake Superior on Pancake Shoal near Coppermine Point.

The WIDLAR's crew was rescued safely despite the battering that the wreck suffered in the heavy seas. Abandoned to the underwriters, the ship spent the winter on Pancake Shoal but was refloated during 1921 by the Reid Wrecking Company and taken to Batchawana, Ontario for temporary patching. She was eventually towed to Port Arthur for full repairs. On October 12, 1922, while at the Port Arthur shipyard, she was purchased by the Mathews Steamship Company Ltd., Toronto. Renamed b) BAYTON (C. 141675) she was taken to Collingwood for further repairs.

The Mathews Steamship Company Ltd. went into receivership on January 8, 1931 and BAYTON ran spasmodically in 1931, 1932 and 1933 under charter to Toronto Elevators Ltd. Along with the remaining Mathews boats, BAYTON was purchased late in 1933 by Capt. Robert Scott Misener, who registered her to his Colonial Steamships Ltd., of Port Colborne, Ontario. In 1952, she was reboilered with second-hand boilers taken from the wartime corvette H.M.C.S. DUNDAS.

BAYTON received a new pilothouse during the winter of 1957-58, and was transferred in 1959 to Scott Misener Steamships Ltd. Suffering a variety of problems related to her advanced age, she was retired in 1965 and was sold to Marine Salvage Ltd., Port Colborne, which had her towed to its Ramey's Bend scrapyard. There, in 1966, the boilers were removed for installation in SHELTER BAY (2). BAYTON was towed from Port Colborne on September 5, 1966 and taken to Burns Harbor, Indiana where she was sunk along with several other old steamers as part of a breakwater Her hull broke in two sections during 1967, but still lies today in the same location.

	a) FRANCIS WIDLAR	b) Bayton
BUILT:	1904 American Shipbuilding Co., Cleveland, Ohio	
HULL NUMBER:	421	
LENGTH:	416.0	
BREADTH:	50.0	
DEPTH:	28.0	
GRT:	4,682	
REGISTRY NUMBER:	US. 200910	
ENGINES:	22", 35", 58" Diameter x 40" Stroke Triple Expansion	
ENGINE BUILDER:	Shipyard	

BAYTON in Mathews colors in 1926

In Lake St. Clair, July 15, 1950

BAYTON upbound in Lake Huron, June 9, 1960

At Ramey's Bend awaiting scrap with GEORGE H. INGALLS in 1966

402

HORACE S. WILKINSON

This steel bulk freighter was a first in lake transportation in the 1960's as an experiment which, by all accounts, was a failure for many reasons. Nevertheless, she was born a modern laker when launched on April 21, 1917 at Toledo, Ohio by the Toledo Shipbuilding Company for the Great Lakes Steamship Company as HORACE S. WILKINSON. For many years she served nearly flawlessly as a modern carrier for her owners who were proud to possess a ship of her durability. The vessel was a good and profitable carrier.

Wilson Marine Transit Company took over the entire Great Lakes Steamship Company fleet in 1957, divesting itself of a few smaller boats to Republic Steel and the T. J. McCarthy Steamship Company after the purchase. HORACE S. WILKINSON became a member of the Wilson fleet.

Hoping to reduce operating costs and extend the usefulness of the vessel, Wilson converted it to a barge at Fraser Shipyards, Inc., Superior, Wisconsin in 1963. Her new dimensions were: 535.8 x 60.0 x 27.0; 7,598 gross tons. Engine and cabins were removed and the ship's stern notched. The plan was to push the barge in confined areas and tow it on the open lake. After several years, the barge was renamed b) WILTRANCO I. The experiment did not meet the owner's expectations and the vessel was laid up after the 1964 season in Buffalo, New York. The BRIAN McALLISTER had been her tug.

The WILTRANCO I was chartered to Bulk Navigation & Transportation Company in 1966 and 1967, primarily for the Lake Erie coal trade, and was pushed/towed by the new tug FRANCES A. SMALL, built for this particular barge. The vessel met with a few mishaps that did not endear her to the sailing community. She was awkward to handle while being pushed and stubborn while being towed. On one occasion she sank in the Black Rock Canal at Buffalo, New York and, on another, was blown aground and abandoned near Hamburg, New York. Clyde Van Enkevort of the Great Lakes Marine Salvage Company succeeded in salvaging the barge late in 1969 and she was later purchased by the Escanaba Towing Company.

The barge was renamed c) WILTRANCO and returned to service in 1970, the tug LEE RUEBEN now her consort. Escanaba Towing discontinued operations in 1973 and their vessels were sold at auction. WILTRANCO was eventually acquired by Marine Salvage Ltd., of Port Colborne, Ontario and was resold for dismantling overseas. The WILTRANCO arrived at Santander, Spain on September 21, 1973 in tow of the tug FAIRPLAY X, along with another laker, J. CLARE MILLER. Both vessels were cut up soon after arrival.

HORACE S. WILKINSON at Conneaut about 1925

a) **HORACE S. WILKINSON**
   b) **Wiltranco I**
   c) **Wiltranco**

BUILT:	1917
	Toledo Shipbuilding Co.,
	Toledo, Ohio
HULL NUMBER:	137
LENGTH:	588.3
BREADTH:	60.0
DEPTH:	27.0
GRT:	8,338
REGISTRY NUMBER:	US. 215122
ENGINES:	21½", 30½", 43", 61" Diameter
	x 42" Stroke
	Quadruple Expansion
ENGINE BUILDER:	Shipyard

403

HORACE S. WILKINSON upbound under the Blue Water Bridge, May 19, 1960

As a barge in 1963

WILTRANCO I with tug BRIAN McALLISTER leaving Fraser Shipyard

WILTRANCO downbound in the St. Mary's River, August 12, 1970

H. W. WILLIAMS

In 1885, Henry W. Williams of Benton Harbor, Michigan, a partner in the Graham & Morton firm, left that company and organized a new line between South Haven, Michigan and Chicago, Illinois, starting with the rebuilt CITY OF ST. JOSEPH (1883) which had been damaged by fire the previous year.

The H. W. WILLIAMS, the first new boat constructed for this line, was built at South Haven in 1888 by John Martel, and immediately went on the South Haven-Chicago run where she remained for twenty-two years. In 1897, she was lengthened and rebuilt to 170.8 x 35.2 x 11.5; 691 gross tons. Mr. Williams died in 1901. The company went through a number of changes, being reorganized in 1909 as the "Chicago and South Haven Steamship Company." In July of that year, the H. W. WILLIAMS, a wooden passenger and freight vessel, was sold to Andrew H. Crawford of Saugatuck, Michigan and became the first boat of the Crawford Transportation Company running between Saugatuck and Chicago.

She was renamed b) TENNESSEE in 1910. Her years on this run, however, were short. The Crawford Transportation Company failed in 1912 and, in the spring of 1913, TENNESSEE was sold to Pere Marquette Line Steamers of Manistee, Michigan. She was renamed c) PERE MARQUETTE 8 and assigned to a coastal run from Pentwater to Frankfort, Michigan stopping at Ludington, Manistee, Onekema and Arcadia. The boat was laid up at Manistee following the season of 1924 and burned to a total loss the night of October 26, 1927.

H. W. WILLIAMS on Lake Michigan

Leaving South Haven

TENNESSEE in Lake Michigan

	BUILT:	1888
		John Martel,
		South Haven, Mich.
	LENGTH:	140.0
a) H. W. WILLIAMS	BREADTH:	28.0
b) Tennessee	DEPTH:	10.3
c) Pere Marquette 8	GRT:	249
	REGISTRY NUMBER:	US. 95952
	ENGINES:	18", 36" Diameter x 30" Stroke
		Fore & Aft Compound
	ENGINE BUILDER:	Wilson & Hendrie
		Montague, Michigan

PERE MARQUETTE 8 in Manistee Harbor

J. T. WING

CHARLES F. GORDON ashore on the East Coast

J. O. WEBSTER on the reef at Key Sal, Bahamas, B.W.I.

J. T. WING at a dock at Port Huron

The last commercial schooner on the Great Lakes, the J. T. WING had an interesting and varied career. The three-masted wooden schooner CHARLES F. GORDON was built by Beazley Brothers at Weymouth, Nova Scotia in 1919 for Richard Beazley of Halifax, Nova Scotia (C. 41455). She was intended as a general cargo vessel but was abandoned to the underwriters five years later when she ran aground in the Bahamas. The schooner was salvaged by J. O. Webster who named her after himself in 1923 b) J. O. WEBSTER (US. 223574) and sailed her for a few years for his Webster Marine Corporation out of Miami, Florida.

Alexander Stockwell of Boston, Massachusetts took over in 1927. He apparently ran the vessel in various and sometimes illegal pursuits until the ship stranded on May 13, 1931 at Norwalk Island, Connecticut. The WEBSTER was not ruined but did no more business for awhile. She does not appear in the List of Merchant Vessels of the U.S. until 1937, when Grant H. Piggott, chairman of the board of the J. T. Wing Company, purchased her and renamed her c) J. T. WING after Jefferson Thurber Wing, founder of the company. From 1939 to 1943, she was unofficially named SSS OLIVER S. PERRY, as a sea scout training vessel which spent most of her time laid up at Marine City, Michigan where she sank at her moorings. Raised in 1943, she was pressed into service again by the Chippewa Timber Company of Sault Ste. Marie, Michigan.

After World War II, the J. T. WING lay rotting in a slip next to the J. W. Westcott Company and adjacent to the Detroit fire tug station just below the Ambassador Bridge. By public subscription, the J. T. WING was purchased by the City of Detroit and towed to a specially dug slip on Belle Isle where her hull was embedded in earth to become Detroit's first marine museum. Here the vessel was refurbished and marine displays gathered for viewing.

Because her timbers were showing signs of deterioration and because a larger building was needed to house the growing number of marine artifacts that were accumulating, the J. T. WING was abandoned. The marine displays were removed and preparation was made to remove the vessel. She was deliberately set afire with a crowd of 6,000 watching on November 3, 1956. A completely new building was constructed, with the help of the Dossin Family of Detroit, and now takes the place of the last commercial schooner on the Great Lakes. The Dossin Marine Museum is a fitting place to keep alive the memory of the J. T. WING and all the other Great Lakes vessels which have passed away.

SSS OLIVER H. PERRY

At the dock at Marine City

Working on the J. T. WING to make her a museum ship

a) Charles F. Gordon   b) J. O. Webster   c) J. T. WING
   d) SSS Oliver H. Perry   e) J. T. Wing

BUILT:	1919 Beazley Brothers, Weymouth, Nova Scotia
LENGTH:	140.5
BREADTH:	33.5
DEPTH:	14.0
GRT:	431
REGISTRY NUMBER:	US. 223574

Detroit's first Marine Museum at Belle Isle

WINONA

This steel bulk carrier and package freighter was built in 1906 by Swan, Hunter and Wigham Richardson Ltd. at Wallsend-on-Tyne, England, for the Winona Steamship Company Ltd., Hamilton, which was managed by R. O. and A. B. McKay. She first appeared on the lakes in September, 1906, and, on October 4, 1906, while on her first trip bound from Fort William to Midland with grain she stranded near Giant's Tomb Island in Georgian Bay. She was released the following day and was taken to Owen Sound for repairs. She cleared Owen Sound on November 16, 1906, but the next day stranded in a blizzard on the Duck Island, near the western tip of Manitoulin Island. Refloated and taken to Collingwood, she was abandoned to the underwriters, but was later repurchased by her former owner and was taken to Detroit for repairs in 1907.

WINONA was taken over by the MacKays' new firm, the Inland Navigation Company Ltd., Hamilton, in 1908 and her owner became known as Inland Lines Ltd. when the fleet was acquired by James Playfair in 1910. WINONA was chartered briefly to the Canada Atlantic Transit Company, but further ownership changes lay waiting for her.

The Playfair interests were merged with the Richelieu and Ontario Navigation Company Ltd., and then into Canada Steamship Lines Ltd., Montreal, when that organization was formed in 1913.

Requisitioned for salt water service in 1915, WINONA carried coal from Great Britain to Sweden from 1918 until 1920, and was returned to the lakes by C.S.L. in 1921. She ran on the lakes and east coast until she was idled by the Great Depression. Reactivated in 1939, she laid up at Toronto that fall with storage coal, but was unloaded and moved to the east coast in November in anticipation of war service on salt water.

WINONA was requisitioned by the British government in 1940 and was sunk that year as a blockship as part of the defense of Zeebrugge, Belgium. Raised and repaired, she was later sold to Chinese owners for Far East service. Acquired by the Lien Yih Steamship Company Ltd., Shanghai, she was renamed b) EDDIE in 1947. Later registered to the Eddie Steamship Company Ltd., she met her end on September 7, 1956, when she stranded and broke in two at Aparri, Luzon in the Philippine Islands.

WINONA downbound in the St. Clair River

a) WINONA	**b) Eddie**		*DEPTH:*	21.3
			GRT:	2,085
BUILT:	1906		*REGISTRY NUMBER:*	C. 122851
	Swan, Hunter & Wigham Richardson Ltd.,		*ENGINES:*	20½", 33", 54" Diameter x
	Wallsend-on-Tyne, England			36" Stroke
HULL NUMBER:	771			Triple Expansion
LENGTH:	252.0		*ENGINE BUILDER:*	MacColl & Pollock Ltd.
BREADTH:	43.5			Sunderland, England

WINONA leaving the locks at the Soo

WINONA at the Soo Locks

WINSLOW (2)

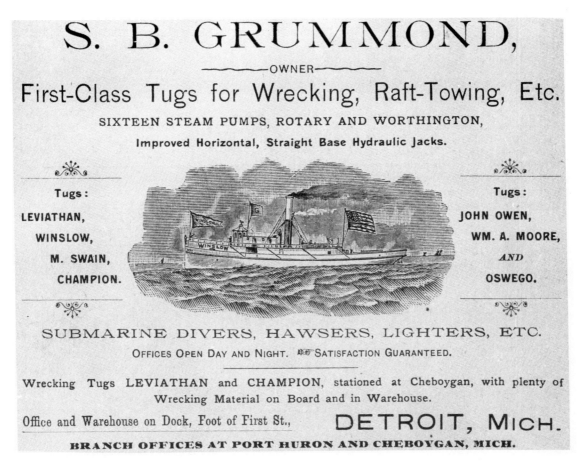

Advertisement for Grummond tugs

WINSLOW in the Davidson drydock at Bay City

The powerful tug WINSLOW was built in 1865 for N. C. and H. J. Winslow of Cleveland, Ohio to replace a similar vessel which had been lost the preceding Fall. The first tug, which bore the same name, was wrecked near the Cleveland piers in a gale on November 7, 1864, and her wreck was raised, but found worthless, so the machinery was refurbished and installed in the new hull just a few months later. The first WINSLOW was only three years old when it was lost.

The new boat became a quick favorite in the towing and rafting business. On her first job, she towed a raft from Penetanguishene to Port Maitland with 240 cribs of timber, enough to fill nineteen canal-size schooners. In 1871 she brought down eleven loaded barges from Saginaw in a single tow.

The WINSLOW was purchased by Ballentine & Crawford of Detroit, Michigan in 1868 and employed largely in towing the barges owned by that firm. In 1873, she was sold to the Grummond tug fleet out of Detroit. Grummond used her for wrecking as well as river towing and rafting; she was usually stationed at the Straits of Mackinac. She suffered a fire at Detroit in November, 1887 which damaged her upper works, but she was soon returned to service.

In April of 1892, the tug was sold to Benjamin Boutell of Bay City, who operated her in his "Saginaw Bay Towing Company" with a variety of other tugs. Boutell rebuilt the WINSLOW in 1892-93, extending her second deck all the way to the stern and increasing her tonnage to 290 gross (129.0 x 22.0 x 17.4). The cabin was also enlarged at this time, the original engines rebuilt as a steeple compound (22" and 40" x 30", 375 horsepower), and the color scheme changed to black.

Boutell ran the ship until 1902, when he disposed of her to the Reid Towing & Wrecking Company of Sarnia, Ontario (C. 96855). In 1907, she was owned by F. F. Pardee of Sarnia. During her last years the WINSLOW was associated with several major salvage jobs, but she ended her days when she went up in smoke at Meldrum Bay, Manitoulin Island on August 21, 1911. The wreck was removed in 1938.

WINSLOW at Tobermory

Assisting MARTIN MULLEN after accident

BUILT:	1865
	Quayle & Martin,
	Cleveland, Ohio
LENGTH:	129.3
BREADTH:	21.9
DEPTH:	10.9
GRT:	237
REGISTRY NUMBER:	US. 26243
SECOND ENGINES:	22", 40" Diameter x
	30" Stroke
	Steeple Compound
ENGINE BUILDER:	Marine Iron Works
	Bay City, Michigan, 1892
	30" x 30"
	Low Pressure
	Original Builder:
	Unknown

WISCONSIN

In all the long history of the Goodrich Transit Company, just one vessel had a "broken" service record, beginning and ending her career under the company's flag, but sailing under several different names and owners during the interim period. This was the iron freight and passenger propellor WISCONSIN of 1881.

During the late 1870's, cross-lake service between Grand Haven, Michigan and Milwaukee, Wisconsin was handled by the Northwestern Transportation Company, under contract with the Detroit, Grand Haven and Milwaukee Railroad. This contract expired in May, 1880 and was then awarded to the Goodrich Transit Company, who put MENOMINEE and DEPERE on the route. Three new iron steamers were ordered from the Wyandotte, Michigan yard of the Detroit Dry Dock Company, the propellors WISCONSIN and MICHIGAN and the sidewheeler CITY OF MILWAUKEE. These were built during the Winter of 1880-81, and entered service the spring of 1881.

The sisters, WISCONSIN and MICHIGAN, being designed for cross-lake winter service, were among the first Lake vessels to be built with double bottoms and fitted with ballast tanks. They were also equipped with reversing gear on their engines, and had full-length passenger cabins.

At the end of the 1882 season, the Detroit, Grand Haven and Milwaukee Railroad did not renew their contract with Goodrich, having decided to operate their own cross-lake service. At about the same time, the Flint and Pere Marquette Railroad, which had been using Goodrich service between Ludington, Michigan and Milwaukee, came to the same decision and ordered construction of the first of their own fleet. The three new Goodrich boats, being thus made surplus, were sold to the D.G.H.&M. for their service between Grand Haven and Milwaukee, beginning April 28, 1883.

On March 20, 1885, the MICHIGAN, having been caught in an ice floe for 40 days, was crushed by the ice and sank, her crew escaping over the ice. The WISCONSIN was also badly damaged by ice but survived, though she had to go into drydock for extensive repairs.

In the spring of 1886, the D.G.H.&M. Railroad again made arrangements to have their cross-lake traffic handled by another company. CITY OF MILWAUKEE was sold to Graham & Morton of Benton Harbor, Michigan, and WISCONSIN was sold to the newly-formed Crosby Transportation Company, which then operated NYACK and WISCONSIN between Muskegon, Grand Haven and Milwaukee, handling the business of the G.R.&I. Railroad, as well as that of the D.G.H.&M.

At the end of the 1898 season, the WISCONSIN was put in the yards and overhauled. She resumed service in early February, 1899, renamed b) NAOMI. She had been back in service for little more than a week when she rescued the crew of the sinking JOHN V. MORAN, a big Crosby package freighter running the same course toward Grand Haven.

A few years later, NAOMI herself was in deep trouble. In the early morning hours of May 21, 1907, enroute from Grand Haven to Milwaukee, she caught fire in mid-lake and was very nearly destroyed. Fortunately, three other steamers were in the vicinity, the KANSAS, D.G. KERR and SAXONA. The KERR, being a steel boat, pushed right up to the burning NAOMI and took off those of the passengers and crew who had not made it into the lifeboats. The KANSAS picked up those in the small boats, and later received the others from the KERR. Nothing could be done about checking the fire, so KANSAS took the survivors to Grand Haven, and the two freighters stood by until the fire burned itself out and the hull cooled down sufficiently. The KERR then took the hull in tow and made way to Grand Haven, arriving about 11 o'clock. NAOMI was later towed to the shipyard of Manitowoc, Wisconsin, where she was completely rebuilt with all-steel upperworks. She was also bustled at this time, increasing her beam by six feet. (Dimensions: 203.9 x 41.1 x 11.7; 1,907 gross tons.) She did not re-enter service until August, 1909, renamed c) E.G. CROSBY (1).

In July of 1918, the E.G. CROSBY was taken over for war duty by the U.S. Shipping Control Committee, was renamed d) GENERAL ROBERT M. O'REILLY, and apparently served for a short time as a hospital ship in New York harbor. A little more than a year later in 1920, her brief service ended, she was back in Lake Michigan this time in the hands of the Chicago, Racine and Milwaukee Line as e) PILGRIM.

She continued in this service, running with the steamer ILLINOIS for three seasons, until June, 1922, when the assets of the Seymour-owned line were taken over by Goodrich Transit Company, and PILGRIM returned to her original owners. Goodrich kept her on this same route between Chicago and Milwaukee, but gave her back her original name f) WISCONSIN in 1924.

On the early morning of October 29, 1929, running 14 miles off Kenosha, Wisconsin in a bad storm, she started to take water. She called for help and finally came to anchor, with fishermen and Coast Guardsmen taking off more than 60 survivors. At 7:10 A.M., her fires out, she went down, with a loss of 16 lives, including her Captain and Chief Engineer.

WISCONSIN in Goodrich colors

WISCONSIN in D.G.H. & M. Ry. colors

NAOMI in the ice

	BUILT:	1881
		Detroit Dry Dock Co.,
		Wyandotte, Mich.
a) Wisconsin	HULL NUMBER:	49
b) Naomi	LENGTH:	203.9
c) E. G. Crosby (1)	BREADTH:	35.1
d) General Robert M. O'Reilly	DEPTH:	11.7
e) Pilgrim	GRT:	1,181
f) WISCONSIN	REGISTRY NUMBER:	US. 80861
	ENGINES:	27", 44", Diameter x
		40" Stroke
		Fore & Aft Compound
	ENGINE BUILDER:	Dry Dock Engine Works
		Detroit, Michigan

NAOMI in Crosby Transportation Co. colors

Crosby Transportation Co.,
Milwaukee-Grand Haven
and Muskegon, Mich.
"Grand Haven Route."

Excursion on Steamer
"E. G. CROSBY"

E. G. CROSBY

GENERAL ROBERT M. O'REILLY

PILGRIM, back in Goodrich colors

418

AUGUSTUS B. WOLVIN

AUGUSTUS B. WOLVIN being unloaded

Nicknamed "the Yellow Kid" because her hull was painted a brilliant yellow, almost orange, the steel bulk freighter AUGUSTUS B. WOLVIN was launched on April 9, 1904 at Lorain, Ohio by the American Shipbuilding Company. It was the largest vessel ever built on the Great Lakes up to that time. This new vessel was said "to revolutionize ship building and Captain Wolvin is responsible for it." He and James C. Wallace of the American Shipbuilding Company had produced a first. She had several unique features that immediately afterwards became standard for lake bulk carrier construction:

"Her cargo hold was hopper shaped to accommodate the new hulett ore unloaders. The shape between the sides of the ship and the sides of the hopper was used for water ballast and extended up the sides to the height of the main deck stringer. The supporting hold stanchions were done away with completely. In their place, a system of girder arches was substituted to provide support to the main deck and the sides of the ship. The thirty-three hatches were spaced with twelve feet centers. She was flush-decked, with only the pilothouse and texas deck forward and the coam-

ings around the engine and boiler openings and dining room skylight aft to break the continuous line of the spar deck."

"Freshwater Whales" by Dr. Richard J. Wright

The WOLVIN entered service that year for Capt. Wolvin's Duluth-based Acme Steamship Company and quickly set cargo records. She was surpassed by longer vessels shortly thereafter but became well known and photographed by sightseers because of her unique color scheme. In 1916, the Interlake Steamship Company, Pickands Mather and Company, managers, took over ownership. In the meantime, she lost her vivid colors and took on the basic iron-ore red, so familiar to most Great Lakes vessels. When new forward cabins and aft superstructure were added, her gross tonnage became 7,403.

In 1966, the WOLVIN was transferred to Canadian registry to the Labrador Steamship Company Ltd., a Canadian subsidiary of Pickands Mather (C. 326401). She did not last long in hauling iron ore from St. Lawrence River ports to Lake Erie ore docks. She was sold for scrap in 1967 and arrived in Santander, Spain with the SASKADOC on September 24, 1967 for dismantling.

BUILT: 1904
American Shipbuilding Co.,
Lorain, Ohio
HULL
NUMBER: 330
LENGTH: 540.0
BREADTH: 56.0
DEPTH: 32.0
GRT: 6,585
REGISTRY
NUMBER: US. 200883
ENGINES: 18½", 28½", 43½", 66"
Diameter x 42" Stroke
Quadruple Expansion
ENGINE
BUILDER: Shipyard

AUGUSTUS B. WOLVIN at Lorain

In Lake St. Clair, August 13, 1938

420

AUGUSTUS B. WOLVIN in the St. Mary's River, August 28, 1958

In the Labrador S.S. colors, July 4, 1966

WYANDOTTE (1892)

On January 28, 1892 Everett N. Clark, the administrator of the Clark Estate, entered into an agreement with the Detroit Dry Dock Company to have Frank E. Kirby draw up a set of plans for a new steel passenger and freight propeller to be named JOHN P. CLARK in honor of an ardent riverboat enthusiast who had passed away in 1880. This hull was built at Wyandotte, Michigan and launched stern first July 16, 1892. It was christened WYANDOTTE instead of CLARK as originally intended with no reason given for the change of name. On October 20, 1892 the WYANDOTTE was delivered to Clark, Ashley, Atchinson et al. of Detroit, Michigan and the vessel began her trips from Detroit to Wyandotte, Grosse Isle, Amherstburg, Ontario and Sugar Island on June 15, 1893.

Besides her regular run downriver each day, WYANDOTTE ran many excursions out of Detroit to Chatham, Wallaceburg, Port Huron, Put-In-Bay and the Lake Erie Islands. In 1903, she was registered to Alice Atchinson, Detroit with Ashley & Dustin as agents. In 1904, the vessel was chartered to run from Buffalo, New York to Crystal Beach, Ontario. Her one mishap occurred when she sank at the dock on March 11, 1904 but was raised on the 14th with no damage.

On March 1, 1905 the WYANDOTTE was sold to the Long Island Railroad with the Montauk Steamboat Company as their operators. She left for New York City on May 27, 1905 after being housed in on the main deck and strengthened throughout. She had been the first vessel to be lifted by the new floating dry dock of the Great Lakes Engineering Works. The vessel arrived at New York in 15 days. Her run was from Orient Point, Long Island to New London, Connecticut and in the winter from New York to New Haven. When the line started to carry automobiles, she was found too small for the route and was sold in 1923 to Theodore H. Kramer of New York. She was sent to Panama as a ferry and placed under Panamanian registry, renamed b) PIZARRO, a name that does not appear on registries but was on the ship.

She came back in 1925 under American registry as c) WYANDOTTE. In 1926, the vessel was renamed again d) CITY OF FORT MYERS, owned by Barron Collier and operated out of Fort Myers, Florida until sold in 1933 to the Tri-State Steamship Company owned by the George Cox Shipyards of New Orleans, Louisiana. These people named her e) DOLPHIN. Her enrollment was surrendered October 30, 1940 at New Orleans as "hull dismantled and cut up."

WYANDOTTE in the Detroit River

a) WYANDOTTE
b) Pizarro
c) Wyandotte
d) City of Fort Myers
e) Dolphin

BUILT:	1892 Detroit Dry Dock Co., Wyandotte, Mich.
HULL NUMBER:	109
LENGTH:	155.6
BREADTH:	35.0
DEPTH:	9.0
GRT:	320
REGISTRY NUMBER:	US. 81406
ENGINES:	16", 24", 38" Diameter x 24" Stroke Triple Expansion
ENGINE BUILDER:	Dry Dock Engine Works Detroit, Michigan

WYANDOTTE at New London, Connecticut

PIZARRO at New York

CITY OF FORT MYERS

WYANDOTTE (1907)

The first ship fitted with continuous conveying apparatus, known as a self-unloader, was the wooden vessel HENNEPIN (1), which was fitted with this type of conveying machinery for handling crushed stone in 1902. A little later, another and larger wooden steamer, the TOPEKA, was similarly converted. In 1907, the steel steamer WYANDOTTE was designed by Babcock & Penton, Cleveland, Ohio and New York for the Michigan Alkali Company to carry crushed limestone from the quarries at Alpena, Michigan to Detroit and Wyandotte. The Great Lakes Engineering Works, Ecorse, Michigan launched this self-unloader, the first such vessel built on the Great Lakes, on July 2, 1908.

Her first cargo was coal from Sandusky, Ohio to Alpena on her maiden voyage, August 5, 1908. The Wyandotte Steamship Company, a division of Michigan Alkali, operated the vessel. In 1910, she was lengthened by the Great Lakes

Engineering Works; new dimensions: 346.0 x 45.2 x 24.0; 2,450 gross tons. The vessel operated without serious incidents for her entire life. In 1942, Wyandotte Chemical Corporation took over the operation when it bought out Michigan Alkali. In 1948, they painted the hull green, emblazoned their name on the sides of the vessels in the fleet and changed the smoke stack color from all black with a red Indian to a silver stack with a black top, keeping the red Indian.

From 1963 to 1966, she lay in ordinary, first at Wyandotte and then at Detroit, until sold to Hudson Waterways Corporation in 1965. They in turn sold her to the U.S. Maritime Commission as "trade-in tonnage" in June, 1966. She was resold to Transeastern Associates and then to Marine Salvage Ltd. of Port Colborne, Ontario where she was dismantled in late 1966.

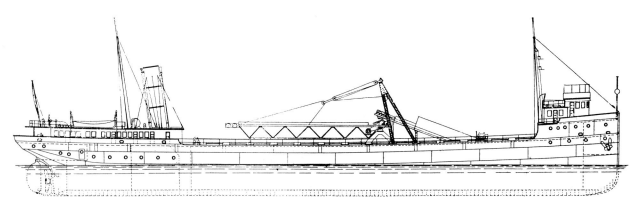

Profile of the WYANDOTTE

Before lengthening, 1908

WYANDOTTE dumping stone into a crib for a new lighthouse in upper Lake Huron

BUILT:	1908
	Great Lakes Engineering Works,
	Ecorse, Mich.
HULL NUMBER:	54
LENGTH:	286.0
BREADTH:	45.2
DEPTH:	24.0
GRT:	2,095
REGISTRY NUMBER:	US. 205458
ENGINES:	18", 31", 50" Diameter x
	36" Stroke
	Triple Expansion
ENGINE BUILDER:	Shipyard

Downbound in the Fighting Island channel, June 22, 1954

WYANDOTTE in the Detroit River, April 9, 1953

INDEX

VESSEL	PAGE
VESSEL	PAGE

VESSEL	PAGE	VESSEL	PAGE